The *Best* of COUNTRY COOKING
2005

Editor: Beth Wittlinger
Art Director: Kathy Crawford
Executive Editor/Books: Heidi Reuter Lloyd
Associate Editor: Jean Steiner
Editorial Assistant: Barb Czysz
Food Editor: Janaan Cunningham
Senior Recipe Editor: Sue A. Jurack
Recipe Editor: Janet Briggs
Food Photography: Dan Roberts, Rob Hagen
Set Stylists: Julie Ferron, Sue Meyers
Associate Set Stylist: Jennifer Bradley Vent
Senior Vice President, Editor in Chief: Catherine Cassidy
President: Barbara Newton
Chairman and Founder: Roy Reiman

For additional copies of this book or information on other books, write *Taste of Home* Books,
P.O. Box 908, Greendale WI 53129, call toll-free 1-800/344-2560 to order with a credit card
or visit our Web site at **www.reimanpub.com**.

PICTURED ON COVER AND ABOVE. From the top: Turkey with Herb Stuffing (p. 174), Buttermilk Lemon Pie (p. 116) and Savory Green Beans (p. 88).

A Year's Worth of Homemade Country Classics

TRY SOMETHING NEW TODAY using recipes from *The Best of Country Cooking 2005*. The eighth in our popular cookbook series, this year's edition serves up 358 country favorites.

This giant collection includes the very best recipes from a year's worth of recent issues of *Country Woman, Country, Country EXTRA, Reminisce* and *Reminisce EXTRA* magazines. All the recipes you'll find are proven favorites of a family just like yours.

You see, these recipes came directly from the personal recipe files of hundreds of everyday cooks across the country. Each and every dish has been sampled and approved by the toughest critic around—a hungry family! Then our Test Kitchen staff (and some lucky taste-testers) try out every recipe, too. So you can be doubly confident each dish is one for the files because it is already a winner.

This book begins with an appealing assortment of 34 Snacks & Beverages. The next time you have family, friends or co-workers clamoring for one of your homemade treats, look to this chapter. For example, Carol Smith's prize-winning Cheesy Beef Taco Dip (p. 6) is always a hit with guests of this Sanford, North Carolina cook.

This year, we also included a special Breakfast & Brunch chapter featuring 33 mouth-watering recipes. Whether you host a special holiday gathering or just want something different for a weekend treat, this chapter has some of the best recipes you could ask for.

You can also take your pick of this beautiful book's 40 recipes included in the Main Dishes chapter. It's filled with wonderful comfort foods like Red-Eye Roast Beef (p. 47) from Basye, Virginia cook Carol Stevens.

In addition, this tried-and-true treasury contains a savory selection of 60 Soups, Salads & Sandwiches. This chapter even features a special section on gelatin, with tips and recipes for wonderful ways to serve up this wobbly treat!

The Side Dishes & Condiments chapter is filled with 22 family-pleasing complements. Plus, you'll find a selection of corn favorites like Corn Pudding Stuffed Tomatoes (p. 87) from Jean Smalls of Cooper City, Florida.

Everyone will save room for a sweet treat when you select any of this book's 73 scrumptious cakes, pies, cookies and more that span two big chapters. In addition to the chapters for main dishes and desserts, you can find even more within our special meal chapters. That includes:

• Thirty-Minute Meals—Six complete meals (18 recipes in all) that are ready to eat in less than half an hour.

• Memorable Meals—Six complete meals featuring 24 favorite recipes from home cooks.

• Cooking for Two—A separate chapter with 6 complete meals plus 30 other dishes properly proportioned to serve two people.

Want more? *The Best of Country Cooking 2005* offers A Basketful of Corn Tips (p. 86), A Host of Cupcake Hints (p. 101), Delightful Drink Ideas (p. 10) and so much more!

As you page through *The Best of Country Cooking 2005*, watch for the special symbol at right. It signifies a "best of the best" recipe representing a winner of a coast-to-coast cooking contest sponsored by one of our magazines.

Finally, throughout this colorful collection are helpful kitchen tips from everyday cooks plus dozens of "restricted diet" recipes marked with this check ✓ that use less fat, sugar or salt.

See why we call this book *The Best*? Just wait until you and your family have tasted it for yourselves!

CONTENTS

Snacks & Beverages...4

Breakfast & Brunch...18

Main Dishes...34

Soups, Salads & Sandwiches...54

Side Dishes & Condiments...80

Cookies, Candies & Bars...90

Cakes, Pies & Desserts...98

Cooking for Two...128

Meals in Minutes...152

Our Most Memorable Meals...164

Index begins on page 176

PARTY PLANNING *can be fun when you have a great selection of wonderful dips, beverages, snacks and more.*

SNACK-TASTIC. Clockwise from top left: Citrus Iced Tea (p. 6), Peanut Butter Chocolate Fondue (p. 5), Party Cheese Balls (p. 5) and Sweet 'n' Salty Party Mix (p. 5).

Snacks & Beverages

PEANUT BUTTER CHOCOLATE FONDUE

(Pictured at left)

Beverly Olthaus, Cincinnati, Ohio

When the family wanted to do a little celebrating over the years, I would make this fondue. It's fun to gather around the table to get a taste of it.

> 1 cup (6 ounces) semisweet chocolate
>   chips
> 1/2 cup sugar
> 1/2 cup milk
> 1/2 cup creamy peanut butter
> 4 large firm bananas, cut into 3/4-inch
>   slices
> 1 pint whole strawberries

In a heavy saucepan, cook and stir the chocolate chips, sugar, milk and peanut butter over low heat until smooth. Transfer to a fondue pot and keep warm. Serve with bananas and strawberries. **Yield:** 12 servings.

SWEET 'N' SALTY PARTY MIX

(Pictured at left)

Candice Lumley, Charles City, Iowa

These crunchy munchies are sure to rank high with your family and friends. The combination of sweet and salty flavors is just right.

> 1 package (12 ounces) Corn Chex
> 1 package (10 ounces) Cheerios
> 1 package (10 ounces) Honeycombs cereal
> 1 package (10 ounces) pretzel sticks,
>   broken
> 1-3/4 cups sugar
> 1-1/2 cups vegetable oil
> 1-1/4 cups butter, melted
> 3 tablespoons soy sauce
> 2 tablespoons garlic salt

In a large bowl, combine cereal and pretzels. In another bowl, combine the remaining ingredients; stir until sugar is dissolved. Pour over cereal mixture and toss to coat. Transfer to a large roasting pan. Bake, uncovered, at 275° for 1-1/4 hours or until crispy, stirring every 15 minutes. Cool. Store in an airtight container. **Yield:** 10 quarts.

PARTY CHEESE BALLS

(Pictured at left)

Shirley Hoerman, Nekoosa, Wisconsin

These tangy cheese balls are guaranteed to spread cheer at your next gathering. The ingredients create a colorful presentation and a savory combination of flavors. As a grandmother who loves to cook, I send many pantry presents off to college.

> 1 package (8 ounces) cream cheese,
>   softened
> 2 cups (8 ounces) shredded cheddar
>   cheese
> 1 jar (5 ounces) sharp American
>   cheese spread
> 1 jar (5 ounces) pimiento cheese
>   spread
> 3 tablespoons finely chopped onion
> 1 tablespoon lemon juice
> 1 teaspoon Worcestershire sauce
> Dash garlic salt
> 1/2 cup chopped pecans, toasted
> 1/2 cup minced fresh parsley
> Assorted crackers

In a mixing bowl, combine the cream cheese, cheddar cheese, cheese spreads, onion, lemon juice, Worcestershire sauce and garlic salt. Beat until blended. Cover and refrigerate for 15 minutes or until easy to handle.

Shape into two balls; roll one ball in pecans and one in parsley. Cover and refrigerate.

Remove from the refrigerator 15 minutes before serving with crackers. **Yield:** 2 cheese balls (1-3/4 cups each).

PARSLEY POINTERS

Thoroughly wash fresh parsley and shake off any excess moisture. Then wrap it in paper towels and store in a plastic bag for up to 1 week. To revive wilted parsley, cut off 1/2 in. from the stem and stand the parsley in a glass of ice water. Refrigerate for at least 1 hour.

CITRUS ICED TEA

(Pictured on page 4)

Amanda Briggs, Greenfield, Wisconsin

I found this refreshing iced tea recipe in a 1932 women's magazine that my grandmother had. The lime adds a nice accent flavor.

    2-1/2 cups water
    1/2 cup plus 2 tablespoons sugar
      1 cup orange juice
      3 tablespoons lemon juice
      1 tablespoon lime juice
      1 teaspoon grated lime peel
ADDITIONAL INGREDIENT
(for each serving):
    3/4 cup brewed tea

In a large saucepan, bring the water and sugar to a boil. Reduce heat; add juices and lime peel. Simmer, uncovered, for 30 minutes. Strain syrup; refrigerate for 2 hours. **Yield:** 2 cups syrup (8 servings).

   To prepare one serving: Fill a glass with ice; add tea. Stir in 1/4 cup syrup.

CHEESY BEEF TACO DIP

(Pictured above)

Carol Smith, Sanford, North Carolina

For a warm, hearty snack with a bit of a kick, try this recipe. It's a hit with my family, and guests rave about it, too. Ideal for parties, it makes a big potful. The only "utensil" you'll need to serve it with is a brimming bowl of tortilla chips.

      2 pounds ground beef
      1 large onion, finely chopped
      1 medium green pepper, finely chopped
      1 pound process cheese (Velveeta), cubed
      1 pound pepper Jack cheese, cubed
      1 jar (16 ounces) taco sauce
      1 can (10 ounces) diced tomatoes and
        green chilies, drained
      1 can (4 ounces) mushroom stems and
        pieces, drained and chopped
      1 can (2-1/4 ounces) sliced ripe olives,
        drained
Tortilla chips

In a large skillet, cook the beef, onion and green pepper over medium heat until meat is no longer pink; drain. Stir in the cheeses, taco sauce, tomatoes, mushrooms and olives. Cook and stir over low heat until cheese is melted. Serve warm with tortilla chips. **Yield:** 10 cups.

LAYERED THREE-CHEESE SPREAD

(Pictured below)

Brenda Smith, Jackson, Michigan

I first made this spread for a baby shower, and it was a huge success. This appetizer tastes like a club sandwich and looks picture-perfect when served. The cream cheese layer can be made ahead of time.

1 package (3 ounces) cream cheese,
  softened
1/2 cup sour cream
1/2 cup mayonnaise
1/2 teaspoon chicken bouillon granules
1/8 teaspoon cayenne pepper
  2 tablespoons grated Parmesan cheese
  3 bacon strips, cooked and crumbled
  1 medium tomato, seeded and
    chopped
1/2 cup shredded Swiss cheese
1/2 cup cubed cooked chicken *or*
    turkey
  2 tablespoons minced fresh parsley
Crackers *or* tortilla chips

In a small mixing bowl, combine the cream cheese,
sour cream, mayonnaise, bouillon and cayenne;
mix well. Cover and refrigerate over-night.

Spread onto a 10-in. serving plate. Sprinkle
with Parmesan cheese, bacon, tomato, Swiss
cheese, chicken and parsley. Serve with crackers
or chips. **Yield:** 10-15 servings.

CHUTNEY STUFFED EGGS

Mrs. Patrick Dare, Fergus, Ontario

*My aunt shared this recipe with me many years ago.
The chutney is a very tasty addition to the eggs!*

  12 hard-cooked eggs
   6 bacon strips, cooked and finely
     crumbled
 1/4 cup chutney, chopped
   3 tablespoons mayonnaise

Cut eggs in half lengthwise. Remove yolks and set
whites aside. In a bowl, mash the yolks. Add the
bacon, chutney and mayonnaise; mix well. Pipe
or spoon into egg whites. Refrigerate until serving. **Yield:** 12 servings.

FANCY FRUIT PIZZA

(Pictured above right)

Suzanne Gruenbacher, Colwich, Kansas

*Sugar cookie dough makes a fun foundation for this
fantastic fruit pizza. The tender crust complements the
sweetened cream cheese and colorful "toppings."
After you serve up the last slice, be prepared to make
another pizza.*

  1 tube (18 ounces) refrigerated sugar
    cookie dough
  1 package (8 ounces) cream cheese,
    softened

1/3 cup sugar
1/2 teaspoon vanilla extract
  2 medium firm bananas, sliced
  2 teaspoons lemon juice
  1 can (20 ounces) pineapple chunks,
    drained
  1 pint fresh strawberries, halved
  2 kiwifruit, peeled and sliced
  1 can (11 ounces) mandarin oranges,
    drained
1/3 cup orange marmalade
  1 tablespoon water

On a greased 14-in. pizza pan, press cookie dough
into a 12-in. circle. Bake at 375° for 10-12 minutes or until golden brown. Cool completely on
a wire rack.

In a small mixing bowl, beat the cream cheese,
sugar and vanilla until smooth. Spread over the
crust. Toss the bananas with lemon juice. Arrange
the pineapple, strawberries, bananas, kiwi and
oranges over the cream cheese mixture. Refrigerate for 1 hour.

Combine marmalade and water; drizzle over
fruit. **Yield:** 12 servings.

DEVILED HAM STUFFED EGGS

(Pictured above)

Margaret Walker, Pace, Florida

I make these stuffed eggs once a month for a fellow-ship meal at church—and I've yet to bring one back home! Different from typical versions, these hard-cooked eggs get a subtle crunch from chopped veggies, and deviled ham adds zing.

    8 hard-cooked eggs
1/4 cup canned deviled ham spread
1/4 cup finely chopped green onions
1/4 cup sweet pickle relish
1/3 cup finely chopped celery
1/3 cup mayonnaise
    1 teaspoon prepared mustard
1/8 teaspoon salt
1/8 teaspoon pepper
Paprika

Slice eggs in half lengthwise; remove yolks and set whites aside. In a small bowl, mash yolks with a fork. Add the next eight ingredients; mix well. Stuff or pipe into egg whites. Refrigerate until serving. Sprinkle with paprika. **Yield:** 8 servings.

WESTERN BLACK BEAN DIP

Pat Cassity, Boise, Idaho

This hearty bean dip is full of flavors from the South-west. After one taste, you'll know how good it is and wonder how it can be good for you, too!

✓ **Uses less fat, sugar or salt. Includes Nutritional Analysis and Diabetic Exchanges.**

    1 can (15 ounces) black beans, rinsed and drained
1/2 cup plus 1 tablespoon chopped green onions, *divided*
1/2 cup plus 1 tablespoon chopped tomato, *divided*
1/2 cup salsa
    3 garlic cloves, minced
1/2 teaspoon chili powder
    1 teaspoon canola oil
1/4 cup shredded reduced-fat Mexican cheese blend, *divided*
1/4 cup minced fresh cilantro
Baked tortilla chips

In a large nonstick skillet, saute the beans, 1/2 cup onions, 1/2 cup tomato, salsa, garlic and chili powder in oil for 4-6 minutes or until heated through, gently mashing the beans while heating. Remove from the heat.

Stir in 3 tablespoons cheese and the cilantro. Transfer to a serving dish; top with the remaining cheese, onions and tomato. Serve warm with chips. **Yield:** 1-1/2 cups.

Nutritional Analysis: One serving (1/4 cup dip) equals 97 calories, 2 g fat (1 g saturated fat), 3 mg cholesterol, 354 mg sodium, 13 g carbohydrate, 5 g fiber, 6 g protein. **Diabetic Exchanges:** 1 starch, 1/2 fat.

SMOKED SALMON SPREAD

Susan L. Pettett, Vancouver, Washington

Growing up in a small coastal town on the Washington Plate Peninsula, my daily staples were fish and shellfish. I'm always asked to bring this dip to family events. It's also great the next day on grilled sourdough bread with olives and tomatoes.

 Uses less fat, sugar or salt. Includes Nutritional Analysis and Diabetic Exchanges.

    1 package (8 ounces) reduced-fat cream cheese
    1 cup fat-free mayonnaise
    2 packages (3 ounces *each*) smoked salmon, flaked
1/4 cup finely chopped onion
    1 teaspoon Worcestershire sauce
1/2 teaspoon garlic powder
1/4 teaspoon lemon juice
Assorted crackers and party breads

In a mixing bowl, beat cream cheese and mayonnaise until smooth. Stir in the salmon, onion, Worcestershire sauce, garlic powder and lemon juice. Cover and refrigerate for at least 2 hours. Serve with crackers and breads. **Yield:** 2-1/2 cups.

HONEY BANANA PUNCH

(Pictured below)

Patricia Stephens, Monticello, Kentucky

Here's a great punch recipe I got from a beekeepers' association. The mix of banana, pineapple and citrus gives it a light, sunny flavor. With its pretty honey color, it makes an elegant beverage for special events.

- 2 cups frozen orange juice concentrate
- 5 ripe bananas, cut into chunks
- 1 can (46 ounces) pineapple juice
- 2 cups water
- 3/4 cup honey
- 1/2 cup sugar
- 1/3 cup sugar sweetened lemonade soft drink mix
- 4 liters lemon-lime soda, chilled

In a blender, combine orange juice concentrate and bananas; cover and process until smooth.

Pour into a large bowl; add the pineapple juice, water, honey, sugar and soft drink mix. Stir until sugar is dissolved. Pour into two 2-qt. freezer containers. Cover and freeze until the mixture is slushy.

To serve, transfer each portion of fruit slush to a large pitcher. Add 2 liters of soda to each pitcher; stir to blend. **Yield:** 7-1/2 gallons (30 1-cup servings).

CARAMEL CRUNCH

(Pictured above)

Mary Koogler, Mitchellville, Iowa

Our whole family has a sweet tooth, so this caramel-drizzled mix of popcorn, almonds and cereal goes quickly. My "off-limits" batches are divided into plastic bags, tied with ribbons and shared with all the snackers on my Christmas list.

- 9 cups popped popcorn
- 9 cups Crispix cereal
- 1 cup slivered almonds
- 1 cup butter, cubed
- 1/2 cup light corn syrup
- 2 cups packed brown sugar
- 1/2 teaspoon baking soda

In a very large heatproof bowl, combine the popcorn, cereal and almonds. In a saucepan, melt the butter; stir in corn syrup and brown sugar.

Cook and stir over medium heat until mixture comes to a boil. Reduce heat to medium-low. Cook 5 minutes longer, stirring occasionally. Remove from the heat. Stir in baking soda. (Mixture will foam up and get lighter in color.) Carefully pour over popcorn mixture; stir to coat evenly.

Transfer to two 15-in. x 10-in. x 1-in. baking pans coated with a nonstick cooking spray. Bake at 250° for 45 minutes, stirring every 15 minutes. Spread on waxed paper to cool. Store in airtight containers. **Yield:** about 4-1/2 quarts.

Delightful Drink Ideas

HERE are some handy hints to help you out when preparing drinks for summertime fun...

- To prevent glasses of punch from being watered down by ordinary ice cubes, try juice cubes instead. Simply fill ice cube trays with fruit juice and pop them in the freezer.
- Try enhancing ice cubes this way—place berries, maraschino cherries or mint leaves in ice cube trays, then fill with water and freeze.
- Planning to add scoops of sherbet or an ice ring to your beverage? Be sure to choose a large enough bowl. If you don't have one that will hold everything, pour in some of the punch and save the rest to replenish the bowl later.
- Want to add pizzazz to your punch bowl? Decorate the edges with fresh fruit. Just cut halfway through berries or slices of orange or lemon, then slip them over the edge.
- Use stalks of celery or pieces of carrot as stir sticks in cups of vegetable juice.
- Knowing how much to make can be a challenge. Our Test Kitchen experts offer this rule of thumb: Plan on each person drinking two 8-ounce glasses per hour.
- If you'll be serving iced drinks, use a pitcher with a pinched pouring lip. It will prevent excess ice from falling into the glass as you pour.
- Whether your blender is on the fritz or you don't have one, you can still make blended drinks. Simply shake the beverage up in a jar with a tight-fitting lid.

FESTIVE CHEESE BEACH BALL

(Pictured above)

Florence McClelland, Fredonia, New York

Made to resemble a beach ball, this appetizer always rounds up compliments. It's filled with a variety of cheeses, and each cut through the ball gives guests a taste along with garnishes of their choice.

6 packages (8 ounces *each*) cream cheese, softened, *divided*
2 cups (8 ounces) crumbled blue cheese
2 cups (8 ounces) shredded cheddar cheese
1/2 cup chopped green onions
1 garlic clove, minced
TOPPINGS:
1/4 cup cooked tiny shrimp
2 tablespoons chopped stuffed olives
2 tablespoons crumbled cooked bacon
2 tablespoons chopped sweet yellow pepper
2 tablespoons chopped green onions
2 tablespoons chopped ripe olives
2 tablespoons chopped pimientos
2 tablespoons minced fresh parsley
Assorted crackers

In a mixing bowl, combine two packages of cream cheese and the blue cheese; set aside. In another mixing bowl, combine two packages of cream cheese and the cheddar cheese; set aside. In a third bowl, beat the remaining cream cheese; add the onions and garlic.

In a 2-qt. bowl lined with plastic wrap, layer each portion of cream cheese. Invert onto a serving platter; remove plastic wrap and shape into a ball. With a sharp knife, score eight sections on the ball. Sprinkle each section with one of the toppings and press lightly. Serve with crackers. **Yield:** 7 cups.

STRAWBERRY PUNCH

Sherry Couture, Lowell, Michigan

Here is a dreamy creamy punch that's packed with flavor. I combine frozen strawberries with strawberry soda, ginger ale and ice cream.

      1 package (16 ounces) frozen
         unsweetened whole strawberries,
         thawed
      1 bottle (2 liters) strawberry soda, chilled
      1 bottle (2 liters) ginger ale, chilled
Vanilla ice cream

In a 6-qt. punch bowl, combine the strawberries, soda and ginger ale. Just before serving, add scoops of ice cream. **Yield:** about 5 quarts.

FROSTED RUBY PUNCH

(Pictured below)

Sandi Pichon, Slidell, Louisiana

With its crimson ice ring and dollops of sherbet, this punch is pretty enough for parties. To make the ice ring, I freeze cranberry juice in a mold. It's perfect for a bridal shower or tea party.

      4 cups cranberry juice
  1-1/2 cups sugar
  1-1/2 cups lemon juice
      1 cup orange juice
      4 cups ginger ale, chilled
      1 quart raspberry sherbet

Pour cranberry juice into a 5-cup ring mold. Freeze overnight. In a punch bowl, combine sugar, lemon juice and orange juice until sugar is dissolved; stir in the ginger ale. Remove ice ring from mold; float in punch. Place scoops of sherbet around ring. **Yield:** 8 servings.

HOT CHEESE SPREAD

(Pictured above)

Marilyn Kumpon, Binghamton, New York

Served with a variety of crackers, this cheese dip is a big hit at parties any time of the year.

- 2 cups (8 ounces) shredded sharp cheddar cheese
- 1 large onion, chopped
- 1 cup mayonnaise
- Assorted crackers *or* breadsticks

In a bowl, combine the cheese, onion and mayonnaise; mix well. Spoon into a greased 1-qt. baking dish. Cover and bake at 350° for 25-30 minutes or until bubbly around the edges; stir. Serve with crackers or breadsticks. **Yield:** 2 cups.

Editor's Note: Reduced-fat or fat-free mayonnaise may not be substituted for regular mayonnaise in this recipe.

BANANA SHAKES

Marsha Gail Overholser, Ash Grove, Missouri

This is a favorite of mine during the hot summer months. I can whip up these shakes in no time!

- 1 cup milk
- 2 tablespoons peanut butter
- 1 tablespoon honey
- 2 large ripe frozen bananas

In a blender, combine all ingredients; cover and process until blended. Pour into chilled glasses. Serve immediately. **Yield:** 2-3 servings.

HERBED GARLIC BREAD

(Pictured below)

Wendy Smith, Hartford, Wisconsin

I use either French or Vienna bread for this recipe. The Parmesan cheese complements the garlic nicely.

- 1 unsliced loaf (1 pound) French bread
- 1/2 cup butter, softened
- 2 tablespoons grated Parmesan cheese
- 2 tablespoons minced fresh parsley
- 4 garlic cloves, minced
- 1/2 teaspoon dried oregano
- 1/8 teaspoon garlic salt

Slice bread, but not all the way through, leaving slices attached at the bottom. In a small mixing bowl, cream butter. Add the Parmesan cheese, parsley, garlic, oregano and garlic salt; mix well. Spread between slices.

Wrap loaf in a large piece of heavy-duty foil (about 28 in. x 18 in.). Bake at 325° for 15-20 minutes or until heated through. **Yield:** 8-10 servings.

SUGARED PECANS

Suzanne Brown, Blue Jay, California

For a number of years, our neighbor gave us these wonderful treats at Christmas. I finally obtained the recipe and make them for others, too.

- 1 egg white
- 1 tablespoon orange juice
- 3 cups pecan halves
- 1/2 cup sugar
- 1/2 teaspoon salt

1 teaspoon ground cinnamon
1/2 teaspoon ground nutmeg
1/2 teaspoon ground cloves

In a mixing bowl, beat egg white and orange juice until frothy. Add nuts; stir gently to coat. Combine the remaining ingredients. Add to nut mixture and stir gently to coat. Spread onto a greased 15-in. x 10-in. x 1-in. baking pan.

Bake, uncovered, at 300° for 30 minutes or until lightly browned, stirring every 10 minutes. Cool. Store in an airtight container. **Yield:** 3 cups.

CHOCOLATE BANANA SMOOTHIES

Katherine Lipka, Galesburg, Michigan

In an effort to lose weight, I wanted to find a healthy, sweet and filling beverage. I came up with this smoothie recipe that fits the bill.

 Uses less fat, sugar or salt. Includes Nutritional Analysis and Diabetic Exchanges.

2 cups cold 2% milk
1 package (1.4 ounces) sugar-free instant chocolate pudding mix
2 tablespoons vanilla extract
2 large ripe frozen bananas, sliced
2 cups coarsely crushed ice cubes

In a blender, combine the milk, pudding mix and vanilla; cover and process until blended. Add the bananas and ice; cover and process until smooth. Pour into chilled glasses; serve immediately. **Yield:** 4 servings.

Nutritional Analysis: One serving (1 cup) equals 166 calories, 3 g fat (2 g saturated fat), 10 mg cholesterol, 360 mg sodium, 31 g carbohydrate, 2 g fiber, 6 g protein. **Diabetic Exchanges:** 1 fruit, 1 fat-free milk.

MEXICAN CORN DIP

(Pictured above right)

Laura Cameron, Delaware, Ohio

This dip goes fast at office parties or any gathering. Mildly spicy, it's easy to alter if you want it to have more of a kick. Make sure your corn chips are large enough to scoop up a hearty helping.

2 cups (8 ounces) shredded cheddar cheese
1 can (11 ounces) yellow and white whole kernel corn, drained
1 can (11 ounces) Mexicorn, drained
4 ounces pepper Jack cheese, shredded
1/4 cup chopped green onions

1 can (4 ounces) chopped green chilies
1 jalapeno pepper, seeded and chopped
3/4 cup mayonnaise
3/4 cup sour cream
1/8 teaspoon sugar
Additional chopped green onions, optional
Tortilla *or* corn chips

In a large bowl, combine the first seven ingredients. In a small bowl, combine the mayonnaise, sour cream and sugar; stir into corn mixture. Cover and refrigerate overnight. Garnish with additional green onions if desired. Serve with chips. **Yield:** 8-10 servings.

Editor's Note: When cutting or seeding hot peppers, use rubber or plastic gloves to protect your hands. Avoid touching your face.

PEANUT BUTTER MILKSHAKES

Joyce Turley, Slaughters, Kentucky

Using just a handful of everyday ingredients and a blender, you can whip up a creamy treat in seconds. It's a delicious after-school snack. Peanut butter fans will love it.

1 cup milk
2 cups vanilla ice cream
1/2 cup peanut butter
2 tablespoons sugar

In a blender, combine all ingredients; cover and process for 30 seconds or until smooth. Stir if necessary. Pour into chilled glasses; serve immediately. **Yield:** 3 servings.

Beverages Add Flavor To Any Occasion

 RASPBERRY MINT COOLER

(Pictured below)

Patricia Kile, Greentown, Pennsylvania

This beverage is lovely in the summer when mint and raspberries are fresh.

    3 cups water
    1 to 1-1/2 cups chopped fresh mint
    3/4 cup sugar
    3 packages (10 ounces *each*) frozen
        sweetened raspberries, thawed
2-1/4 cups lemonade concentrate
    6 cups cold water
Crushed ice

In a large saucepan, bring water, mint and sugar to a boil. Stir until sugar is dissolved. Remove from the heat; let stand for 5 minutes. Add the raspberries and the lemonade concentrate; gently mash raspberries.

Line a strainer with four layers of cheesecloth; place over a 1-gal. container. Slowly pour raspberry mixture into strainer; discard pulp and mint. Add cold water to the raspberry juice; stir well. Serve over ice. **Yield:** 3-1/2 quarts.

PEACHES 'N' CREAM SMOOTHIES

(Pictured below)

Kathy Kittell, Lenexa, Kansas

With five active teenagers in the house, I often serve them this smoothie as a pick-me-up in the afternoon or as a quick breakfast on hectic mornings.

DELICIOUS DRINKS include (left to right) Punch Delight, Peaches 'n' Cream Smoothies and Raspberry Mint Cooler.

1/2 cup milk
2 cups (16 ounces) peach yogurt
1 medium ripe peach, peeled and sliced
2 cups vanilla ice cream
2-1/2 teaspoons sugar

In a blender, combine all ingredients; cover and process until smooth. Pour into chilled glasses; serve immediately. **Yield:** 4 servings.

PUNCH DELIGHT

(Pictured below left)

Barbara Koehnke, Fremont, Wisconsin

When we celebrated my mother's 75th birthday, we wanted a punch everyone could enjoy. This delightful combination of lemonades, juice and soda was perfect and so easy to make. All of our guests loved it.

1 can (12 ounces) frozen orange juice concentrate, thawed
1 can (12 ounces) frozen lemonade concentrate, thawed
1 can (12 ounces) frozen pink lemonade concentrate, thawed
2 liters Mello Yellow soda, chilled
2 liters 50/50 *or* lemon-lime soda, chilled
Ice cubes

In a large punch bowl, combine the concentrates. Gradually stir in sodas. Add ice. **Yield:** 5 quarts.

GRAPE JUICE CRUSH

Joy Butler, Pincher Creek, Alberta

I've served this drink for more than 20 years and always get compliments. For parties, I often dip small clusters of grapes in sugar and perch them on the edge of each glass for a garnish.

3/4 cup grape juice concentrate
3/4 cup lemonade concentrate
1 can (6 ounces) frozen orange juice concentrate, thawed
6 cups water
4 cups cold ginger ale
Crushed ice

In a 1-gal. container, combine the concentrates and water; stir well. Refrigerate until well chilled. Just before serving, slowly add the ginger ale. Serve over ice. **Yield:** about 3 quarts.

FRUITY THIRST QUENCHER

Bernice Morris, Marshfield, Missouri

This beverage gets plenty of flavor from powdered drink mix, juice and crushed pineapple. During the summer, I keep a jug of it in the fridge. It tastes so good on hot days.

4 cups water
3/4 cup sugar
1 envelope (.15 ounce) unsweetened strawberry starfruit soft drink mix *or* unsweetened soft drink mix of your choice
1/2 cup orange juice
1/4 cup lemon juice
1/2 cup crushed pineapple

In a 3-qt. pitcher, combine the water, sugar and soft drink mix. Stir until sugar and mix are dissolved. Add the orange juice, lemon juice and pineapple; mix well. Refrigerate until serving. **Yield:** about 5 cups.

PEAR COOLER

Jeri Clayton, Sandy, Utah

My daughter and I had eaten a cold fruit soup while on vacation. When we got home, we tried to create our own version—and wound up with this smoothie. Everyone enjoys it.

1 can (15-1/4 ounces) sliced pears, undrained
2 cups ice cubes
1 envelope whipped topping mix
1/4 to 1/2 teaspoon vanilla *or* almond extract, optional

In a blender or food processor, combine first three ingredients. Add extract if desired. Cover and process until smooth. Pour into chilled glasses; serve immediately. **Yield:** 3 servings.

1 package (25.6 ounces) nonfat dry milk powder
2-1/2 cups confectioners' sugar
1 cup powdered nondairy creamer
25 peppermint candies, crushed

ADDITIONAL INGREDIENT
(for each serving):
1 cup milk

In a large bowl, combine the first five ingredients; mix well. Store in an airtight container in a cool dry place for up to 6 months. **Yield:** 53 servings (17-2/3 cups total).

To prepare hot drink: Warm milk; stir in 1/3 cup mix until dissolved. **Yield:** 1 serving.

CHEESY CORN DIP

Pat Habiger, Spearville, Kansas

We like to munch on this tasty dip before dinner is ready. I also take it along to tail-gating or card-playing parties.

1 package (8 ounces) cream cheese, softened
2 tablespoons ranch salad dressing mix
1 can (8-3/4 ounces) whole kernel corn, drained
1/2 cup finely chopped sweet red pepper

ORANGE SPICED TEA

(Pictured above)

This sweet steeped beverage from our Test Kitchen staff is the perfect complement to a plate of scones. If you like, garnish the tea with the orange slices and cinnamon sticks.

4 cups boiling water
7 orange-flavored tea bags
3 cinnamon sticks (3 inches)
1/4 cup honey
Orange slices and additional cinnamon sticks

Place boiling water in a teapot. Add the tea bags and cinnamon sticks. Cover and let steep for 5 minutes.

Discard the cinnamon sticks and tea bags. Stir in the honey. Garnish each teacup with an orange slice and another cinnamon stick if desired. **Yield:** 4 servings.

MINT COCOA MIX

(Pictured at right)

LaVonne Hegland, St. Michael, Minnesota

I've made this beverage mix many times as Christmas gifts for neighbors and our three sons' teachers. The mint flavor makes the warm drink so refreshing.

1 package (30 ounces) instant chocolate drink mix

2 tablespoons chopped ripe olives
1 tablespoon finely chopped jalapeno
  pepper
Tortilla chips *or* **raw vegetables**

In a mixing bowl, combine cream cheese and salad dressing mix. Fold in the corn, red pepper, olives and jalapeno. Serve with tortilla chips or vegetables. **Yield:** about 1-1/2 cups.

Editor's Note: When cutting or seeding hot peppers, use rubber or plastic gloves to protect your hands. Avoid touching your face.

TASTY CHEESE SPREAD

Lynda Hensley, Lima, Ohio

We especially like to use this dip for Christmas gift-giving. It can be packaged in small holiday tins or pint-size jars and tied with ribbons.

    2 containers (16 ounces *each*) sharp
      cheddar cheese spread
    2 cups (16 ounces) sour cream
    1 package (8 ounces) cream cheese,
      softened
  1/2 teaspoon salt
  1/4 to 1/2 teaspoon garlic powder
Crackers *and/or* **celery**

In mixing bowl, beat the cheese spread, sour cream, cream cheese, salt and garlic powder. Serve with crackers and/or celery. **Yield:** 8 cups.

GREEN BEAN FRITTERS

(Pictured above right)

Sharon Dyck, Roxton Falls, Quebec

A few years ago during bean season, a friend of mine shared this recipe with me. It is now a must-have at our place every summer.

    2 green onions
  3/4 pound fresh green beans, trimmed
    1 teaspoon salt, *divided*
    6 eggs, *separated*
  2/3 cup all-purpose flour
  1/4 teaspoon pepper
Oil for deep-fat frying
SALSA:
    2 medium tomatoes, seeded and chopped
    3 tablespoons finely chopped onion
    1 jalapeno pepper, seeded and chopped
    2 tablespoons minced fresh parsley
    1 garlic clove, minced
    1 tablespoon olive oil
    1 tablespoon cider vinegar

Salt and pepper to taste

Cut green tops from onions (save white portion for another use). Cut tops into narrow strips; soften in boiling water for 30 seconds. Drain and rinse in cold water. Wrap each strip around a bundle of eight green beans; gently tie in a knot.

Place 1/2 in. of water in a large skillet; add bean bundles and 1/2 teaspoon salt. Bring to a boil. Reduce heat; cover and simmer for 8-10 minutes or until beans are crisp-tender. Drain on paper towels. In a mixing bowl, beat egg yolks until lemon-colored. Stir in flour, pepper and remaining salt.

In another mixing bowl, beat egg whites until stiff peaks form. Fold into flour mixture.

In an electric skillet or deep-fat fryer, heat oil to 375°. Dip bean bundles in batter; fry a few at a time for 7 minutes or until golden brown. Drain on paper towels. In a bowl, combine salsa ingredients. Serve with fritters. **Yield:** 10 servings.

Editor's Note: When cutting or seeding hot peppers, use rubber or plastic gloves to protect your hands. Avoid touching your face.

FRYING TIPS

Don't fork it over! While frying fritters, turn the pieces with tongs or a slotted spoon to help keep the pieces together.

EYE-OPENING breakfasts and brunch treats are a sure way to get your family or guests smiling as they start their day.

EGG-CELLENT DISHES. Clockwise from top: Apple Oven Pancake, Sausage Garden Quiche and Breakfast Pizza (all recipes on p.19).

Breakfast & Brunch

SAUSAGE GARDEN QUICHE

(Pictured at left)

Janet Jackson, Bakers Mills, New York

This quiche is my favorite! I sometimes omit the sausage and add more garden-fresh ingredients.

    5 eggs
    3/4 cup milk
    1/2 cup chopped fresh spinach
    1/3 cup shredded cheddar cheese
    1 tablespoon dried minced onion
    1 tablespoon minced chives
    1/8 teaspoon salt
    1/8 teaspoon garlic powder
Dash pepper
Pastry shell (9 inches), baked
    6 brown-and-serve sausage links
    3 slices fresh tomato, halved

In a bowl, whisk eggs and milk. Stir in the next seven ingredients. Carefully pour into crust. Cook sausage according to package directions. Arrange sausage in a spoke pattern in egg mixture; place tomato slices between links.

Bake, uncovered, at 350° for 30-35 minutes or until a knife inserted near the center comes out clean. Let stand for 10 minutes before cutting. **Yield:** 6 servings.

APPLE OVEN PANCAKE

(Pictured at left)

Carol Gillespie, Chambersburg, Pennsylvania

Here's a puffed pancake that wins raves. It looks so pretty with apple slices peeking through.

    3 large Granny Smith or other tart apples,
      peeled and sliced
    1 cup raisins
    1/4 cup packed brown sugar
    1 tablespoon honey
    1/2 teaspoon ground cinnamon
    1/4 teaspoon ground nutmeg
    2 tablespoons butter
    4 eggs
    1 cup milk
    1 cup all-purpose flour
    1 tablespoon sugar

    1/4 teaspoon salt
    2 teaspoons lemon juice, *divided*
    3 tablespoons confectioners' sugar

In a bowl, combine the first six ingredients. Melt butter in a 12-in. ovenproof skillet. Add apple mixture to skillet; saute for 15 minutes or until tender.

In a blender, combine the eggs, milk, flour, sugar and salt; cover and process for 10 seconds or until smooth. Pour over apple mixture; gently lift apple mixture, letting egg mixture flow underneath.

Bake, uncovered, at 425° for 15-20 minutes or until pancake is puffy and golden brown. Sprinkle with lemon juice and confectioners' sugar if desired. Cut into wedges. Serve warm. **Yield:** 6 servings.

BREAKFAST PIZZA

(Pictured at left)

Jean Beggs, Mears, Michigan

This pizza is perfect for brunch. Put it together the night before, refrigerate and bake it in the morning.

    2 cans (7-1/2 ounces each) refrigerated
      buttermilk biscuits, separated into 20
      biscuits
    2 cans (4 ounces each) mushroom stems
      and pieces, drained
    1 large onion, diced
 4-1/2 teaspoons butter
    1 pound bulk pork sausage, cooked and
      drained
   12 eggs
    3 cups (12 ounces) shredded mozzarella
      cheese

Cover the bottom of a greased 13-in. x 9-in. x 2-in. baking pan with biscuits; set aside. In a large skillet, saute mushrooms and onion in butter for 3-5 minutes or until tender; add sausage.

In bowl, whisk eggs. Coat skillet with nonstick cooking spray. Add eggs; cook and stir over medium heat until nearly set. Add sausage and vegetable mixture. Cook; stir until completely set.

Spread egg mixture over biscuits. Sprinkle with cheese. Cover and bake at 400° for 12 minutes. Uncover; bake 10-13 minutes longer or until cheese is melted and biscuits are golden brown. **Yield:** 6-8 servings.

Nutritional Analysis: One serving (2 blintzes) equals 326 calories, 10 g fat (5 g saturated fat), 129 mg cholesterol, 759 mg sodium, 39 g carbohydrate, 1 g fiber, 19 g protein. **Diabetic Exchanges:** 2 starch, 2 lean meat, 1/2 fat-free milk, 1/2 fat.

CURRANT JELLY SCONES

(Pictured below)

These golden goodies dotted with red jelly are rich and delicious. Plus, they're quick to prepare—no kneading is required. Our Test Kitchen staff is happy to share this tasty recipe with you.

> 2 cups all-purpose flour
> 1/4 cup sugar
> 3 teaspoons baking powder
> 1/2 teaspoon salt
> 1/2 cup cold butter
> 1 egg
> 1/2 cup half-and-half cream
> 1 teaspoon grated orange peel
> 4 teaspoons currant jelly

In a bowl, combine the flour, sugar, baking powder and salt; cut in butter until mixture resembles coarse crumbs. Combine the egg, cream and orange peel. Stir into dry ingredients just until moistened.

On a greased baking sheet, pat dough into an 8-in. circle; cut into eight wedges. Do not separate wedges. Make a thumbprint in each wedge, about 1/4 in. deep. Fill indentation with jelly. Bake at 400° for 13-15 minutes or until golden brown. Serve warm. **Yield:** 8 servings.

SWEET CORN BLINTZES

(Pictured above)

Paula Marchesi, Lenhartsville, Pennsylvania

I often make a double batch of these blintzes to take to work. I always come home with an empty platter!

> ✓ **Uses less fat, sugar or salt. Includes Nutritional Analysis and Diabetic Exchanges.**

> 1 cup fresh *or* frozen corn, thawed
> 1/2 cup fat-free half-and-half
> 1/2 cup all-purpose flour
> 2 eggs
> 2 tablespoons butter, melted
> 1/2 teaspoon salt
> 1/4 teaspoon pepper
> 1-1/2 cups (12 ounces) 2% cottage cheese, drained
> 1/4 cup sugar
> **Confectioners' sugar, optional**

Place the corn and half-and-half in a blender; cover and process until smooth. Add the flour, eggs, butter, salt and pepper; cover and process until blended. Cover and refrigerate for 1 hour.

Heat an 8-in. nonstick skillet coated with nonstick cooking spray; pour about 3 tablespoons batter into the center of skillet. Lift and tilt pan to evenly coat bottom. Cook until top appears dry; turn and cook 15-20 seconds longer. Remove to a wire rack. Repeat with remaining batter, using additional nonstick cooking spray as needed. When cool, stack crepes with waxed paper or paper towels in between.

In a small bowl, combine the cottage cheese and sugar. Spoon 2 tablespoonfuls down the center of each crepe; roll up. Place in a 13-in. x 9-in. x 2-in. baking dish. Bake, uncovered, at 350° for 8-10 minutes or until heated through. Sprinkle with confectioners' sugar if desired. **Yield:** 4 servings.

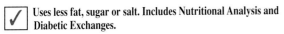

SAUSAGE EGG BAKE

Jeanette Brower, Huber Heights, Ohio

The original recipe for this was so rich and full of fat, I made it only a few times. Lighter ingredients now allow me to enjoy it often.

✓ **Uses less fat, sugar or salt. Includes Nutritional Analysis and Diabetic Exchanges.**

- 12 ounces reduced-fat pork and turkey breakfast sausage links, cut into pieces
- 2 cups egg substitute
- 2 cups 1% milk
- 1/2 teaspoon salt
- 1/2 teaspoon pepper
- 12 slices whole wheat bread, cut into 1-inch cubes
- 1 cup cubed reduced-fat process cheese (Velveeta)

In a large nonstick skillet, cook sausage over medium heat until no longer pink; drain if necessary. In a large bowl, combine the egg substitute, milk, salt and pepper. Add the bread, sausage and cheese; mix well.

Transfer to a 13-in. x 9-in. x 2-in. baking dish coated with nonstick cooking spray. Cover and refrigerate overnight.

Remove from the refrigerator 30 minutes before baking. Bake, covered, at 350° for 40 minutes. Uncover; bake 10-15 minutes longer or until cheese is bubbly and bread is lightly browned. **Yield:** 8 servings.

Nutritional Analysis: One serving equals 244 calories, 9 g fat (5 g saturated fat), 40 mg cholesterol, 960 mg sodium, 18 g carbohydrate, 1 g fiber, 25 g protein. **Diabetic Exchanges:** 3 lean meat, 1 starch.

PEPPERONI CHEESE BAKE

(Pictured above right)

Sharon Deur, Fremont, Michigan

We have this cheesy, pepperoni-filled casserole monthly because it is a welcome dish for me after working full time. It requires very little prep time so it's easy to make in a jiffy, but it's also chock-full of protein and flavor.

- 2 cups (8 ounces) shredded mozzarella cheese
- 1/2 cup diced pepperoni
- 5 eggs
- 3/4 cup milk
- 1/4 teaspoon dried basil

In a greased 9-in. pie plate, layer the mozzarella cheese and pepperoni. In a bowl, whisk the eggs, milk and basil; pour over the cheese.

Bake at 400° for 20-25 minutes or until a knife inserted near the center comes out clean. Let stand for 10 minutes before cutting. **Yield:** 6-8 servings.

HEARTY POTATO OMELET

Elsie Norton, Mt. Vernon, Illinois

I put this together years ago when my kids were small. It was delicious, economical and nutritious. Now they make it for their own families.

- 1 bacon strip, cut into 1/2-inch pieces
- 4 frozen Tater Tots, thawed
- 2 eggs
- 2 tablespoons water
- 3 tablespoons shredded cheddar cheese

In an 8-in. nonstick skillet, cook bacon over medium heat until crisp. Add Tater Tots and break apart with a spatula. In a small bowl, beat eggs and water; add to skillet. As eggs set, lift edges, letting uncooked portion flow underneath.

When eggs are set, spoon cheese over one side; fold omelet over filling. Cover and let stand for 1-1/2 minutes or until cheese is melted. **Yield:** 1 serving.

Country Jams and Jellies Will Make Smiles Spread for Miles!

ORANGE PINEAPPLE MARMALADE

(Pictured below right)

Stephanie Heise, Rochester, New York

This sweet citrusy marmalade is perfect for spreading on English muffins or biscuits. It also makes a delicious housewarming or hostess gift.

- 2 medium oranges
- 2 cans (8 ounces *each*) crushed pineapple, drained
- 4 cups sugar
- 2 tablespoons lemon juice

Grate outer peel from oranges and set aside. Peel off and discard white membrane from oranges and section the fruit, discarding any seeds. In a food processor, combine orange peel and orange sections; cover and process until orange is in small pieces.

In a wide-bottomed microwave-safe 2-1/2-qt. bowl, combine the pineapple, sugar, lemon juice and orange mixture. Microwave, uncovered, on high for 3 minutes; stir. Heat for 3 minutes longer (edges will be bubbly); stir. Microwave for 2 to 2-1/2 minutes or until mixture is bubbly in center; stir. Heat 2-1/2 minutes longer; stir. Cool for 10 minutes.

Carefully pour into jars or freezer containers; cool to room temperature, about 1 hour. Cover and let stand at room temperature for 4 hours. Refrigerate for up to 3 weeks or freeze for up to 1 year. **Yield:** 4 cups.

Editor's Note: This recipe does not use pectin. It was tested in an 850-watt microwave.

PEACH RASPBERRY JAM

(Pictured at right)

Mrs. Donn White, Wooster, Ohio

Back when my children were young, I put up about 100 jars of jams and jellies each summer, including this freezer version. Although I don't make that many now, I do stir up a batch to give to neighbors at Christmastime.

- 1-1/4 cups finely chopped peaches
- 2 cups fresh raspberries
- 2 tablespoons lemon juice
- 4 cups sugar
- 3/4 cup water
- 1 package (1-3/4 ounces) powdered fruit pectin

Place peaches in a large bowl. In a small bowl, mash the raspberries; strain to remove seeds if desired. Add raspberries and lemon juice to peaches. Stir in sugar. Let stand for 10 minutes.

In a small saucepan, bring water and pectin to a full rolling boil. Boil for 1 minute, stirring constantly. Add to fruit mixture; stir for 2-3 minutes or until the sugar is dissolved.

Pour into jars or freezer containers; cool to room temperature, about 30 minutes. Cover and let stand overnight or until set, but not longer than 24 hours. Refrigerate for up to 3 weeks or freeze for up to 1 year. **Yield:** about 5 cups.

ORANGE PEAR JAM

(Pictured at right)

Delores Ward, Decatur, Indiana

Full of fruity flavor, this delightful jam is a great toast topper. I came up with the recipe when a neighbor gave me an armload of pears. Everyone really likes it because it has such a great combination of flavors.

- 7 cups sugar
- 5 cups chopped peeled fresh pears
- 1 cup crushed pineapple, drained
- 2 tablespoons lemon juice
- 2 packages (3 ounces *each*) orange gelatin

In a Dutch oven or large kettle, combine the sugar, pears, pineapple and lemon juice. Bring to a full rolling boil over high heat, stirring constantly. Reduce heat; simmer for 15 minutes, stirring frequently. Remove from the heat; stir in gelatin until dissolved.

Pour into jars or containers; cool to room temperature, about 1 hour. Cover and let stand overnight or until set, but not longer than 24 hours. Refrigerate for up to 3 weeks. **Yield:** about 7 cups.

APRICOT PINEAPPLE JAM

Carol Radil, New Britain, Connecticut

Dried apricots, crushed pineapple and grapefruit juice create a memorable jam. The juice is what makes the jam taste so good.

12 ounces dried apricots
1 cup water
1 can (20 ounces) crushed pineapple, undrained
1/2 cup grapefruit juice
3 cups sugar

In a large saucepan, bring apricots and water to a boil. Reduce heat; cover and simmer for 15 minutes or until apricots are very tender. Mash. Add pineapple, grapefruit juice and sugar. Simmer, uncovered, for 1 hour or until thick and translucent, stirring frequently.

Pour into jars or freezer containers; cool to room temperature, about 1 hour. Cover and let stand overnight or until set, but not longer than 24 hours. Refrigerate for up to 3 weeks or freeze for up to 1 year. **Yield:** 5 cups.

Editor's Note: This recipe does not use pectin.

TOAST TOPPERS. Clockwise from top right are Orange Pineapple Marmalade, Peach Raspberry Jam and Orange Pear Jam.

5 cups chopped peeled fresh tomatoes
4 cups sugar
1 tablespoon lemon juice
2 packages (3 ounces *each*) raspberry gelatin

In a large saucepan or Dutch oven, combine the tomatoes, sugar and lemon juice. Cook and stir over high heat until mixture comes to a boil. Reduce heat; simmer, uncovered, for 25 minutes. Remove from the heat. Skim off foam if necessary. Stir in gelatin until completely dissolved.

Pour into jars or containers; cool to room temperature, about 1 hour. Cover and let stand for 3 hours or until set, but not longer than 24 hours. Refrigerate for up to 3 weeks. **Yield:** about 5-1/2 cups.

SURPRISE RASPBERRY JAM

(Pictured above)

Elizabeth Baker, Birdsboro, Pennsylvania

Family and friends will never guess the secret ingredient in this jam—tomatoes! I got the recipe from a co-worker, and it is just delicious.

ORANGE JELLY

Mary Rice, Maysville, Oklahoma

For a change of pace, give this yummy jelly made from frozen orange juice a try. I've given it as gifts to friends and family—and many times the jars have been returned for refills.

2-1/3 cups water
1 can (12 ounces) frozen orange juice concentrate, thawed

Helpful Bread-Spread Tips

HERE ARE HINTS to help make jellies and jams:
- Use firm, ripe fruit. Overripe fruit will cause jelly or jam to be soft and watery, while under-ripe fruit will make it too firm and hard to spread.

- You can use frozen fruit—just make sure it's thoroughly thawed first.

- Don't reduce the sugar in recipes or use sugar substitutes. If you do, the jam or jelly will not set up right.

  If you want to make a low-sugar jam or jelly, look for pectin specifically designed for lower sugar recipes and follow the recommended sugar amounts on the pectin box.

- Do not double recipes—the spread may not set properly. If a larger yield is desired, make two separate batches.

- The containers you use should be clean, moisture- and vapor-resistant and should not be larger than 1 pint (2 cups).

- Recipes that call for gelatin should not be frozen or they may become thin after thawing. They can be stored in the refrigerator for up to 3 weeks.

- Frozen jam and jelly can be stored for up to 1 year. If a recipe is not frozen, it can be kept in the refrigerator for as long as 3 weeks.

- Freezer jams and jellies should be thawed in the refrigerator. Once they've been opened, you can store them in the fridge for up to 3 weeks.

- Keep in mind that freezer jams and jellies are generally less firm than those that aren't frozen. You'll also find that freezer spreads are brighter in color and taste more like fresh fruit.

1 package (1-3/4 ounces) powdered fruit
    pectin
4-1/2 cups sugar

In a Dutch oven or large kettle, combine the water, orange juice concentrate and pectin. Cook and stir until mixture comes to a full rolling boil. Add sugar; return to a full rolling boil. Boil for 2 minutes, stirring constantly. Remove from the heat; skim off foam if necessary.

Pour into jars or freezer containers; cool to room temperature, about 1 hour. Cover and let stand overnight or until set, but not longer than 24 hours. Refrigerate for up to 3 weeks or freeze for up to 1 year. **Yield:** 6 cups.

ITALIAN SAUSAGE STRATA
(Pictured below)

Amanda Reid, Oakville, Iowa

When our family sits down for breakfast on days when this do-ahead dish is on the menu, I can relax and join them.

1/2 cup butter, softened, *divided*
12 to 16 slices day-old bread, crusts
    removed
1/2 pound fresh mushrooms, sliced
2 cups sliced onions
Salt and pepper to taste
1 pound bulk Italian sausage,
    cooked and drained
3 cups (12 ounces) shredded cheddar
    cheese

5 eggs
2-1/2 cups milk
1 tablespoon Dijon mustard
1 teaspoon ground nutmeg
1 teaspoon ground mustard
2 tablespoons minced fresh parsley

Using 1/4 cup butter, spread one side of each bread slice with butter. Place half of the bread, butter side down, in a greased 13-in. x 9-in. x 2-in. baking dish.

In a large skillet, saute the mushrooms and onions in remaining butter. Sprinkle with salt and pepper. Spoon half of the mushroom mixture over bread in the prepared pan. Top with half of the sausage and cheddar cheese. Layer with the remaining bread, mushroom mixture, sausage and cheddar cheese.

In a bowl, combine the eggs, milk, Dijon mustard, nutmeg and ground mustard. Pour over cheese. Cover and refrigerate overnight.

Remove from the refrigerator 30 minutes before baking. Bake, covered, at 350° for 50 minutes. Uncover; bake 10-15 minutes longer or until a knife inserted near the center comes out clean. Sprinkle with parsley. **Yield:** 12 servings.

CORNY EGGS

Pamelyn Hooley, Goshen, Indiana

I developed this recipe myself a few years ago. The bacon, onion, green pepper, hominy, eggs and cheese makes it a great combination for brunch. I like to serve portions of it along with slices of toast and glasses of juice.

1/2 pound sliced bacon, diced
1/4 cup chopped onion
1/4 cup chopped green pepper
12 eggs, beaten
1 can (15-1/2 ounces) hominy,
    drained
1/2 cup sour cream
1/4 teaspoon pepper
1 cup (4 ounces) shredded cheddar
    cheese

In a large skillet, cook bacon over medium heat until crisp; remove to paper towels. Drain, reserving 1 tablespoon drippings. In the drippings, saute onion and green pepper for 2-3 minutes or until tender. Add bacon.

In a large bowl, combine the eggs, hominy, sour cream and pepper; stir until blended. Pour over bacon mixture; cook and stir over medium heat until eggs are set. Sprinkle with cheese. **Yield:** 6-8 servings.

rest in a warm place for 20 minutes.

Punch dough down. Turn onto a floured surface; roll into a 22-in. x 14-in. rectangle. For filling, combine butter, confectioners' sugar and nuts. Spread lengthwise over half of the dough. Fold dough over filling, forming a 22-in. x 7-in. rectangle. Cut into 7-in. x 3/4-in. strips. Twist each strip 4 or 5 times and shape into a ring. Pinch ends together. Place on two greased 15-in. x 10-in. x 1-in. baking pans. Cover and let rise for 30 minutes or until doubled.

Bake at 375° for 17-20 minutes or until golden brown. Remove to wire racks. Meanwhile, in a saucepan, combine glaze ingredients over medium heat. Bring to boil; boil and stir for 3 minutes or until thickened. Remove from the heat. Drizzle over warm rolls. **Yield:** about 2 dozen.

ORANGE-HAZELNUT SPIRAL ROLLS
(Pictured above)

Loraine Meyer, Bend, Oregon

By adapting a popular coffee cake recipe, I came up with these scrumptious rolls. I make them for family throughout the year.

　　5 to 5-1/2 cups all-purpose flour
　　1 cup mashed potato flakes
　1/4 cup sugar
　　2 packages (1/4 ounce *each*) quick-rise
　　　yeast
　　1 teaspoon salt
　　2 teaspoons grated orange peel
　　1 cup milk
　1/2 cup butter, cubed
　1/2 cup sour cream
　1/4 cup water
　　2 eggs
FILLING:
　1/3 cup butter, softened
　　1 cup confectioners' sugar
　　1 cup ground hazelnuts
GLAZE:
　1/2 cup sugar
　1/4 cup orange juice concentrate
　1/4 cup sour cream
　　2 tablespoons butter

In a large mixing bowl, combine 4 cups flour, potato flakes, sugar, yeast, salt and orange peel. In saucepan, heat milk, butter, sour cream and water to 120°-130°. Add to dry ingredients; beat just until moistened. Add eggs; beat until smooth. Stir in enough remaining flour to form stiff dough.

Turn onto floured surface; knead until smooth and elastic, about 6-8 minutes. Place in greased bowl, turning once to grease top. Cover; let dough

HAM 'N' CORN FRITTERS
(Pictured below)

Nelda Cronbaugh, Belle Plaine, Iowa

Here's an old-fashioned recipe that's welcome at any meal. The pretty golden fritters are a perfect addition to a down-home breakfast or brunch in place of typical pancakes.

　　2 eggs
　1/3 cup milk
1-1/4 cups all-purpose flour
　　1 tablespoon sugar
　　2 teaspoons baking powder
　1/2 teaspoon salt
Dash pepper
　　1 cup fresh *or* frozen corn, cooked
　　　and drained
　　1 cup chopped fully cooked ham
Oil for deep-fat frying

26

Separate eggs; let stand at room temperature for 30 minutes. In a mixing bowl, beat egg yolks until slightly thickened. Beat in milk.

Combine the flour, sugar, baking powder, salt and pepper; add to yolk mixture and mix well. Stir in the corn and ham. In a small mixing bowl, beat egg whites on high speed until stiff peaks form. Fold into the corn mixture.

In an electric skillet or deep-fat fryer, heat oil to 375°. Drop batter by heaping tablespoonfuls, a few at a time, into hot oil. Fry until golden brown, about 1 minute on each side, turning with a slotted spoon. Drain on paper towels. **Yield:** 2 dozen.

PEACH COFFEE CAKE

Barbara Gerriets, Emporia, Kansas

This recipe has been a family favorite for many years. I especially like making it for Christmas.

  2 packages (1/4 ounce *each*) active dry
    yeast
1/2 cup warm water (110° to 115°)
1/2 cup warm milk (110° to 115°)
1/2 cup butter, softened
1/2 cup sugar
  2 teaspoons salt
  3 eggs
  5 to 5-1/2 cups all-purpose flour
FILLING:
1/4 cup butter, melted
1-1/2 cups peach preserves
  1 cup chopped pecans
2/3 cup sugar
  2 teaspoons ground cinnamon
GLAZE:
1-1/2 cups confectioners' sugar
1-1/2 teaspoons vanilla extract
  2 to 3 tablespoons milk

In a mixing bowl, dissolve yeast in water. Add the milk, butter, sugar, salt, eggs and 2 cups flour; beat on low speed for 3 minutes. Stir in enough remaining flour to form a soft dough.

Turn onto a floured surface; knead until smooth and elastic, about 6-8 minutes. Place in a greased bowl, turning once to grease top. Cover and let rise in a warm place until doubled, about 1 hour.

Punch dough down. Turn onto a lightly floured surface; divide in half. Roll each portion into a 20-in. x 10-in. rectangle. Spread with butter; top with preserves and pecans. Combine sugar and cinnamon; sprinkle over the top. Roll up jelly-roll style, starting at a long end. Pinch seams to seal and tuck ends under. Place seam side down on a greased baking sheet, curving ends to make a U shape. With scissors, make cuts every 1-1/2 in.

Cover and let rise in a warm place for 45 minutes. Bake at 350° for 25-30 minutes or until golden brown. Remove from pans to wire racks. Combine the glaze ingredients; drizzle over warm coffee cakes. Cool. **Yield:** 2 coffee cakes.

SPINACH FETA STRATA

(Pictured above)

Pat Lane, Pullman, Washington

This is a fairly new recipe for me, but my family loved it the first time I made it. A friend shared it with me.

 10 slices French bread (1 inch thick) *or* 6
    croissants, split
  6 eggs
1-1/2 cups milk
  1 package (10 ounces) frozen chopped
    spinach, thawed and squeezed dry
1/2 teaspoon salt
1/4 teaspoon ground nutmeg
1/4 teaspoon pepper
1-1/2 cups (6 ounces) shredded Monterey
    Jack cheese
  1 cup crumbled feta cheese *or* shredded
    mozzarella cheese

In a greased 13-in. x 9-in. x 2-in. baking dish, arrange French bread or croissant halves with sides overlapping. In a bowl, combine the eggs, milk, spinach, salt, nutmeg and pepper; pour over bread. Sprinkle with cheeses. Cover and refrigerate for 8 hours or overnight.

Remove from the refrigerator 30 minutes before baking. Bake, uncovered, at 350° for 40-45 minutes or until lightly browned. Serve warm. **Yield:** 12 servings.

OMELET BISCUIT CUPS

(Pictured below)

Leila Zimmer, York, South Carolina

My husband's a busy farmer and sometimes eats his breakfast on the run. He's able to take these omelet biscuit cups with him in his truck or tractor cab.

    1 tube (12 ounces) large refrigerated
      buttermilk biscuits
    4 eggs
1/4 cup milk
1/8 teaspoon salt
1/8 teaspoon pepper
    1 cup diced fully cooked ham
3/4 cup shredded cheddar cheese, *divided*
1/3 cup chopped canned mushrooms
    1 tablespoon butter

Press biscuits onto the bottom and up the sides of greased muffin cups; set aside. In a large bowl, beat the eggs, milk, salt and pepper. Add ham, 1/4 cup cheese and mushrooms; mix well. In a skillet, melt butter; add the egg mixture. Cook and stir until eggs are nearly set. Spoon into biscuit cups.

Bake at 375° for 10-15 minutes or until biscuits are golden brown. Sprinkle with the remaining cheese. Bake 2 minutes longer or until cheese is melted. **Yield:** 5 servings.

SOUR CREAM BANANA BREAD

Marge Schoessler, Warden, Washington

This recipe is very quick and easy to prepare (as well as light). I bake several at once and store them in the freezer.

✓ **Uses less fat, sugar or salt. Includes Nutritional Analysis and Diabetic Exchanges.**

1-1/2 cups all-purpose flour
    1 cup sugar
    1 teaspoon baking soda
1/2 teaspoon salt
    1 cup mashed ripe bananas (about 3
      medium)
1/2 cup egg substitute
1/2 cup canola oil
1/2 cup fat-free sour cream
    1 teaspoon vanilla extract

Coat a 9-in. x 5-in. x 3-in. loaf pan with non-stick cooking spray and dust with flour; set aside. In a large bowl, combine the flour, sugar, baking soda and salt. Combine the bananas, egg substitute, oil, sour cream and vanilla; stir into the dry ingredients just until moistened.

Pour into prepared pan. Bake at 350° for 55-65 minutes or until a toothpick comes out clean. Cool for 10 minutes before removing from pan to a wire rack. **Yield:** 1 loaf (18 slices).

Nutritional Analysis: One slice equals 186 calories, 7 g fat (1 g saturated fat), 1 mg cholesterol, 332 mg sodium, 28 g carbohydrate, 1 g fiber, 3 g protein. **Diabetic Exchanges:** 1 starch, 1 fruit, 1 fat.

ZUCCHINI YEAST BREAD

Marion Lowery, Medford, Oregon

This recipe combines the texture of sweet dough bread and the flavor of zucchini bread. It's wonderful toasted for breakfast.

    1 tablespoon active dry yeast
1/2 cup warm water (110° to 115°)
1/3 cup warm milk (110° to 115°)
1/3 cup sugar
    3 tablespoons butter, softened
    3 tablespoons grated orange peel
1/2 teaspoon salt
1-1/2 cups shredded unpeeled
      zucchini
1/3 cup raisins
1-1/2 cups whole wheat flour
    2 teaspoons ground cardamom
1-2/3 to 2-1/3 cups all-purpose flour

In a large mixing bowl, dissolve yeast in warm water. Beat in the milk, sugar, butter, orange peel and salt; mix well. Add the zucchini, raisins, whole wheat flour, cardamom and enough all-purpose flour to form a soft dough.

Turn onto a floured surface; knead until smooth and elastic, about 6-8 minutes. Place in a greased bowl, turning once to grease top. Cover and let rise in a warm place until doubled, about 1-1/4 hours.

Punch dough down; shape into a loaf. Place in a greased 9-in. x 5-in. x 3-in. loaf pan. Cover and let rise until doubled, about 45 minutes. Bake at 375° for 40-45 minutes or until golden brown. Remove from pan to cool on a wire rack. **Yield:** 1 loaf.

POTATO VEGETABLE QUICHE

(Pictured above)

Lori Hiscock, Kalamazoo, Michigan

Of all the recipes Mom used to make, this was one of her best. When I make it, I'm reminded of home.

3 cups frozen shredded hash brown potatoes, thawed

1 egg, lightly beaten
1/4 cup grated Parmesan cheese
FILLING:
1-1/2 cups sliced zucchini
3/4 cup diced sweet red pepper
1 tablespoon butter
1/2 cup diced fully cooked ham
2 eggs, lightly beaten
1/4 cup milk
1-1/2 teaspoons dried basil
Salt and pepper to taste
3/4 cup shredded Monterey Jack cheese

In a bowl, combine the hash browns, egg and Parmesan cheese. Press onto the bottom and up the sides of a greased 9-in. pie plate. Bake at 400° for 16-20 minutes or until golden brown.

Meanwhile, in a skillet, saute zucchini and red pepper in butter until crisp-tender. Remove from the heat; stir in the ham, eggs, milk, basil, salt and pepper. Pour into crust. Sprinkle with Monterey Jack cheese.

Bake at 400° for 15-20 minutes or until a knife inserted near the center comes out clean. Let stand for 5 minutes before cutting. **Yield:** 4-6 servings.

wire rack. Repeat with remaining batter. When cool, stack crepes with paper towels in between.

In a small skillet, cook butter and brown sugar over medium heat until sugar is dissolved. Add bananas; toss to coat. Remove from the heat; keep warm.

In a small bowl, combine sour cream and confectioners' sugar. Spread over each crepe. Spoon banana filling over sour cream filling; sprinkle with almonds. Roll up crepes; sprinkle with additional confectioners' sugar and toasted almonds. **Yield:** 1 dozen.

BACON-ONION CRESCENT BUNS

(Pictured below)

Helen Wilson, San Benito, Texas

These savory crescents are a hit with everyone. They're very tasty served alongside many main dishes as well as for brunch.

      4-3/4 to 5-1/4 cups all-purpose flour
      1/2 cup sugar
        1 package (1/4 ounce) active dry yeast
      1/2 teaspoon salt
        1 cup milk
      1/2 cup butter, cubed
      1/2 teaspoon caraway seeds
        3 eggs
        1 pound sliced bacon, diced
        1 small onion, finely chopped
      1/8 teaspoon white pepper
        2 tablespoons water

CREAMY BANANA CREPES

(Pictured above)

Parrish Smith, Lincoln, Nebraska

My husband and I enjoy taking turns fixing weekend breakfasts. These crepes are frequently on our menus. The sweet-and-sour banana filling is delicious. You'll want to have them for lunch, dinner and dessert!

      3/4 cup water
      3/4 cup milk
        2 eggs
        2 tablespoons butter, melted
      1/2 teaspoon vanilla extract
        1 cup all-purpose flour
        1 tablespoon sugar
      1/2 teaspoon salt
    BANANA FILLING:
        3 tablespoons butter
        3 tablespoons brown sugar
        3 medium firm bananas, cut
          into 1/4-inch slices
    SOUR CREAM FILLING:
        1 cup (8 ounces) sour cream
        2 tablespoons confectioners' sugar
      1/2 cup slivered almonds, toasted
    Additional confectioners' sugar and toasted
      almonds

In a mixing bowl, combine the water, milk, eggs, butter and vanilla. Combine the flour, sugar and salt; add to milk mixture and mix well. Cover and refrigerate for 1 hour.

Heat an 8-in. nonstick skillet over medium heat; pour 3 tablespoons batter into the center of skillet. Lift and tilt pan to evenly coat bottom. Cook for 1-2 minutes or until top appears dry; turn and cook 15-20 seconds longer. Remove to a

In a mixing bowl, combine 2 cups flour, sugar, yeast and salt. In a saucepan, heat the milk and butter to 120°-130°. Add to dry ingredients; beat on medium speed for 2 minutes. Add caraway seeds and 2 eggs; mix well. Stir in enough remaining flour to form a stiff dough. Turn onto a floured surface; knead until smooth and elastic, about 6-8 minutes. Place in a greased bowl, turning once to grease top. Cover and let rise in a warm place until doubled, about 1 hour.

Meanwhile, in a large skillet, cook bacon over medium heat until crisp. Remove with a slotted spoon to paper towels. Saute onion in the drippings; remove onion with a slotted spoon and set aside. When cool, combine the bacon, onion and pepper; set aside.

Punch dough down. Turn onto a lightly floured surface; divide into four portions. Roll each into a 12-in. circle; cut into 12 wedges. Sprinkle a heaping teaspoonful of bacon mixture over each wedge. Roll up from the wide end. Place point end down 2 in. apart on greased baking sheets. Cover and let rise, about 30 minutes.

In a small bowl, beat water and remaining egg; brush over rolls. Bake at 350° for 12-14 minutes or until golden brown. Refrigerate leftovers. **Yield:** 4 dozen.

hot griddle. Turn when bubbles form on top; cook until second side is golden brown. Serve with blueberry sauce. **Yield:** 11 pancakes and 1-1/2 cups sauce.

BANANA PANCAKES

Helen Dresen, Cross Plains, Wisconsin

I prefer this recipe for pancakes to plain ones any day! The blueberry sauce is the perfect topper.

BLUEBERRY SAUCE:
    1 can (6 ounces) pineapple juice
    1 tablespoon quick-cooking tapioca
    2 tablespoons sugar
    2 cups fresh *or* frozen blueberries, thawed
PANCAKES:
    1 cup biscuit/baking mix
    1 egg, beaten
  1/2 cup milk
    1 teaspoon vanilla
    3 medium ripe bananas, cut into 1/4-inch slices

For the sauce, combine the pineapple juice and tapioca in a saucepan; let stand for 5 minutes. Stir in the sugar. Bring to a boil; cook and stir for 2 minutes or until slightly thickened. Add blueberries. Return to a boil; cook and stir for 5-10 minutes or until sauce reaches desired thickness.

For pancakes, in a large bowl, combine the biscuit mix, egg, milk and vanilla. Fold in the bananas. Pour batter by 1/4 cupfuls onto a greased

APRICOT-DATE MINI LOAVES

(Pictured above)

Marilyn Miner, Santa Margarita, California

By using a prepared muffin mix, it's easy to make a loaf of this apricot-date bread for yourself and extras to give to friends.

    1 package (19.1 ounces) cinnamon swirl muffin mix
  1/2 teaspoon baking powder
    2 eggs, lightly beaten
  2/3 cup orange juice
  1/2 cup chopped dried apricots
  1/2 cup chopped dates

Set aside cinnamon swirl and topping packets from muffin mix. In a bowl, combine the dry muffin mix and baking powder. Make a well in the center; add eggs and orange juice. Stir just until moistened. Fold in apricots and dates. Pour into four greased 5-3/4-in. x 3-in. x 2-in. loaf pans.

Squeeze contents of cinnamon swirl packet over batter; cut through with a knife to swirl. Sprinkle with the topping.

Bake at 350° for 25-28 minutes or until a toothpick inserted near the center comes out clean. Cool for 10 minutes before removing from pans to wire racks. **Yield:** 4 loaves.

The recipe for these pancakes developed several years ago when our four children were still living at home. It was one of their favorite breakfast items for many years.

> 3 cups biscuit/baking mix
> 2 tablespoons sugar
> 2 tablespoons cornmeal
> 2 eggs
> 2 cups milk
> 1 can (15-1/4 ounces) whole kernel corn, drained
> 3 bacon strips, cooked and crumbled
> Maple syrup

In a large bowl, combine the biscuit mix, sugar and cornmeal. Combine the eggs and milk; stir into dry ingredients just until moistened. Stir in corn and bacon.

Pour batter by 1/4 cupfuls onto a greased hot griddle. Turn when bubbles form on top; cook until second side is golden brown. Serve with syrup. **Yield:** about 20 pancakes.

ARTICHOKE CHEESE OVEN OMELET
(Pictured above)

Bonnie Hawkins, Burlington, Wisconsin

Every Saturday for 10 years, my husband has gotten together with his "breakfast club"—good friends who take turns cooking for the group in their homes. The "boys" all love his cheesy artichoke omelet, and he appreciates the easy cleanup.

> 3/4 cup salsa
> 1 can (14 ounces) water-packed artichoke hearts, drained and chopped
> 1 cup (4 ounces) shredded Monterey Jack cheese
> 1 cup (4 ounces) shredded cheddar cheese
> 1/4 cup grated Parmesan cheese
> 6 eggs, beaten
> 1 cup (8 ounces) sour cream
> Chopped fresh tomatoes, sliced ripe olives and minced chives, optional

Spread salsa in a greased 9-in. deep-dish pie plate. Top with the artichoke hearts and cheeses. In a bowl, whisk the eggs and sour cream. Pour over the cheeses.

Bake, uncovered, at 350° for 25-30 minutes or until a knife inserted near the center comes out clean. Let stand for 5 minutes before cutting. Garnish with tomatoes, olives and chives if desired. **Yield:** 6-8 servings.

CORN AND BACON PANCAKES
Pearl Sheler, Milan, Michigan

RAISIN SWEET POTATO BREAD
(Pictured below)

Gloria Wilson, Florence, Alabama

This is a tasty bread with a moist center and crunchy crust. My mother asked me to make it for her 90th birthday party. Everyone asked for the recipe.

> 2 cups self-rising flour
> 2 cups sugar

3 teaspoons ground cinnamon
1/2 teaspoon ground nutmeg
1/4 teaspoon ground cloves
1-1/2 cups mashed cooked sweet potatoes
1 cup vegetable oil
3 eggs
3 teaspoons vanilla extract
3/4 cup raisins

In a bowl, combine the flour, sugar, cinnamon, nutmeg and cloves. Combine the sweet potatoes, oil, eggs and vanilla; stir into the dry ingredients just until moistened. Fold in raisins. Transfer to two greased 8-in. x 4-in. x 2-in. loaf pans.

Bake at 350° for 55-60 minutes or until a toothpick inserted near the center comes out clean. Cool for 10 minutes before removing from pans to wire racks. **Yield:** 2 loaves.

Editor's Note: For *each* cup of self-rising flour, place 1-1/2 teaspoons baking powder and 1/2 teaspoon salt in a measuring cup. Add all-purpose flour to measure 1 cup.

Bake at 350° for 40-45 minutes or until golden brown. Remove from pans to wire racks to cool. **Yield:** 2 loaves.

Maple Oatmeal Bread

(Pictured above right)

Marian Tobin, Underhill, Vermont

This is one of my favorite recipes, especially since it features maple syrup. Vermont produces more maple syrup than any other state.

1 cup hot brewed coffee
3/4 cup boiling water
1/2 cup maple syrup
1/3 cup vegetable oil
1 cup old-fashioned oats
1/2 cup sugar
2 teaspoons salt
2 packages (1/4 ounce *each*) active dry yeast
1/4 cup warm water (110° to 115°)
2 eggs, lightly beaten
5-1/2 to 6 cups bread flour

In a bowl, combine the first seven ingredients. Cool to 110°-115°. In a large mixing bowl, dissolve yeast in warm water. Add the oat mixture, eggs and 2 cups flour; mix well. Stir in enough remaining flour to form a soft dough.

Turn onto a floured surface; knead until smooth and elastic, about 6-8 minutes. Place in a greased bowl, turning once to grease top. Cover; let rise in a warm place until doubled, about 1 hour.

Punch dough down. Turn onto a lightly floured surface; divide in half. Shape into loaves. Place in two greased 9-in. x 5-in. x 3-in. loaf pans. Cover and let rise until doubled, about 30 minutes.

Simple Souffle

Rosemarie McCormack, Pagosa Springs, Colorado

My children, who are vegetarian, rave about this souffle. Plus, I can make it for breakfast, brunch or as a side dish.

 Uses less fat, sugar or salt. Includes Nutritional Analysis and Diabetic Exchanges.

1 can (10-3/4 ounces) reduced-fat reduced-sodium cream of mushroom soup, undiluted
1 cup (4 ounces) shredded reduced-fat cheddar cheese
3 eggs, *separated*
3 egg whites
1 tablespoon fine dry bread crumbs

In a saucepan, combine soup and cheese. Cook and stir over low heat until the cheese is melted. Cool. In a mixing bowl, beat egg yolks until thick and lemon-colored; stir into soup mixture.

In another mixing bowl, beat six egg whites on high speed until stiff peaks form; fold into soup mixture. Spoon into a 2-qt. straight-sided baking dish coated with nonstick cooking spray and dusted with bread crumbs.

Bake, uncovered, at 375° for 40-45 minutes or until the souffle is risen and golden brown. Serve immediately. **Yield:** 4 servings.

Nutritional Analysis: One serving equals 202 calories, 10 g fat (5 g saturated fat), 179 mg cholesterol, 640 mg sodium, 11 g carbohydrate, 2 g fiber, 15 g protein. **Diabetic Exchanges:** 2 lean meat, 1 fat, 1/2 starch.

FINE DINING *is a breeze when you have satisfying recipes that are easy to prepare and oh, so tasty!*

ERUPTING WITH FLAVOR. From top to bottom: Lemonade Chicken and Aloha Pork Chops (recipes on p. 35).

Main Dishes

ALOHA PORK CHOPS

(Pictured at left)

Betty Jean Nichols, Eugene, Oregon

I enjoy adapting recipes to suit my tastes. In this one, I give everyday pork chops extra flair by simmering them in a tangy sauce.

      4 boneless pork loin chops (3/4 inch thick)
      1 tablespoon lemon-pepper seasoning
      1 teaspoon plus 2 tablespoons olive oil, *divided*
      1 cup sweet-and-sour sauce
      1 can (20 ounces) pineapple chunks, drained
   1/2 medium green pepper, julienned
   1/2 cup chopped red onion
      6 cups cold cooked rice
   1/4 cup stir-fry sauce
Parsley, optional

Sprinkle pork chops with lemon-pepper. In a large skillet, brown chops on both sides in 1 teaspoon oil over medium-high heat; remove and set aside. Drain skillet; add sweet-and-sour sauce and pineapple chunks. Bring to a boil. Reduce heat; return chops to skillet. Simmer, uncovered, for 5 minutes or until meat juices run clear.

Meanwhile, in another skillet, saute the green pepper and onion in remaining oil for 2 minutes. Add rice and stir-fry sauce; cook and stir for 4 minutes or until lightly browned. Transfer to a serving platter; top with pork mixture. Garnish with parsley if desired. **Yield:** 4 servings.

LEMONADE CHICKEN

(Pictured at left)

Olivia Logan, Delphi, Indiana

It doesn't take a seasoned cook to turn out this scrumptious entree. Try it with limeade or orange juice instead.

      1 can (12 ounces) frozen lemonade concentrate, thawed
      2 tablespoons brown sugar
      2 tablespoons soy sauce

      1 teaspoon garlic powder
      1 teaspoon chopped fresh mint *or* 1/4 teaspoon dried mint flakes
      6 bone-in chicken breast halves (about 4 pounds)

In a large resealable bag, combine the first five ingredients. Remove half of the marinade to a small bowl; cover and refrigerate for basting. Add chicken to the bag; seal and turn to coat. Refrigerate overnight, turning occasionally.

Drain and discard marinade from chicken. Grill, covered, over medium heat for 20 minutes, turning occasionally. Baste with reserved marinade. Grill 5-10 minutes longer or until juices run clear, basting and turning several times. **Yield:** 6 servings.

MICROWAVE MEAT LOAF

Becky Cain, Hutchinson, Kansas

I often fix this meat loaf since it's such a time-saver. It's also great in summer because I don't need to heat up the oven.

      1 can (8 ounces) tomato sauce
   1/4 cup packed brown sugar
      1 teaspoon prepared mustard
      1 egg, lightly beaten
      1 medium onion, chopped
   1/4 cup cracker crumbs (about 6 crackers)
      1 teaspoon salt
   1/4 teaspoon pepper
1-1/2 pounds ground beef

In a small bowl, combine tomato sauce, brown sugar and mustard; set aside. In a large bowl, combine the egg, onion, cracker crumbs, salt, pepper and 3/4 cup of the sauce mixture. Crumble beef over mixture and mix well.

Shape into a uniform round loaf in a greased microwave-safe 9-in. pie plate. Cover with waxed paper. Microwave on high for 20-22 minutes or until meat is no longer pink and a meat thermometer reads 160°, turning dish a quarter turn every 5 minutes. Drain; top with remaining sauce mixture. Let stand for 5 minutes before slicing. **Yield:** 6 servings.

Editor's Note: This recipe was tested in an 850-watt microwave.

On a lightly floured surface, roll pastry into a 10-in. square. Sprinkle with remaining rosemary; press into pastry. Place over filling; flute edges and cut slits in top. Brush with egg. Bake, uncovered, at 400° for 25-30 minutes or until crust is golden brown. **Yield:** 6 servings.

MACARONI 'N' CHEESE PIZZA
(Pictured below)

Edna Havens, Bartlesville, Oklahoma

Here's a fun and flavorful dish that will please those who like pizza and macaroni and cheese. It will likely top the popularity poll for most-requested recipes. Feel free to experiment with other pizza toppings.

     8 ounces uncooked elbow macaroni
     3 eggs
     1 cup (4 ounces) shredded cheddar
         cheese
     1 pound ground beef
  3/4 cup chopped onion
     1 can (15 ounces) pizza sauce
     1 can (4 ounces) mushroom stems and
         pieces, drained
    28 pepperoni slices
     1 cup (4 ounces) shredded Mexican
         cheese blend *or* additional cheddar
         cheese

Cook macaroni according to package directions; drain. In a bowl, beat the eggs; stir in cheddar cheese and macaroni. Spread onto a greased 14-in. pizza pan. Bake at 375° for 15 minutes.

VEGETABLE BEEF POTPIE
(Pictured above)

Trudy Williams, Shannonville, Ontario

This old-fashioned main dish is tried-and-true comfort food. The golden crust and savory filling make such a pretty presentation.

     1 pound ground beef
  1/2 teaspoon pepper
  1/4 teaspoon salt
     2 cups frozen pearl onions, thawed
1-1/2 cups baby carrots, halved
     1 medium parsnip, peeled, halved
         lengthwise and sliced
     2 tablespoons butter
     3 garlic cloves, minced
  1/4 cup all-purpose flour
1-1/3 cups beef broth
4-1/2 teaspoons red wine vinegar
4-1/2 teaspoons Dijon mustard
     3 teaspoons minced fresh rosemary,
         divided
     1 sheet frozen puff pastry, thawed
     1 egg, beaten

In a large skillet, cook beef over medium heat until no longer pink; drain. Stir in pepper and salt; remove and set aside. In the same skillet, saute the onions, carrots and parsnip in butter for 7 minutes. Add garlic; cook 2 minutes longer or until vegetables are crisp-tender. Stir in flour.

Combine the broth, vinegar and mustard; gradually stir into vegetable mixture. Bring to a boil; cook and stir for 2-3 minutes or until thickened. Stir in beef mixture and 2 teaspoons rosemary; heat through. Transfer to a greased 8-in. square baking dish.

Meanwhile, in a large skillet, cook beef and onion over medium heat until meat is no longer pink; drain. Add pizza sauce; mix well. Spread over macaroni crust. Sprinkle with mushrooms, pepperoni and Mexican cheese.

Bake for 15-20 minutes or until the cheese is melted. Let stand for 5-10 minutes before slicing. **Yield:** 6-8 servings.

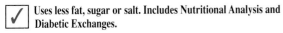

PORK WITH SOUR CREAM SALSA

Lea Baker, Pacific Grove, California

This pork chop supper packs just the right amount of zip. The salsa is a great accompaniment to the pork.

> ✓ **Uses less fat, sugar or salt. Includes Nutritional Analysis and Diabetic Exchanges.**

  1 tablespoon chili powder
  1 tablespoon red wine vinegar
1/4 teaspoon ground cumin
  6 boneless pork loin chops (4 ounces *each*)
SALSA:
  2 medium tomatoes, chopped
  1 can (4 ounces) chopped green chilies, drained
1/2 cup minced fresh cilantro
1/2 cup chopped onion
  2 garlic cloves, minced
3/4 teaspoon salt
1/2 teaspoon red wine vinegar
1/2 teaspoon olive *or* canola oil
1/4 teaspoon pepper
1/4 teaspoon crushed red pepper flakes
1/8 teaspoon ground cumin
1/2 cup fat-free sour cream

Combine the chili powder, vinegar and cumin; rub over pork chops. In a bowl, combine the first 11 salsa ingredients; set aside. Broil chops 4 in. from the heat for 6 minutes on each side or until no longer pink and juices run clear. Fold sour cream into salsa; serve with pork. **Yield:** 6 servings.

Nutritional Analysis: One serving (1 pork chop with 1/4 cup salsa) equals 214 calories, 9 g fat (3 g saturated fat), 60 mg cholesterol, 407 mg sodium, 9 g carbohydrate, 1 g fiber, 23 g protein. **Diabetic Exchanges:** 3 lean meat, 1/2 starch.

BEEF CABBAGE ROLL-UPS

(Pictured above right)

Irma Finley, Lockwood, Missouri

Cooking up original recipes is a hobby of mine. My version of classic cabbage rolls is delicious served over rice or noodles.

  1 head cabbage
  1 large potato, peeled and shredded
  1 large carrot, shredded
1/2 cup finely chopped celery
1/2 cup finely chopped green pepper
1/2 cup finely chopped onion
  2 eggs, beaten
  2 garlic cloves, minced
3/4 teaspoon salt
1/2 teaspoon pepper
  1 pound ground beef
  2 cans (8 ounces *each*) tomato sauce
1/2 teaspoon dried basil
1/2 teaspoon dried parsley flakes

Cook cabbage in boiling water just until the leaves fall off head. Cut out the thick vein from the bottom of 12 large leaves, making a V-shaped cut; set aside. (Refrigerate remaining cabbage for another use.)

In a large bowl, combine the potato, carrot, celery, green pepper, onion, eggs, garlic, salt and pepper. Crumble beef over mixture; mix well. Shape into 12 logs. Place one log on each cabbage leaf; overlap cut ends of leaf. Fold in sides, beginning from the cut end. Roll up completely to enclose filling. Secure with a toothpick.

Place in a greased 13-in. x 9-in. x 2-in. baking dish. Pour tomato sauce over roll-ups. Sprinkle with basil and parsley.

Cover and bake at 350° for 30-35 minutes or until a meat thermometer reads 160° and the cabbage is tender. **Yield:** 6 servings.

In a small bowl, combine the cornstarch and water until smooth; stir into the stew. Bring to a boil; cook and stir for 2 minutes or until thickened. **Yield:** 6 servings.

Nutritional Analysis: One serving (1-1/3 cups) equals 246 calories, 6 g fat (3 g saturated fat), 37 mg cholesterol, 659 mg sodium, 29 g carbohydrate, 5 g fiber, 18 g protein. **Diabetic Exchanges:** 2 lean meat, 2 vegetable, 1 starch.

BEEF-STUFFED POTATOES

(Pictured below)

Kay Scheidler, Bull Shoals, Arkansas

This is a stuffed potato with a twist. Teenagers like the flavor the green chilies and cheese add.

- 6 medium baking potatoes
- 1 pound ground beef
- 2 tablespoons chopped onion
- 1/3 cup sour cream
- 1 can (4 ounces) chopped green chilies
- 3 tablespoons butter
- 1 tablespoon Worcestershire sauce
- 1 teaspoon salt
- 1/2 teaspoon garlic powder
- 1/2 teaspoon chili powder
- 3/4 cup shredded cheddar cheese

Bake potatoes at 375° for 1 hour or until tender. Cool. Meanwhile, in a large skillet, cook the beef and onion over medium heat until the meat is no longer pink; drain.

Cut a thin slice off the top of each potato. Carefully scoop out pulp, leaving a thin shell; place pulp in a bowl. Add sour cream, chilies, but-

ROOT VEGETABLE BEEF STEW

(Pictured above)

Mary Rea, Orangeville, Ontario

I found this recipe in our local paper a number of years ago. It's so satisfying on a cold winter or fall day.

✓ **Uses less fat, sugar or salt. Includes Nutritional Analysis and Diabetic Exchanges.**

- 1 pound lean ground beef
- 1 medium onion, chopped
- 2 cans (14-1/2 ounces *each*) reduced-sodium beef broth
- 1 medium sweet potato, peeled and cubed
- 1 cup cubed carrot
- 1 cup cubed peeled rutabaga
- 1 cup cubed peeled parsnips
- 1 cup cubed peeled potato
- 2 tablespoons tomato paste
- 1 teaspoon Worcestershire sauce
- 1/2 teaspoon dried thyme
- 1/4 teaspoon salt
- 1/4 teaspoon pepper
- 1 tablespoon cornstarch
- 2 tablespoons water

In a Dutch oven or large kettle, cook beef and onion over medium heat until meat is no longer pink; drain. Add the broth, vegetables, tomato paste, Worcestershire sauce, thyme, salt and pepper. Bring to a boil. Reduce the heat; cover and simmer for 30-40 minutes or until the vegetables are tender.

ter, Worcestershire sauce, salt, garlic powder and chili powder; mash or beat. Stir in meat mixture until combined. Stuff into potato shells.

Place on an ungreased baking sheet. Sprinkle with cheese. Bake at 350° for 10-15 minutes or until heated through. **Yield:** 6 servings.

⊪⊪⊪⊪⊪⊪⊪⊪⊪⊪⊪⊪
Cranberry Kraut Meatballs
(Pictured at right)

Anne Karth, Mt. Prospect, Illinois

The combination of cranberries and sauerkraut gives these meatballs a different flavor.

2-1/2 pounds ground beef
   1 envelope onion soup mix
   1 cup dry bread crumbs
   1 can (16 ounces) whole-berry cranberry sauce
   1 can (14 ounces) sauerkraut, rinsed and drained
1-1/3 cups water
   1 bottle (12 ounces) chili sauce
3/4 cup packed brown sugar
Hot mashed potatoes

In a bowl, combine the beef, soup mix and bread crumbs. Shape into 18 meatballs. Place in an un- greased 13-in. x 9-in. x 2-in. baking dish. In a large saucepan, combine the cranberry sauce, sauerkraut, water, chili sauce and brown sugar. Bring to a boil. Pour over meatballs.

Bake, uncovered, at 350° for 1-1/2 hours or un- til meat is no longer pink. Serve with mashed potatoes. **Yield:** 6 servings.

Great Ground Beef Tips

• Sometimes I use my favorite meatball recipe to make a meat loaf instead.
—*Elaine Schulmeister, Fayette, Iowa*

• A small ice cream scoop will make perfect meatballs that are all the same size.
—*Celeste Cornish, Yucca Valley, California*

• To vary the taste of meat loaf, I like to combine ground beef and ground venison.
—*Leann Williams, Beaverton, Oregon*

• It's easier to roll up a meat loaf jelly-roll style if I roll the meat mixture out on waxed paper. That way, I can lift up the edge of the paper to get it started. —*Ann Bjornson New Norway, Alberta*

• When I make sloppy joes I like to serve them in hot dog buns because they are less messy to eat this way. —*Rosella Buehrer Stryker, Ohio*

• My Mexican hash recipe is also a great filling for stuffed peppers. —*Marianne Hay Lincoln, Illinois*

• I put meatballs on a tray and freeze until they are solid. Then I place them in a large freezer bag and take out only as many as I need each time. —*Christeen DeAnn Mosher, Winslow, Maine*

• For an extra surprise, I sometimes put pieces of string cheese in the middle of my meat loaf before baking it. —*Debbie Hahn Sauk Rapids, Minnesota*

for 10 minutes.

Spread about 1/4 cup barbecue sauce in a greased 13-in. x 9-in. x 2-in. baking dish. Layer with three noodles and half of the beef. Spread with half of the remaining barbecue sauce; sprinkle with half of the mozzarella, cheddar and Colby cheeses. Repeat layers.

Combine cottage cheese and egg; spoon evenly over the top. Bake, uncovered, at 350° for 50-60 minutes or until lightly browned. Let stand for about 10 minutes before cutting. **Yield:** 8 servings.

CREOLE FLOUNDER WITH SEAFOOD SAUCE

(Pictured below)

Melinda Sue Daenen, Pineville, Louisiana

This is one of my family's favorite Creole dishes. The recipe can be made with flounder or sole fillets, but I sometimes use locally caught kingfish bass.

- 1 cup diced onion
- 1 cup diced green pepper
- 2 garlic cloves, minced
- 1/2 cup minced fresh parsley
- 1/2 cup butter
- 1/4 cup all-purpose flour
- 2 cups half-and-half cream
- 8 ounces Mexican process cheese (Velveeta), cubed
- 2 tablespoons lemon *or* lime juice

BARBECUE LASAGNA

(Pictured above)

Hazel Selle, Miles City, Montana

This hearty dish is a nice change of pace from more traditional lasagna. The barbecue flavor is fantastic!

- 1-1/2 pounds ground beef
- 1 cup ketchup
- 1 medium green pepper, chopped
- 1 medium onion, chopped
- 1/2 cup packed brown sugar
- 1/4 cup lemon juice
- 2 tablespoons cider vinegar
- 2 tablespoons Worcestershire sauce
- 1 tablespoon prepared mustard
- 1 garlic clove, minced
- 1 teaspoon salt
- 1/2 teaspoon pepper
- 1/8 teaspoon chili powder
- 1/8 teaspoon lemon-pepper seasoning
- 6 lasagna noodles, cooked and drained
- 2 cups (8 ounces) shredded mozzarella cheese
- 1 cup (4 ounces) shredded sharp cheddar cheese
- 1 cup (4 ounces) shredded Colby *or* mild cheddar cheese
- 1 cup (8 ounces) small-curd cottage cheese
- 1 egg

In a skillet, cook beef over medium heat until no longer pink; drain. For barbecue sauce, combine the next 13 ingredients in a large saucepan. Bring to a boil. Reduce heat; simmer, uncovered,

2 cans (6 ounces *each*) crabmeat,
   drained, flaked and cartilage removed
   or 2 cups chopped imitation crabmeat
1/4 cup Creole mustard *or* other spicy
   mustard
8 flounder *or* sole fillets (about 2 pounds)
1-1/2 teaspoons Creole seasoning
2 pounds cooked shrimp, peeled and
   deveined

In a large skillet, saute the onion, green pepper, garlic and parsley in butter until tender. Stir in flour until blended. Gradually add the cream. Bring to a boil; cook and stir for 2 minutes or until thickened. Reduce heat. Stir in cheese and lemon juice; cook and stir until cheese is melted. Add crab. Cover and keep warm.

Spread mustard on both sides of fillets. Sprinkle with Creole seasoning. Place on a greased broiler pan. Broil 4-6 in. from the heat for 3-5 minutes on each side or until fish flakes easily with a fork. Top each fillet with four to five shrimp; serve over crab sauce. **Yield:** 4-5 servings.

fiber, 26 g protein. **Diabetic Exchanges:** 3 lean meat, 2 vegetable, 1/2 starch, 1/2 fat.

DEVILED SWISS STEAK

Melissa Gerken, Zumbrota, Minnesota

This main dish is satisfying all by itself. But you can also serve this Swiss steak over hot mashed potatoes, pasta or rice.

✓ Uses less fat, sugar or salt. Includes Nutritional Analysis and Diabetic Exchanges.

1/2 cup all-purpose flour
1 tablespoon ground mustard
1/2 teaspoon salt
1/8 teaspoon pepper
2 beef flank steaks (1 pound *each*),
   halved
2 tablespoons butter
1 cup thinly sliced onion
1 can (28 ounces) stewed tomatoes
2 tablespoons Worcestershire sauce
1 tablespoon brown sugar

In a large resealable plastic bag, combine the flour, mustard, salt and pepper. Add steaks and shake to coat. In a large nonstick skillet, brown steaks on both sides in butter. Transfer to a 5-qt. slow cooker. Top with onion.

In a bowl, combine the tomatoes, Worcestershire sauce and brown sugar; pour over meat and onion. Cover and cook on low for 6-8 hours or until meat is tender. **Yield:** 8 servings.

Nutritional Analysis: One serving equals 286 calories, 12 g fat (6 g saturated fat), 66 mg cholesterol, 575 mg sodium, 17 g carbohydrate, 2 g

HEARTY CHICKEN STRATA

(Pictured above)

Sara Yoder, Mount Hope, Ohio

My great-grandparents made this traditional Amish recipe on Sundays when they had company, and it's still one of my family's favorite dishes.

10 cups bread cubes (1/2-inch cubes)
2 cups diced cooked chicken
1 cup diced potatoes
1 cup diced celery
1/2 cup diced carrots
1/4 cup minced fresh parsley
4 cups milk
2 cups chicken broth
5 eggs, beaten
1/4 cup butter, melted
1 teaspoon salt
1/2 teaspoon pepper
1 to 2 jars (12 ounces *each*) chicken
   gravy, warmed, optional

Arrange bread cubes in a single layer on large baking sheets. Bake at 350° for 20-30 minutes until golden brown and crisp. Place in a large bowl; add the chicken, potatoes, celery, carrots and parsley. Combine the milk, broth, eggs, butter, salt and pepper; pour over bread mixture and stir to coat.

Transfer to a greased 13-in. x 9-in. x 2-in. baking dish. Bake, uncovered, at 350° for 45 minutes; stir. Bake 45 minutes longer or until a knife inserted near the center comes out clean. Serve with gravy if desired. **Yield:** 12-14 servings.

SHRIMP CREOLE
(Pictured below)

Johnnie McLeod, Bastrop, Louisiana

A true Cajun dish, this recipe is even better if refrigerated overnight to allow the flavors to blend.

　1/4 cup all-purpose flour
　1/2 cup vegetable oil
　　1 medium onion, chopped
　　1 medium green pepper, chopped
　　1 celery rib, chopped
　　1 garlic clove, minced
　　1 can (14-1/2 ounces) stewed tomatoes
　　1 can (6 ounces) tomato paste
　　4 bay leaves
　　1 tablespoon Worcestershire sauce
　1/2 teaspoon hot pepper sauce
Salt and pepper to taste
　　2 pounds fresh *or* frozen uncooked
　　　medium shrimp, peeled and deveined
Hot cooked rice

In a heavy skillet, combine the flour and oil until smooth. Cook and stir over medium heat until flour is a rich deep brown. Add the onion, green pepper, celery and garlic; cook until vegetables are tender, about 5 minutes. Stir in the tomatoes, tomato paste, bay leaves, Worcestershire sauce, hot pepper sauce, salt and pepper. Cover and simmer for 45-50 minutes.

Add shrimp. Simmer, uncovered, for 5-6 minutes or until shrimp turn pink. Discard bay leaves. Serve over rice. **Yield:** 4-6 servings.

GRILLED HERBED PORK ROAST

Marie Daley, Charles City, Iowa

During the summer, we enjoy cooking outdoors on our gas grill, and this is one of our favorite ways to prepare pork.

　　2 tablespoons dill seed, crushed
　　1 tablespoon fennel seed, crushed
　　1 teaspoon dried oregano
　　1 teaspoon lemon-pepper seasoning
　1/2 teaspoon garlic powder
　1/4 teaspoon onion powder
　　1 boneless pork loin roast (3-1/2 to 4
　　　pounds)

Combine the seasonings; rub over pork roast. Prepare grill for indirect heat; place a pan of water in the center.

Grill roast, covered, for 1-1/2 to 2 hours or until a meat thermometer reads 160°. Let stand for 10 minutes before slicing. **Yield:** 10-12 servings.

 ## CORN BREAD TACO BAKE

Vicki Good, Oscoda, Michigan

The corn bread and beef bake together in the same casserole dish, making this entree convenient. It's packed with tempting seasonings, and the cheese and onions make an attractive topping. Everyone who tries it likes it.

1-1/2 pounds ground beef
　　1 can (15-1/4 ounces) whole kernel corn,
　　　drained
　　1 can (8 ounces) tomato sauce
　1/2 cup water
　1/2 cup chopped green pepper
　　1 envelope taco seasoning
　　1 package (8-1/2 ounces) corn
　　　bread/muffin mix
　　1 can (2.8 ounces) french-fried onions,
　　　divided
　1/3 cup shredded cheddar cheese

In a large skillet, cook beef over medium heat until no longer pink; drain. Stir in corn, tomato sauce, water, green pepper and taco seasoning; mix well. Spoon into a greased 2-qt. baking dish.

Prepare corn bread mix according to package directions for corn bread. Stir in half of the onions. Spread over beef mixture.

Bake, uncovered, at 400° for 20 minutes. Sprinkle with cheese and remaining onions. Bake 3-5 minutes longer or until cheese is melted and a toothpick inserted into corn bread layer comes out clean. **Yield:** 6 servings.

COUNTRY CHICKEN

(Pictured above)

Lillian Beckham, San Antonio, Texas

I've been making this recipe for about 30 years, and it's still my husband's favorite chicken dinner.

      1 broiler/fryer chicken (3 to 4 pounds),
        cut up
  1/4 cup vegetable oil
  1/4 pound thick-sliced bacon, cut
        into 1-inch pieces
      1 cup chopped green pepper
  1/2 cup chopped onion
      2 cups water
      1 cup sliced fresh mushrooms
  1/2 cup diced fresh tomato
      2 tablespoons minced fresh parsley
      2 garlic cloves, minced
      1 bay leaf
      1 teaspoon salt
  1/4 teaspoon dried thyme
  1/4 teaspoon pepper
      3 tablespoons all-purpose flour
      3 tablespoons chicken broth
Hot cooked noodles

In a skillet, brown chicken in oil. Remove and set aside. Drain drippings. In same skillet, cook bacon over medium heat until almost crisp. Add green pepper and onion; saute until tender. Drain. Return chicken to skillet. Add next nine ingredients. Bring to a boil. Reduce heat; cover and simmer 30-40 minutes until meat juices run clear.

Remove chicken; keep warm. Discard bay leaf. In a small bowl, combine flour and broth until smooth. Stir into cooking juices. Bring to a boil; cook and stir 2 minutes or until thickened. Serve over chicken and noodles. **Yield:** 6 servings.

PORK ROAST WITH TANGY SAUCE

(Pictured below)

Janice Christofferson, Eagle River, Wisconsin

Everyday dinners are considered a hit in our home when I plan them around this hearty roast. The juicy meat and pleasant sauce are delectable together.

  2-1/2 teaspoons chili powder, ***divided***
    1/2 teaspoon salt
    1/2 teaspoon garlic salt
      1 rolled boneless pork loin roast
        (3-1/2 to 4 pounds)
      1 cup apple jelly
      1 cup ketchup
      2 tablespoons white vinegar

In a bowl, combine 1/2 teaspoon chili powder, salt and garlic salt; rub over roast. Place roast fat side up on a rack in a shallow roasting pan. Bake, uncovered, at 350° for 1-1/2 hours.

In a saucepan, combine jelly, ketchup, vinegar and remaining chili powder. Bring to a boil; cook and stir until jelly is melted and mixture is smooth. Reduce heat; simmer, uncovered, 2 minutes.

Brush 1/4 cup jelly mixture over roast. Bake 10-15 minutes longer until a meat thermometer reads 160°. Remove roast to a serving platter; let stand 10-15 minutes. Skim fat from drippings. Stir in remaining jelly mixture; heat through. Slice roast; serve with sauce. **Yield:** 10-12 servings.

wrap. Flatten to 3/4-in. thickness. Remove plastic; sprinkle with salt and pepper. Spoon stuffing over two tenderloins. Top with remaining tenderloins; tie with kitchen string.

Place on a rack in a shallow roasting pan. Cover and bake at 350° for 20 minutes. Brush with half of the molasses. Bake, uncovered, 45-50 minutes longer or until a meat thermometer inserted into meat reads 160°, brushing once with remaining molasses. Let stand for 5 minutes.

Meanwhile, in a small saucepan, combine cornstarch, bouillon and water until smooth. Bring to a boil; cook and stir for 2 minutes or until thickened. Add mushrooms and browning sauce if desired. Slice pork; serve with gravy. **Yield:** 8-10 servings.

Crawfish-Stuffed Pork Tenderloins

(Pictured above)

Kim Bunting, Colfax, Louisiana

This is a great main dish to serve to company. The meat is so moist and bakes to a nice golden brown, while the flavorful stuffing inside adds extra color.

    6 green onions, chopped
  3/4 cup chopped green pepper
  1/4 cup butter
  1/2 teaspoon chicken bouillon granules
  1/2 cup boiling water
    2 cups seasoned stuffing croutons
    1 pound cooked crawfish tails *or* cooked
      medium shrimp, peeled and deveined
    4 pork tenderloins (1 pound *each*)
  1/2 teaspoon salt
  1/4 teaspoon pepper
  1/4 cup molasses
GRAVY:
    5 teaspoons cornstarch
    2 teaspoons beef bouillon granules
    1 cup plus 2 tablespoons cold water
    1 can (4 ounces) mushroom stems and
      pieces, undrained
  1/4 teaspoon browning sauce, optional

In a skillet, saute onions and green pepper in butter until tender. Dissolve bouillon in boiling water. Place the croutons in a large bowl; add onion mixture and bouillon mixture. Stir in crawfish tails; set aside.

Cut a lengthwise slit down the center of each tenderloin to within 1/2 in. of bottom. Open tenderloins so they lie flat; cover with plastic

Sweet and Sour Ham

Joyce Peugh, Woodstock, Maryland

This quick-to-fix meal makes great use of leftover ham. It's also good with cooked chicken or beef.

✓ Uses less fat, sugar or salt. Includes Nutritional Analysis and Diabetic Exchanges.

    1 can (20 ounces) pineapple chunks
    3 tablespoons brown sugar
    2 tablespoons cornstarch
  1/2 teaspoon ground ginger
  1/2 cup water
    3 tablespoons white vinegar
    2 cups cubed fully cooked ham
    1 small green pepper, cut into julienne
      strips
  1/4 cup thinly sliced halved onion
    1 tablespoon canola oil
Hot cooked rice

Drain pineapple, reserving juice and pineapple chunks. In a bowl, combine the brown sugar, cornstarch and ginger. Stir in the water, vinegar and reserved juice until smooth; set aside.

In a large nonstick skillet, saute the ham, green pepper and onion in hot oil over medium-high heat for 3 minutes or until ham is lightly browned and vegetables are crisp-tender. Stir reserved pineapple chunks into skillet; heat through. Stir juice mixture. Gradually stir into skillet. Bring to a boil; cook and stir for 1-2 minutes or until thickened. Serve over rice. **Yield:** 4 servings.

Nutritional Analysis: One serving (1 cup stir-fry, calculated without rice) equals 288 calories, 7 g fat (2 g saturated fat), 39 mg cholesterol, 946 mg sodium, 36 g carbohydrate, 2 g fiber, 18 g protein. **Diabetic Exchanges:** 2 lean meat, 1-1/2 fruit, 1 starch.

SNOWCAPPED SALMON

(Pictured below)

Ella Hosmer, Central, Alaska

The name of this recipe is suggestive of my state's wondrous beauty. Alaska is known for its salmon, and this is one of my favorite ways to prepare it.

  1 tablespoon all-purpose flour
  4 salmon fillets (6 ounces *each*)
  2 egg whites
  1 cup mayonnaise
  1 teaspoon ground mustard
  1/4 cup grated Parmesan cheese

Sprinkle flour over salmon. Place in a greased 11-in. x 7-in. x 2-in. baking dish. In a small mixing bowl, beat egg whites until stiff peaks form. In another bowl, combine the mayonnaise and mustard; fold in egg whites. Spoon over salmon. Sprinkle with cheese. Bake, uncovered, at 350° for 25-30 minutes or until fish flakes easily with a fork. **Yield:** 4 servings.

Editor's Note: Reduced fat or fat-free mayonnaise may not be substituted for regular mayonnaise in this recipe.

ROASTED GARLIC TOMATO PIZZA

(Pictured above right)

Ann Boulay, Omaha, Nebraska

There's nothing fancy about this appetizing entree. Its naturally good ingredients speak for themselves. We especially enjoy it in summer when the tomatoes and basil are fresh from our garden.

  3 cups all-purpose flour
  1/4 cup grated Parmesan cheese

  1 package (1/4 ounce) active dry yeast
  1 teaspoon sugar
  1 teaspoon salt
  1 cup warm water (120° to 130°)
4-1/2 teaspoons olive oil
TOPPING:
  1 large whole garlic bulb
  2 to 3 teaspoons olive oil, *divided*
  3 plum tomatoes, thinly sliced
  1/4 teaspoon salt
  1/4 teaspoon pepper
  2 cups (8 ounces) shredded mozzarella
    cheese
  3 tablespoons julienned fresh basil

In a mixing bowl, combine 1-1/2 cups flour, Parmesan cheese, yeast, sugar and salt. Add water and oil; beat just until moistened. Stir in enough remaining flour to form a stiff dough.

Turn onto a floured surface; knead until smooth and elastic, about 6-8 minutes. Place in a greased bowl, turning once to grease top. Cover; let rise in a warm place until doubled, about 1 hour.

Meanwhile, remove papery outer skin from garlic (do not peel or separate cloves). Cut top off bulb. Brush with 1 teaspoon oil. Wrap in heavy-duty foil. Bake at 425° for 30-35 minutes or until softened. Cool for 10-15 minutes. Squeeze roasted garlic onto a cutting board; thinly slice.

Punch dough down. On a lightly floured surface, roll dough into a 15-in. circle. Transfer to a greased 14-in. pizza pan. Build up edges slightly; prick dough thoroughly with a fork. Brush dough with remaining oil.

Layer with tomatoes, roasted garlic, salt, pepper and mozzarella cheese. Bake at 450° for 18-20 minutes or until golden brown. Sprinkle with basil. **Yield:** 8 servings.

In a large bowl, combine the flour, cornmeal, sugar, baking powder, cayenne, chili powder and salt. Combine the milk, oil and egg; stir into dry ingredients just until moistened. Stir in the cheeses. Spread into a greased 15-in. x 10-in. x 1-in. baking pan. Bake at 400° for 10-12 minutes or until a toothpick comes out clean.

In a large skillet, cook beef over medium heat until no longer pink; drain. Stir in water and one envelope of taco seasoning. Bring to a boil. Reduce the heat; simmer, uncovered, for 5 minutes. Set aside.

In a small bowl, combine the sour cream and remaining taco seasoning; mix well. Spread over crust. Sprinkle with the beef mixture and half of the cheeses. Combine the corn, beans and salsa; spoon over cheese. Sprinkle with remaining cheese. Broil 5-6 in. from heat for 5-10 minutes or until cheese is melted. **Yield:** 12-15 servings.

CREAMED HAM IN TOAST CUPS
(Pictured below)

Catherine Crandall, Amity, Oregon

My grandmother taught me many of her recipes in show-and-cook sessions. Usually, we had this dish on Mondays, following a Sunday lunch of ham, peas and corn. These buttery cups are one of my favorite ways to use leftover ingredients.

> 8 slices bread
> 1/2 cup butter, softened, *divided*
> 1/4 cup all-purpose flour

SOUTHWESTERN PIZZA
(Pictured above)

Caroline Grooms, Dickinson, North Dakota

I dreamed up this pizza for a New Year's Eve party at church. My craving for corn bread and black bean and corn salsa was the inspiration.

> 1-1/4 cups all-purpose flour
> 3/4 cup cornmeal
> 1/4 cup sugar
> 2 teaspoons baking powder
> 1 teaspoon cayenne pepper
> 1 teaspoon chili powder
> 1/2 teaspoon salt
> 1 cup milk
> 1/4 cup vegetable oil
> 1 egg
> 3/4 cup *each* shredded cheddar and
> Monterey Jack cheese
> TOPPING:
> 1-1/2 pounds ground beef
> 2/3 cup water
> 2 envelopes taco seasoning, *divided*
> 2 cups (16 ounces) sour cream
> 1-3/4 cups (10 ounces) *each* shredded
> cheddar and Monterey Jack cheese,
> *divided*
> 1 can (15-1/4 ounces) whole kernel corn,
> drained
> 1 can (15 ounces) black beans, rinsed and
> drained
> 1 cup salsa

1/8 teaspoon white pepper
1 cup milk
1 cup heavy whipping cream
2 cups chopped fully cooked ham
1 cup frozen green peas, thawed
1 cup whole kernel corn
Paprika

Remove and discard crusts from bread; using a rolling pin, flatten to 1/8-in. thickness. Butter both sides of each slice, using 1/4 cup of butter.

Press into eight greased muffin cups or 6-oz. custard cups. Bake at 350° for 15-18 minutes or until golden brown. Meanwhile, in a saucepan, melt the remaining butter. Stir in flour and pepper. Gradually stir in milk and cream. Bring to a boil; cook and stir for 2 minutes or until thickened. Reduce heat. Stir in the ham, peas and corn. Cook and stir for 5 minutes or until heated through. Pour into warm toast cups; sprinkle with paprika. **Yield:** 4 servings.

Editor's Note: This recipe is best made with a soft-textured bread such as Wonderbread.

The addition of hot sauce zips up this cut of meat. It takes me back to spicy dinners I enjoyed as a child in the Southwest. I like to use the leftovers in different dishes—including barbecued beef sandwiches, quesadillas and burritos.

1 boneless beef eye of round roast
   (about 3 pounds)
1 tablespoon vegetable oil
2-1/4 cups water, *divided*
1 envelope onion soup mix
3 tablespoons cider vinegar
2 tablespoons Louisiana hot sauce
2 tablespoons all-purpose flour

In a Dutch oven, brown roast on all sides in oil over medium-high heat; drain. Combine 3/4 cup water, soup mix, vinegar and hot sauce; pour over roast. Cover and bake at 325° for 2-3 hours or until tender. Transfer to a serving platter and keep warm. Let stand for 10-15 minutes before slicing.

For gravy, combine flour and remaining water until smooth; stir into meat juices. Bring to a boil; cook and stir for 2 minutes or until thickened. Serve with meat. **Yield:** 10-12 servings.

PORK TENDERLOIN WITH HERB SAUCE

Linda Wheeler, Harrisburg, Pennsylvania

This tenderloin was such a hit at our Easter dinner, I continued to serve it all summer for family and guests. The basting sauce would be delicious with other grilled meats as well.

3/4 cup red wine vinegar
1/4 cup butter
2 tablespoons Worcestershire sauce
2 teaspoons seasoned salt
1-1/2 teaspoons dried parsley flakes
1-1/2 teaspoons dried oregano
1 teaspoon garlic powder
1/4 teaspoon pepper
2 pork tenderloins (about 3/4
   pound *each*)

In a saucepan, combine the first eight ingredients. Cook for 3 minutes or until butter is melted. Grill pork tenderloins, covered, over medium heat for 18-20 minutes or until a meat thermometer reads 160°, basting with herb sauce and turning occasionally. Let stand for 5 minutes before cutting. **Yield:** 6 servings.

RED-EYE BEEF ROAST
(Pictured above right)

Carol Stevens, Basye, Virginia

MIND THE MARINADE

Always discard sauces used for marinating and basting uncooked meat. If you want to serve some sauce with dinner, set aside the desired amount before using it on raw meat.

▪▪▪▪▪▪▪▪▪▪▪▪

CATFISH CREOLE

(Pictured above)

Val Keithley, Hammond, Indiana

A friend gave me this recipe, and it's been a family favorite since the first time I made it.

  1/4 cup *each* chopped onion, celery and
     green pepper
    2 garlic cloves, minced
    2 teaspoons olive oil
  3/4 cup chicken broth
    1 tablespoon tomato paste
  1/2 teaspoon salt
  1/2 teaspoon *each* dried basil, oregano and
     thyme
  1/8 teaspoon *each* white, black and cayenne
     pepper
Dash paprika
  1/2 cup diced fresh tomato
    1 pound catfish *or* orange roughy fillets
Hot cooked rice
Minced fresh parsley

In a small skillet, saute the onion, celery, green pepper and garlic in oil until tender. Add the broth, tomato paste and seasonings. Bring to a boil. Reduce heat; simmer, uncovered, for 5 minutes or until heated through. Stir in tomato.

Arrange the fillets in a greased 13-in. x 9-in. x 2-in. baking dish; top with vegetable mixture. Bake, uncovered, at 375° for 15-20 minutes or until fish flakes easily with a fork. Serve over rice; sprinkle with parsley. **Yield:** 4 servings.

▪▪▪▪▪▪▪▪▪▪▪▪

BEANS AND BISCUITS

Sandra McKenzie, Braham, Minnesota

This is one of my husband's favorite dishes. It's easy to prepare and makes a satisfying meal served with a side veggie or fruit.

    1 pound ground beef
    2 green onions, chopped
    1 garlic clove, minced
    1 can (28 ounces) baked beans, drained
  1/2 cup barbecue sauce
  1/4 cup packed brown sugar
  1/4 cup ketchup
    1 tablespoon prepared mustard
    1 tube (4-1/2 ounces) refrigerated
     buttermilk biscuits
  1/2 cup shredded cheddar cheese

In a skillet, cook beef, onions and garlic over medium heat until meat is no longer pink; drain. Add beans, barbecue sauce, brown sugar, ketchup and mustard. Simmer 5 minutes or until heated through.

Transfer to a greased 11-in. x 7-in. x 2-in. baking dish. Separate biscuits and cut in half; arrange over beef mixture. Bake, uncovered, at 400° for 18 minutes or until biscuits are golden. Sprinkle with cheese; bake 2-3 minutes longer or until cheese is melted. **Yield:** 4-6 servings.

Editor's Note: This recipe was tested with Pillsbury buttermilk biscuits, which has six biscuits in a 4-1/2-ounce tube.

▪▪▪▪▪▪▪▪▪▪▪▪

APPLE-SMOTHERED PORK CHOPS

Bonnie Riffle, New Lexington, Ohio

When I serve this entree to my guests, I always get lots of compliments—and requests for the recipe.

    6 bone-in pork loin chops (3/4 inch
     thick)
  3/4 teaspoon salt
  1/4 teaspoon rubbed sage
    1 tablespoon vegetable oil
    3 medium tart apples, peeled and sliced
    3 tablespoons molasses
    3 tablespoons all-purpose flour
    2 cups water
    1 tablespoon white vinegar
  1/3 cup golden raisins

Sprinkle pork chops with salt and sage. In a large skillet, brown chops on both sides in oil. Transfer to a greased shallow 3-qt. baking dish. Layer apples over the meat; drizzle with molasses.

Add flour to pan drippings in skillet; stir until blended. Gradually stir in water. Bring to a boil; cook and stir for 2 minutes or until thickened. Remove from heat; stir in vinegar and raisins. Pour over apples and chops. Bake, uncovered, at 350° for 1 hour or until a meat thermometer reads 160°. **Yield:** 6 servings.

PINEAPPLE HAM CASSEROLE
(Pictured below)

Marsha Fleming, Kula, Hawaii

Living in Hawaii, I wanted to share this recipe which features pineapple. It's our most important fruit crop.

- 2 cups uncooked wide egg noodles
- 1/2 cup chopped celery
- 2 tablespoons butter, *divided*
- 1 package (8 ounces) cream cheese, cubed
- 3/4 cup milk
- 2 cups cubed fully cooked ham
- 2 cans (8 ounces *each*) crushed pineapple, drained
- 2 teaspoons Worcestershire sauce
- 1/2 teaspoon salt
- Dash pepper
- 1/4 cup dry bread crumbs

Cook noodles according to package directions; drain. In a large skillet, saute celery in 1 tablespoon butter until tender. Stir in cream cheese and milk; cook and stir until cheese is melted. Add the noodles, ham, pineapple, Worcestershire sauce, salt and pepper.

Transfer to an ungreased 1-1/2-qt. baking dish. Melt remaining butter; toss with bread crumbs.

Sprinkle over top. Bake, uncovered, at 350° for 30-35 minutes or until heated through. **Yield:** 4 servings.

BAKED ORANGE ROUGHY
(Pictured above)

Wendy Clark, Eagleville, Pennsylvania

I did some experimenting to come up with this recipe. It's quick and easy enough to prepare for the family after coming home from work, and tasty enough for company.

- 1/2 cup mayonnaise
- 1/4 cup sour cream
- 1/4 cup sweet pickle relish
- 1 tablespoon Dijon mustard
- 1 cup finely crushed cornflakes
- 1/3 cup grated Parmesan cheese
- 1 teaspoon dried basil
- 1 teaspoon dill weed
- 1 teaspoon paprika
- 1/8 teaspoon pepper
- 1/2 cup milk
- 1-1/2 pounds orange roughy fillets
- Lemon wedges

For tartar sauce, combine the mayonnaise, sour cream, pickle relish and mustard in a small bowl; mix well. Cover and refrigerate.

In a large resealable plastic bag, combine the cornflake crumbs, Parmesan cheese and seasonings. Place the milk in a shallow bowl. Dip fillets in milk, then place in bag and shake to coat.

Arrange in a greased 15-in. x 10-in. x 1-in. baking pan. Bake at 450° for 10-15 minutes or until fish flakes easily with a fork. Serve with tartar sauce and lemon. **Yield:** 6 servings.

JAMBALAYA
(Pictured below)

Glada Marie St. Clair, Crossville, Tennessee

I first tasted this dish at a church potluck. I got the original recipe from my daughter's godfather and adapted it to suit my family's tastes.

- 1 pound fully cooked kielbasa *or* Polish sausage, cut into 1/4-inch slices
- 1 pound boneless skinless chicken breasts, cut into 1-inch cubes
- 2 celery ribs, thinly sliced
- 1 large onion, chopped
- 1 medium green pepper, chopped
- 2 garlic cloves, minced
- 1 can (28 ounces) diced tomatoes, undrained
- 2 cups uncooked rice
- 2 cups water
- 1/2 pound fresh *or* frozen uncooked medium shrimp, peeled and deveined
- 3 tablespoons minced fresh parsley
- 2 tablespoons Worcestershire sauce
- 1 teaspoon salt
- 1/2 teaspoon dried thyme
- 1/4 to 1/2 teaspoon cayenne pepper

In a Dutch oven, saute sausage for 1 minute. Add chicken; saute 2 minutes longer. Add the celery, onion, green pepper and garlic; saute for 2 minutes. Stir in the remaining ingredients.

Bring to a boil. Reduce heat; cover and simmer for 20 minutes. Stir to fluff the rice. Let stand for 5 minutes to absorb any remaining liquid before serving. **Yield:** 8 servings.

PICANTE CRANBERRY MEATBALLS
(Pictured above)

Marge Wyse, Winfield, British Columbia

These zippy ground beef meatballs are my favorites. Cranberry, chili and picante sauce sound like an unusual combination, but the flavors blend deliciously.

- 2 eggs, lightly beaten
- 1/3 cup ketchup
- 1/3 cup minced fresh parsley
- 2 tablespoons soy sauce
- 2 tablespoons dried minced onion
- 1/2 teaspoon garlic powder
- 1/4 teaspoon pepper
- 1 cup crushed saltines (about 30 crackers)
- 2 pounds ground beef

SAUCE:
- 1 can (16 ounces) jellied cranberry sauce
- 1 cup chili sauce
- 1/4 cup picante sauce
- 2 tablespoons brown sugar
- 1 tablespoon lemon juice

Hot cooked noodles, optional

In a bowl, combine the eggs, ketchup, parsley, soy sauce, onion, garlic powder and pepper. Add cracker crumbs. Crumble beef over mixture; mix well. Shape into 1-1/2-in. balls. In a skillet, brown meatballs over medium heat. Transfer to a greased 13-in. x 9-in. x 2-in. baking dish.

In a saucepan, combine the first five sauce ingredients. Cook and stir until cranberry sauce is melted and mixture is heated through. Pour over meatballs. Cover and bake at 350° for 30-35 minutes or until meat is no longer pink. Serve over noodles if desired. **Yield:** 8 servings.

CIDER PORK CHOP DINNER

(Pictured below)

Clyda Conrad, Yuma, Arizona

When autumn arrives, I like to make this recipe for its hearty aromas of pork, vegetables and apple cider.

- 1 teaspoon dried thyme
- 1 teaspoon salt
- 1 teaspoon pepper
- 4 bone-in pork loin chops (1 inch thick)
- 1 tablespoon olive oil
- 2 cups apple cider *or* apple juice
- 4 medium red potatoes, cubed
- 1 medium onion, cut into 1/2-inch pieces
- 1 large carrot, cut into 1/2-inch pieces
- 1 small turnip *or* rutabaga, peeled and cubed
- 2 tablespoons all-purpose flour
- 1/4 teaspoon ground nutmeg
- 3/4 cup half-and-half cream

Combine the thyme, salt and pepper; rub over both sides of pork chops. In a large skillet over medium heat, brown the chops in oil on both sides. Remove and set aside.

Add cider to the pan, stirring to loosen any browned bits. Add vegetables and pork chops. Bring to a boil. Reduce heat; cover and simmer for 1 hour or until meat juices run clear and vegetables are tender, stirring occasionally.

Transfer pork chops and vegetables to a serving platter and keep warm. For gravy, bring the pan juices to a boil; cook, uncovered, until reduced to 3/4 cup. In a small bowl, combine flour, nutmeg and cream until smooth. Stir into reduced liquid. Bring to a boil; cook and stir for 2 minutes or until thickened. Serve with meat and vegetables. **Yield:** 4 servings.

BARBECUED ROUND STEAK

(Pictured above)

Mina Dyck, Boissevain, Manitoba

I found this recipe years ago, and it has become a favorite of my family and friends. The combination of ingredients for the sauce seems to be exactly right.

- 2 pounds boneless beef round steak (1 inch thick), cut into strips
- 2 tablespoons vegetable oil
- 1/2 cup tomato juice
- 1/2 cup ketchup
- 1/4 cup water
- 1/4 cup cider vinegar
- 2 tablespoons Worcestershire sauce
- 2 tablespoons brown sugar
- 2 teaspoons paprika
- 1 teaspoon salt
- 1 teaspoon ground mustard
- 1 garlic clove, minced
- 1/4 teaspoon chili powder
- 1/4 teaspoon pepper
- 4 teaspoons cornstarch
- 2 tablespoons cold water

Hot cooked rice, optional

In a large skillet, brown beef in oil over medium-high heat; drain. In a bowl, combine the next 12 ingredients; pour over the beef. Bring to a boil. Reduce heat; cover and simmer for 1-1/2 to 2 hours or until the meat is tender.

Combine cornstarch and cold water until smooth; stir into meat mixture. Bring to a boil; cook and stir for 1-2 minutes or until thickened. Serve over rice if desired. **Yield:** 6-8 servings.

leaves. Skim fat from pan juices. In a small bowl, combine cornstarch and water until smooth; gradually stir into pan juices. Bring to a boil; cook and stir for 2 minutes or until thickened. Strain; serve with meat. **Yield:** 12-16 servings.

SWORDFISH WITH SAUTEED VEGETABLES

(Pictured below)

Susie Thompson, Dexter, Oregon

My husband says "wow!" when I prepare swordfish this way. The seasonings are just right!

        1/2 cup olive oil
        2 green onions, sliced
        2 teaspoons dried rosemary, crushed
        2 tablespoons lime juice
        2 tablespoons Dijon mustard
        6 swordfish *or* halibut steaks (6 ounces *each*)
VEGETABLES:
        2 small zucchini
        2 small yellow summer squash
    1/4 cup sliced green onions
        2 teaspoons dried rosemary, crushed
        3 tablespoons olive oil
        1 pound small red potatoes, cooked and cut into 1/2-inch slices
        2 cups halved cherry tomatoes
    1/2 to 3/4 teaspoon salt
    1/4 teaspoon pepper

In a large resealable plastic bag, combine the first five ingredients; add swordfish. Seal bag and

SPICED BEEF POT ROAST

(Pictured above)

Florine Bruns, Fredericksburg, Texas

I like to make this pot roast when I have dinner guests. If desired, potatoes and carrots can be added during the final hour of cooking time.

        3 teaspoons salt
    1/2 teaspoon pepper
    1/2 teaspoon ground allspice
    1/4 teaspoon ground mace
        1 boneless beef chuck roast (4 to 5 pounds)
    2-1/4 cups tomato juice
        1 large onion, chopped
        8 tablespoons vegetable oil, *divided*
        3 tablespoons lemon juice
    4-1/2 teaspoons cider vinegar
        2 bay leaves
        3 tablespoons cornstarch
    1/3 cup cold water

Combine salt, pepper, allspice and mace; rub over the roast. In a bowl, combine tomato juice, onion, 6 tablespoons oil, lemon juice and vinegar; mix well. Pour half of the marinade into a large resealable plastic bag; add roast. Seal bag and turn to coat; refrigerate for 8 hours or overnight. Cover and refrigerate remaining marinade.

Drain and discard marinade from meat. In a Dutch oven, brown roast on both sides in remaining oil over medium-high heat; drain. Pour reserved marinade over roast; add bay leaves. Bring to a boil. Reduce heat; cover and simmer for 2-3/4 hours or until meat is tender.

Remove roast and keep warm. Discard bay

turn to coat; refrigerate for 30-45 minutes.

Drain and discard marinade. If grilling the fish, coat grill rack with nonstick cooking spray before starting the grill. Grill swordfish, uncovered, over medium-hot heat or broil 4-6 in. from the heat for 5-7 minutes on each side or until fish flakes easily with a fork.

Cut zucchini and yellow squash lengthwise into 1/4-in. slices, then widthwise into 3-in. pieces. In a large skillet, saute the onions and rosemary in oil for 1-2 minutes or until onions are tender. Add squash; saute for 5-6 minutes or until crisp-tender. Add potatoes and tomatoes; cook just until heated through. Sprinkle with salt and pepper; toss to coat. Serve with the swordfish. **Yield:** 4 servings.

STUFFED ROUND STEAK

Helen Heathcote, Hawk Run, Pennsylvania

When my grown daughter and I have our choice of special meals, we both pick my mom's round steak. The flavor-filled stuffing is wonderful.

    2 boneless beef round steaks (about 1
      pound *each*)
    4 bacon strips, diced
    1 medium onion, chopped
1-1/2 cups stuffing croutons
    2 tablespoons minced fresh parsley
  1/2 teaspoon salt
  1/2 teaspoon celery salt
  1/4 teaspoon rubbed sage
  1/4 teaspoon pepper
    1 cup beef broth
    1 can (8 ounces) tomato sauce
4-1/2 teaspoons cornstarch
    2 tablespoons cold water

Flatten steaks to 1/4-in. thickness; set aside. In a skillet, cook bacon over medium heat until crisp; using a slotted spoon, remove to paper towels. Drain, reserving 3 tablespoons drippings.

Saute onion in the drippings. Add the croutons, parsley, salt, celery salt, sage, pepper and bacon. Spread over each steak to within 1 in. of edges. Roll up jelly-roll style, starting with a long side; tie with kitchen string.

Place in a greased 13-in. x 9-in. x 2-in. baking dish. Pour broth over steaks. Cover and bake at 325° for 1 hour. Drizzle with the tomato sauce.

Bake, uncovered, for 45 minutes or until the meat is tender.

Remove meat to a serving platter and keep warm. Pour drippings and loosened brown bits into a measuring cup; skim fat. In a saucepan, combine cornstarch and water until smooth; gradual-ly stir in drippings. Bring to a boil; cook and stir for 2 minutes or until thickened. Serve with sliced steak. **Yield:** 6-8 servings.

CHICKEN ITALIAN

(Pictured above)

Ann Walsh, Maple Park, Illinois

This hearty chicken dish is sure to please. A friend gave me the recipe years ago, and I've since added a couple ingredients of my own.

    1 can (28 ounces) crushed tomatoes
    1 can (28 ounces) Italian diced tomatoes
    1 cup chicken broth
  1/4 cup red wine vinegar
    1 can (8 ounces) tomato sauce
    1 medium green pepper, julienned
    1 medium sweet red pepper, julienned
    1 medium onion, chopped
    6 garlic cloves, minced
    1 tablespoon brown sugar
    1 teaspoon dried oregano
    1 teaspoon salt
    1 teaspoon pepper
    2 broiler/fryer chickens (3 to 4 pounds
      each), cut up and skin removed
    1 pound Italian sausage links, sliced
Hot cooked spaghetti

In a large roasting pan, combine the first 13 ingredients. Place the chicken and sausage over tomato mixture. Bake, uncovered, at 350° for 2 hours or until chicken is tender and juices run clear, basting occasionally with sauce. Serve over spaghetti. **Yield:** 10 servings.

SO SATISFYING! *A simple meal made up of a cup of soup, side salad and sandwich is just right on days when you don't want a lot of fuss.*

LIGHT BITES. From top: Corn Medley Salad (p. 56), Hearty Chili Mac (p. 55) and Super Bowl Stromboli (p. 55).

Soups, Salads & Sandwiches

HEARTY CHILI MAC

(Pictured at left)

Fannie Wehmas, Saxon, Wisconsin

Luckily, this recipe makes a lot, since everyone is apt to want another bowl. It freezes well and makes excellent leftovers—if there are any.

- 2 pounds ground beef
- 1 medium onion, chopped
- 1 can (46 ounces) tomato juice
- 1 can (28 ounces) diced tomatoes, undrained
- 2 celery ribs, chopped
- 3 tablespoons brown sugar
- 2 tablespoons chili powder
- 1 teaspoon salt
- 1 teaspoon prepared mustard
- 1/4 teaspoon pepper
- 2 cans (16 ounces *each*) kidney beans, rinsed and drained
- 1/2 cup uncooked elbow macaroni

In a Dutch oven or large kettle, cook beef and onion over medium heat until meat is no longer pink; drain. Stir in the tomato juice, tomatoes, celery, brown sugar, chili powder, salt, mustard and pepper. Bring to a boil. Reduce heat; simmer, uncovered, for 1 hour, stirring occasionally.

Add the beans and macaroni; simmer 15-20 minutes longer or until macaroni is tender. **Yield:** 10-12 servings.

SUPER BOWL STROMBOLI

(Pictured at left)

Mary Anita Ruppert, Peterborough, Ontario

Guests will scramble for this warm loaf stuffed with ham, cheese and more. It tends to disappear quickly— you might consider making two.

- 2-1/2 to 3 cups all-purpose flour
- 1 tablespoon sugar
- 1 package (1/4 ounce) active dry yeast
- 1 teaspoon garlic salt
- 1 cup water
- 1 tablespoon butter
- 6 thin slices deli ham
- 6 thin slices cheddar *or* Swiss cheese
- 6 thin slices summer sausage *or* salami
- 2 tablespoons Dijon mustard
- 1/2 cup julienned green pepper
- 1 egg white, lightly beaten
- 1/2 to 1 teaspoon sesame seeds, optional

In a large mixing bowl, combine 1-1/2 cups flour, sugar, yeast and garlic salt. In a saucepan, heat water and butter to 120°-130°. Add to dry ingredients; beat just until moistened. Stir in enough remaining flour to form a soft dough. Turn onto a floured surface; knead until smooth and elastic, about 6-8 minutes.

Place in a greased bowl, turning once to grease top. Cover and let rise in a warm place until doubled, about 1 hour.

Punch dough down. Turn onto a lightly floured surface; roll into a 14-in. x 10-in. rectangle. Place on a greased baking sheet. Place ham down center of rectangle; top with cheese and sausage. Spread mustard over meat; sprinkle with green pepper.

On each long side, cut 1-in.-wide strips about 2-1/2 in. into center. Starting at one end, fold alternating strips at an angle across filling. Pinch ends to seal. Cover and let rise until doubled, about 30 minutes.

Brush with egg white. Sprinkle with sesame seeds if desired. Bake at 400° for 20-25 minutes or until golden brown. Cool on a wire rack for 10 minutes before slicing. Serve warm. **Yield:** 8-10 servings.

YEAST BREAD BASICS

- Heat liquids to 120° to 130° in a saucepan or microwave. Always use a thermometer to check the temperature.
- Allow dough to rise in a warm, draft-free area (80° to 85°) until doubled in size. To determine if the dough has doubled, press two fingers 1/2 in. into the dough. If the dent remains, it's ready to punch down.

CORN MEDLEY SALAD

(Pictured on page 54)

Judy Meckstroth, New Bremen, Ohio

Whenever I need a dish to pass that's guaranteed to please, I put together this easy corn salad. Whether you serve it from a crystal dish, a ceramic crock or a plastic bowl, it will stand out as a mealtime highlight.

- 2/3 cup sugar
- 2/3 cup cider vinegar
- 2/3 cup vegetable oil
- 1 can (15-1/4 ounces) whole kernel corn, drained
- 1 can (15 ounces) whole baby corn, rinsed and drained, halved
- 1 can (11 ounces) yellow and white whole kernel corn, drained
- 1 can (11 ounces) white *or* shoepeg corn, drained
- 1 large sweet red pepper, chopped
- 1 medium red onion, chopped
- 4 to 5 celery ribs, sliced

Leaf lettuce, optional

In a small saucepan, combine the sugar, vinegar and oil. Cook over medium heat for 5 minutes, stirring until sugar is dissolved. Cool completely. In a bowl, combine the corn, red pepper, onion and celery. Add dressing and toss to coat. Cover and refrigerate overnight.

Stir well. Serve with a slotted spoon in a lettuce-lined bowl if desired. **Yield:** 10-12 servings.

BLACK-EYED PEA SALAD

(Pictured above)

Ruth Hunter, Bucks County, Pennsylvania

This is a wonderful recipe to serve any time of the year, but it's especially good with ripe cherry tomatoes picked fresh from the garden.

- 1 package (16 ounces) frozen black-eyed peas
- 1 package (10 ounces) frozen peas, thawed
- 4 green onions, sliced
- 2 celery ribs, diced
- 1 medium sweet yellow pepper, diced
- 2 medium carrots, coarsely chopped
- 1/3 cup chopped fresh mint
- 1/2 cup olive oil
- 1/3 cup white wine vinegar
- 2 garlic cloves, minced
- 1 teaspoon salt
- 1/4 teaspoon pepper
- 1 cup halved cherry tomatoes
- 1/4 pound sliced bacon, cooked and crumbled

Cook black-eyed peas according to package directions; drain and place in a large bowl. Add peas, onions, celery, yellow pepper, carrots and mint.

In a jar with a tight-fitting lid, combine the oil, vinegar, garlic, salt and pepper; shake well. Drizzle over salad; toss to coat. Cover and refrigerate overnight. Top with tomatoes and bacon. **Yield:** 10-12 servings.

DILLY CUCUMBER SALAD

June Stinson, Cedar Bluff, Alabama

In England, where I was born and raised, friends get together twice a year for English tea. We'd serve an assortment of dishes, including this cucumber salad.

- 1 cup sugar
- 1 cup white vinegar
- 1/2 cup water
- 1 tablespoon snipped fresh dill *or* 1 teaspoon dill weed
- 2 teaspoons salt
- 4 medium cucumbers, thinly sliced
- 1/3 cup sour cream

In a saucepan, combine the sugar, vinegar, water, dill and salt. Bring to a boil over medium heat. Remove from the heat. Place cucumbers in a large bowl. Pour vinegar mixture over and toss to coat. Cover and refrigerate overnight.

Drain and discard vinegar mixture. Stir sour cream into cucumbers. Cover and refrigerate until serving. **Yield:** 6-8 servings.

ZIPPY CHICKEN CORN CHOWDER
(Pictured below)

Doris Krise, Edwardsburg, Michigan

In this full-bodied chowder, corn is complemented by a zesty pepper flavor that you can adjust to suit your family's palate. Serve it with warm rolls and a salad for a completely satisfying meal on a chilly winter day.

  2 pounds boneless skinless chicken
    breasts, cubed
  4 tablespoons butter, *divided*
  1 large sweet red pepper, chopped
  2 medium leeks, chopped
  3 tablespoons all-purpose flour
  1 tablespoon paprika
  4 cups chicken broth
  2 medium potatoes, cubed
  4 cups frozen corn
  1 tablespoon Worcestershire sauce
  1 teaspoon salt
1/2 to 1 teaspoon hot pepper sauce
  1 cup half-and-half cream

In a soup kettle or Dutch oven, saute chicken in 2 tablespoons butter until lightly browned; set aside and keep warm. In the same pan, saute the red pepper in remaining butter until tender. Add the leeks; cook for 1 minute. Stir in the flour and paprika until blended. Gradually stir in the broth. Add the potatoes; bring to a boil.

Reduce heat; cover and simmer for 15 min-

utes or until the potatoes are tender. Stir in corn, Worcestershire sauce, salt, hot pepper sauce and reserved chicken; bring to a boil. Reduce heat. Cook, uncovered, for 5-8 minutes or until corn is tender and chicken juices run clear, stirring occasionally. Stir in cream and heat through (do not boil). **Yield:** 10 servings (2-1/2 quarts).

CRANBERRY VELVET FREEZE
(Pictured above)

Pat Seville, Hagerstown, Maryland

Everyone in my family loves this salad. I normally serve it at the holidays when we're all together.

2 cans (16 ounces *each*) whole-berry
  cranberry sauce
2 cans (one 20 ounces, one 8 ounces)
  crushed pineapple, drained
1 package (10-1/2 ounces) miniature
  marshmallows
1 cup green maraschino cherries,
  quartered
1 cup red maraschino cherries,
  quartered
1 teaspoon lemon juice
3 cups heavy whipping cream, whipped

In a bowl, combine the cranberry sauce, pineapple, marshmallows, cherries and lemon juice. Fold in whipped cream.

Spoon into an ungreased 13-in. x 9-in. x 2-in. dish. Cover and freeze overnight. Remove from the freezer 10 minutes before serving. **Yield:** 12-16 servings.

WILD RICE SEAFOOD SALAD

(Pictured below)

Kathleen Zusan, Scandia, Minnesota

With the rich Native American heritage of our state, a Minnesota wild rice recipe is in order. Wild rice grows naturally in our shallow lakes.

- 3 cups cooked wild rice
- 2 packages (5 ounces each) frozen cooked salad shrimp, thawed
- 2 cups flaked imitation crabmeat
- 1/2 cup *each* chopped sweet yellow, green and red peppers
- 1/2 cup chopped onion
- 1/2 cup red wine vinegar
- 1/4 cup olive oil
- 2 teaspoons minced fresh marjoram *or* 1/2 teaspoon dried marjoram
- 2 teaspoons minced fresh tarragon *or* 1/2 teaspoon dried tarragon
- 2 teaspoons minced fresh thyme *or* 1/2 teaspoon dried thyme
- 1 teaspoon salt
- 1/4 teaspoon pepper

In a serving bowl, combine the rice, shrimp, crab, peppers and onion. In a jar with a tight-fitting lid, combine the remaining ingredients; shake well. Pour over rice mixture and toss to coat. Cover and refrigerate for at least 2 hours before serving. **Yield:** 4-5 servings.

SPECIAL EGG SALAD

(Pictured above)

Judy Nissen, Sioux Falls, South Dakota

We enjoy this egg salad as a stuffing for fresh tomatoes or a spread on sandwiches. It could even be used as a dip with your favorite crackers.

☑ Uses less fat, sugar or salt. Includes Nutritional Analysis and Diabetic Exchanges.

- 3 ounces reduced-fat cream cheese
- 1/4 cup fat-free mayonnaise
- 1/2 teaspoon sugar
- 1/4 teaspoon onion powder
- 1/4 teaspoon garlic powder
- 1/8 teaspoon salt
- 1/8 teaspoon pepper
- 6 hard-cooked eggs, chopped
- 12 slices whole wheat bread, toasted
- 6 lettuce leaves

In a small mixing bowl, beat the cream cheese until smooth. Add the mayonnaise, sugar, onion powder, garlic powder, salt and pepper. Fold in the eggs. Cover and refrigerate for 1 hour. Serve on toast with lettuce. **Yield:** 6 servings.

Nutritional Analysis: One serving equals 259 calories, 10 g fat (4 g saturated fat), 225 mg cholesterol, 528 mg sodium, 30 g carbohydrate, 4 g fiber, 13 g protein. **Diabetic Exchanges:** 2 starch, 1-1/2 fat, 1 lean meat.

▰▰▰▰▰▰▰▰▰▰
CHICKEN AND PEAR TOSSED SALAD
(Pictured below)

Jeanette Luttman, Sacramento, California

I got this recipe at a pear festival. It's a great meal to serve on a hot summer day.

- 3/4 pound boneless skinless chicken breasts, cut into 1-1/2-inch slices
- 6 tablespoons olive oil, *divided*
- 1/2 cup walnut halves
- 2 tablespoons chopped green onions
- 2 tablespoons cider vinegar
- Salt and pepper to taste
- 10 cups torn mixed salad greens
- 2 medium ripe pears, peeled and thinly sliced
- 1/4 cup crumbled blue cheese

In a large skillet, cook chicken in 2 tablespoons oil until no longer pink. Remove and keep warm. Add walnuts to skillet; saute for 1 minute. Add green onions and saute until tender. Stir in vinegar; bring to a boil. Remove from heat; stir in salt, pepper and remaining oil.

Place salad greens in a large bowl. Add pears, chicken and walnut mixture; toss. Sprinkle with blue cheese. **Yield:** 10 servings.

▰▰▰▰▰▰▰▰▰▰
APPLE MALLOW SALAD
(Pictured above)

Paula Marchesi, Rocky Point, New York

I enjoy picking fresh apples at local orchards. Using both red and green apples makes this a festive-looking salad to serve at parties, family gatherings and many other occasions.

- 1 can (20 ounces) crushed pineapple
- 1/2 cup sugar
- 1 tablespoon all-purpose flour
- 1 to 2 tablespoons vinegar
- 1 egg, beaten
- 1 carton (12 ounces) frozen whipped topping, thawed
- 2 medium red apples, diced
- 2 medium green apples, diced
- 4 cups miniature marshmallows
- 1 cup honey-roasted peanuts

Drain pineapple, reserving juice; set pineapple aside. In a saucepan, combine sugar, flour, vinegar and reserved juice until smooth. Bring to a boil; cook and stir for 2 minutes or until thickened. Remove from the heat.

Stir a small amount of hot mixture into egg; return all to the pan, stirring constantly. Bring to a gentle boil; cook and stir for 2 minutes. Remove from the heat; cool.

Fold in whipped topping. Fold in the apples, marshmallows and reserved pineapple. Cover and refrigerate for 1 hour. Just before serving, fold in the peanuts. **Yield:** 16-20 servings.

Fun and Festive Gelatin

USE IT AS a side, salad and dessert, gelatin is always a light and refreshing treat.

✦✦✦✦✦✦✦✦✦✦✦✦
PEACHES 'N' CREAM GELATIN

Cyndi Brinkhaus, South Coast Metro, California

Dinner guests are never too full for this luscious treat. It always draws raves.

> 1-1/3 cups graham cracker crumbs
>   (about 22 squares)
>   1/4 cup sugar
>   1/3 cup butter, melted
> TOPPING:
>   1 package (8 ounces) cream cheese,
>   softened
>   1/4 cup sugar
>   1/4 cup milk
>   1 carton (8 ounces) frozen whipped
>   topping, thawed
>   1 can (15-1/4 ounces) sliced peaches,
>   drained
>   1 package (3 ounces) peach gelatin
>   3/4 cup boiling water
> 1-1/4 cups cold water

In a bowl, combine the crumbs, sugar and butter. Press into a 13-in. x 9-in. x 2-in. dish. In a mixing bowl, beat the cream cheese and sugar until smooth; gradually add the milk. Fold in the whipped topping. Spread over crust.

Cut peach slices in half lengthwise; arrange over top. In a bowl, dissolve the gelatin in boiling water; stir in the cold water. Refrigerate for 1-1/2 hours or until slightly thickened. Gently spoon gelatin over peaches; refrigerate until set. Cut into squares. **Yield:** 12-15 servings.

✦✦✦✦✦✦✦✦✦✦✦✦
GELATIN BANANA SPLIT

Dixie Terry, Goreville, Illinois

JOLLY GELATIN. Clockwise from top left are Eggnog Gelatin Mold, Peaches 'n' Cream Gelatin, Gelatin Banana Split and Seven-Layer Gelatin Salad.

Here is a dessert that my younger guests have as much fun assembling as eating.

    2 packages (3 ounces *each*) strawberry
      gelatin
    2 cups boiling water
    1 cup cold water
    6 medium firm bananas
Whipped cream in a can
Chopped nuts, optional

In a small bowl, dissolve gelatin in boiling water. Stir in cold water. Pour into a 13-in. x 9-in. x 2-in. dish. Refrigerate for 2 hours or until firm. Cut gelatin into 1/2-in. cubes. Just before serving, split bananas in half lengthwise. Place two pieces in each serving dish. Top with gelatin cubes, whipped cream and nuts if desired. **Yield:** 6 servings.

SEVEN-LAYER GELATIN SALAD

Melody Mellinger, Myerstown, Pennsylvania

Alternating fruity layers of gelatin with sweetened sour cream creates an eye-catching treat.

    1 package (3 ounces) cherry gelatin
    4 cups boiling water, *divided*
2-1/2 cups cold water, *divided*
    2 envelopes unflavored gelatin
    2 cups milk
    1 cup sugar
    2 cups (16 ounces) sour cream
    2 teaspoons vanilla extract
    1 package (3 ounces) lemon gelatin
    1 package (3 ounces) orange gelatin
    1 package (3 ounces) lime gelatin

In a bowl, dissolve cherry gelatin in 1 cup boiling water. Add 1/2 cup cold water; stir. Pour into a 13-in. x 9-in. x 2-in. dish coated with nonstick cooking spray; refrigerate until set but not firm, about 30 minutes.

In a small saucepan, sprinkle unflavored gelatin over 1/2 cup cold water. Let stand for 1 minute. Stir in milk and sugar. Cook and stir over medium heat until gelatin and sugar are dissolved. Remove from the heat. Whisk in sour cream and vanilla until smooth. Spoon 1-2/3 cups creamy gelatin mixture over the first flavored layer. Chill until set but not firm. Prepare remaining flavored gelatins as directed for cherry gelatin. Alternate-

ly layer flavored gelatins with creamy gelatin layers, allowing each to set before adding next layer. Top with lime gelatin. Refrigerate overnight. Cut into squares. **Yield:** 12-15 servings.

Editor's Note: This salad takes time to prepare since each layer must be set before the next layer is added.

EGGNOG GELATIN MOLD

Irene Johnson, Alexandria, Minnesota

This is my family's all-time favorite Christmas salad. One taste will have you convinced, too!

    3 envelopes unflavored gelatin
    3/4 cup cold water
    4 cups eggnog, *divided*
    1/4 cup sugar
    1/4 teaspoon ground nutmeg
    1 cup heavy whipping cream, whipped
CRAN-APPLE COMPOTE:
    3/4 cup sugar
    1/3 cup water
    1 cup fresh *or* frozen cranberries
    1 teaspoon unflavored gelatin
    3 tablespoons cold water
    1 cup chopped peeled apple
    1/3 cup chopped walnuts

In a large saucepan, sprinkle gelatin over cold water; let stand for 1 minute. Stir 1 cup eggnog, sugar and nutmeg into gelatin mixture. Cook over medium-low heat until gelatin and sugar are dissolved, stirring occasionally. Add remaining eggnog. Refrigerate until slightly thickened, about 1 hour. Fold in cream. Transfer to a 7-cup mold coated with nonstick cooking spray. Refrigerate for at least 4 hours or until firm.

Meanwhile, for compote, in a saucepan, combine the sugar and water. Bring to a boil and stir until sugar is dissolved. Add the cranberries and boil for 5 minutes, stirring occasionally. Sprinkle gelatin over cold water; let stand for 1 minute. Stir into cranberry mixture until gelatin is dissolved. Remove from the heat; stir in apple and walnuts. Transfer to a bowl and refrigerate for at least 2 hours. Serve with the eggnog gelatin. **Yield:** 8-10 servings (2 cups sauce).

Editor's Note: This recipe was tested with commercially prepared eggnog.

HAM AND SWEET POTATO SALAD

(Pictured above)

Carolyn Hayes, Marion, Illinois

A friend shared this recipe with me. It's her favorite salad, and you'll see why when you try it.

    4 to 5 cups cubed peeled sweet potatoes
      1 cup mayonnaise
    1/3 cup orange juice
      1 tablespoon honey
      1 tablespoon grated orange peel
    1/8 teaspoon salt
    1/2 teaspoon grated fresh gingerroot
    1/8 teaspoon ground nutmeg
  1-1/2 cups julienned fully cooked ham
      2 celery ribs, thinly sliced
    1/4 cup chopped dried apricots
      1 whole fresh pineapple
      1 cup chopped pecans

Place the sweet potatoes in a large saucepan and cover with water. Bring to a boil. Reduce heat; cover and simmer for 20 minutes or until tender. Drain and cool. In a large bowl, combine the mayonnaise, orange juice, honey, orange peel, salt, ginger and nutmeg. Stir in the ham, celery, apricots and sweet potatoes.

Stand pineapple upright and cut in half vertically, leaving the top attached. Remove fruit, leaving a 1/2-in. shell. Cut fruit into chunks; stir 1 cup into the salad (save remaining fruit for another use). Cover and refrigerate salad and shells for at least 4 hours. Just before serving, stir pecans into salad. Spoon into pineapple shells. **Yield: 8** servings.

FARMHOUSE CHICKEN SOUP

(Pictured below)

Janice Mitchell, Aurora, Colorado

Over the years, I've changed this recipe bit by bit until my family said it was perfect. I hope your family enjoys it as much as we do!

      1 broiler/fryer chicken (3 to 3-1/2
        pounds)
      2 quarts water
      1 large onion, chopped
    1/2 cup chopped celery
      1 cup diced carrots
      2 garlic cloves, minced
      2 teaspoons salt
    1/2 teaspoon pepper
    1/2 teaspoon poultry seasoning
    1/4 teaspoon crushed red pepper flakes
SPAETZLE:
  1-1/2 cups all-purpose flour
    1/2 teaspoon salt
    1/8 teaspoon baking powder
    1/8 teaspoon ground nutmeg
      2 eggs, well beaten
    1/2 cup milk
      1 tablespoon minced fresh parsley

Place the chicken and water in a Dutch oven or soup kettle. Bring to a boil; reduce heat. Add the onion, celery, carrots, garlic, salt, pepper, poultry seasoning and red pepper flakes. Cover and simmer for 1 hour or until chicken is tender.

Remove chicken from broth; cool. Skim fat from broth. Remove meat from bones; discard

bones and skin. Cut meat into bite-size pieces; return to broth. Cover and simmer.

For spaetzle, combine the flour, salt, baking powder and nutmeg in a small bowl. Stir in the eggs, milk and parsley; blend well. With a rubber spatula, push batter through a large-hole grater or colander into simmering soup. Simmer, uncovered, for 10 minutes or until spaetzle float to the top. **Yield:** 10-12 servings (about 3 quarts).

FRESH FRUIT SALAD

Marcelene Sapp, Finley, Kentucky

The sauce in this salad coats the fruit nicely and lets its fresh flavors shine through.

> 2 **medium red apples, cut into 1/2-inch chunks**
> 2 **medium firm bananas, cut into 1/4-inch slices**
> 1/2 **cup green grapes**
> 1 **can (8 ounces) pineapple chunks, drained**
> 1/4 **cup sugar**
> 1 **tablespoon cornstarch**
> 1/2 **cup water**
> 3 **tablespoons orange juice**
> 4-1/2 **teaspoons lemon juice**

In a bowl, combine the apples, bananas, grapes and pineapple; set aside. In a small saucepan, combine sugar and cornstarch. Add the water, orange juice and lemon juice; stir until smooth. Bring to a boil; cook and stir for 1 minute or until thickened. Pour over fruit; toss gently. Cover and refrigerate until serving. **Yield:** 6 servings.

EASTER LETTUCE SALAD

Tammy Myers, Waupun, Wisconsin

Here's a salad that is so simple yet so tasty, it will impress your holiday guests.

> 1/2 **cup vegetable oil**
> 1/2 **cup sugar**
> 1/3 **cup white vinegar**
> 1/2 **small onion**
> 2 **tablespoons mayonnaise**
> 1 **teaspoon salt**
> 1 **teaspoon ground mustard**
> 1/2 **teaspoon celery seed**
> 9 **cups torn leaf lettuce**
> 6 **hard-cooked eggs, sliced**

In a blender, combine the first eight ingredients; cover and process until blended. Divide lettuce among six salad plates; drizzle with dressing. Top each with a sliced egg. Refrigerate leftover dressing. **Yield:** 6 servings (about 1 cup dressing).

ZESTY ONION BURGERS
(Pictured above)

Mary Welle, Lake Elmo, Minnesota

My mother found this simple recipe on a soup can over 40 years ago. The oniony sandwiches starred in many of our Sunday suppers. I carry on the same tradition today, making them for my husband and our two grown sons.

> 1 **pound ground beef**
> 1 **cup chopped celery**
> 1 **can (10-1/2 ounces) condensed onion soup, undiluted**
> 1/2 **cup water**
> 1/4 **cup ketchup**
> 1 **teaspoon Worcestershire sauce**
> 1 **teaspoon prepared mustard**
> **Dash pepper**
> 6 **hamburger buns, split**
> 3 **tablespoons butter, softened**

In a large skillet, cook beef and celery over medium heat until meat is no longer pink; drain. Add the soup, water, ketchup, Worcestershire sauce, mustard and pepper. Bring to a boil.

Reduce heat; simmer, uncovered, for 20-25 minutes or until thickened, stirring occasionally. Spread cut sides of buns with butter; toast the buns. Top with beef mixture. **Yield:** 4 servings.

2 teaspoons sugar
1/2 teaspoon salt
1/2 teaspoon ground mustard
1/2 teaspoon paprika
1/4 teaspoon dried tarragon
1/4 teaspoon dried oregano
1/4 teaspoon dried thyme
1/8 teaspoon pepper
Dash garlic powder
1 package (16 ounces) frozen baby lima beans, cooked and drained
1/2 cup sliced onion, halved
1/2 cup sliced fresh mushrooms
2 tablespoons diced pimientos

In a jar with a tight-fitting lid, combine the first 11 ingredients; shake well. Cover and refrigerate for at least 1 hour. In a serving bowl, combine the lima beans, onion, mushrooms and pimientos. Add dressing and toss to coat. Cover and refrigerate for 1 hour. **Yield:** 6-8 servings.

CHEDDAR WALDORF SALAD

(Pictured above)

Barba McCarty, Paris, Texas

Wherever I take this one-of-a-kind salad, people eat it until it's gone. I got the original recipe from my mother-in-law and adapted it to fit my tastes. My fondness for cheese and cranberries prompted me to toss them into the delicious mix.

2 large Red Delicious apples, cubed
2 large Golden Delicious apples, cubed
1/2 cup chopped pecans
1/4 cup mayonnaise
3 tablespoons sugar, *divided*
1/4 cup chopped fresh *or* frozen cranberries, thawed
1/4 cup shredded cheddar cheese

In a large bowl, combine the apples and pecans. Combine mayonnaise and 2 tablespoons sugar; add to apple mixture and mix well. Combine cranberries and remaining sugar; sprinkle over apple mixture. Top with cheese. Serve immediately. **Yield:** 6-8 servings.

MARINATED LIMA BEAN SALAD

Sue Thompson, Chester, Maryland

This salad is one of my family's favorites. It tastes even better the next day, after the lima beans have marinated in the dressing.

1/3 cup vegetable oil
2 tablespoons red wine vinegar

TOSSED SALAD WITH CITRUS DRESSING

(Pictured below)

Mary Jane Ruther, Trenton, New Jersey

This is a refreshing salad with a very light dressing. The radishes add nice color.

4 cups torn fresh spinach
4 cups torn leaf lettuce
3 medium navel oranges, peeled and sectioned
2 tablespoons thinly sliced radishes

DRESSING:
- 1/2 cup orange juice
- 1/4 cup lemon juice
- 1/4 cup vegetable oil
- 1/2 teaspoon seasoned salt
- 1/8 teaspoon paprika
- 1/8 teaspoon pepper

In a salad bowl, toss the spinach, lettuce, orange sections and radishes. In a blender, combine the dressing ingredients; cover and process until blended. Serve with salad. Refrigerate any leftover dressing. **Yield:** 8 servings.

CHILLED BLUEBERRY SOUP

(Pictured above)

Sue Tucker, Brush Prairie, Washington

When I serve this fruit soup on a warm summer evening, my guests are always delighted. Compliments abound for this sweet and creamy meal starter.

- 4 cups fresh *or* frozen blueberries
- 3 cups water
- 2/3 cup sugar
- 1/4 teaspoon ground allspice
- 1 carton (16 ounces) plain yogurt
- Sour cream *or* additional yogurt, optional

In a large saucepan, combine the blueberries, water, sugar and allspice. Bring to a boil, stirring occasionally. Remove from the heat. In batches, process blueberry mixture in a blender for 1-2 minutes or until pureed. Strain through a sieve; discard seeds. Cool completely.

In batches, process blueberry mixture and yogurt until smooth. Cover and refrigerate until chilled. Garnish servings with sour cream or yogurt if desired. **Yield:** 6 servings.

REUBEN SANDWICHES

(Pictured below)

Kathryn Binder, Pickett, Wisconsin

My daughter shared this recipe with me. It's become a favorite of our entire family.

- 3/4 cup mayonnaise
- 3 tablespoons chili sauce
- 1 can (14 ounces) sauerkraut, rinsed and well drained
- 12 ounces shredded deli corned beef
- 2 cups (8 ounces) shredded Swiss cheese
- 30 slices rye bread
- 1/2 cup butter, softened
- Thousand Island salad dressing, optional

In a large bowl, combine the mayonnaise, chili sauce, sauerkraut, corned beef and Swiss cheese. Spread over 15 slices of bread, about 1/3 cup on each; top with remaining bread. Lightly butter the outsides of sandwiches.

Toast on a hot griddle for 4-5 minutes on each side or until golden brown. Serve with Thousand Island dressing if desired. **Yield:** 15 servings.

1 pound ground beef
1 small onion, chopped
1 can (16 ounces) chili beans in chili
   sauce
1 can (14-3/4 ounces) cream-style corn
1 can (14-1/2 ounces) diced tomatoes,
   undrained
1 jar (14 ounces) spaghetti sauce
1 envelope taco seasoning
1/4 teaspoon pepper

In a large saucepan, cook beef and onion over medium heat until meat is no longer pink; drain. Stir in the chili beans, corn, tomatoes, spaghetti sauce, taco seasoning and pepper. Bring to a boil. Reduce heat; simmer, uncovered, for 10 minutes. **Yield:** 6-8 servings.

MANDARIN PEANUT RICE SALAD
(Pictured below)

Shirley Reedy, Jacksonville, Arkansas

I learned how to make this salad while visiting England with a friend. When I made it for a family reunion, everyone asked for the recipe.

2 cups cooked rice
2 cups chopped green onions
1 can (15 ounces) mandarin oranges,
   drained
1 cup salted peanuts
1 cup mayonnaise
Salt and pepper to taste
Leaf lettuce

In a bowl, combine the rice, onions, oranges, peanuts, mayonnaise, salt and pepper; mix well.

TACO SANDWICH
(Pictured above)

Melody Stoltzfus, Parkesburg, Pennsylvania

One evening, Mom and I helped each other put together this sandwich using things we had on hand. It's delicious and was an instant hit with our family.

1 unsliced loaf (1 pound) Italian bread
4 ounces cream cheese, softened
1/2 cup salsa
1 pound ground beef
2 tablespoons taco seasoning
1 cup shredded lettuce
1 large tomato, sliced
6 slices American cheese

Cut bread in half lengthwise; hollow out top and bottom of loaf, leaving a 1/2-in. shell (discard removed bread or save for another use). In a mixing bowl, beat cream cheese and salsa until blended. Spread inside bread shell; set aside.

   In a large skillet, cook beef over medium heat until no longer pink; drain. Stir in taco seasoning. Layer lettuce and tomato in bottom of bread shell; top with beef mixture and cheese. Replace bread top. **Yield:** 6 servings.

PANTRY CHILI

Dorothy Russell, Portage, Wisconsin

I love a steaming, hot bowl of this flavorful chili in the cold winter months. It's conveniently made with items I keep in my pantry.

Soups, Salads & Sandwiches

Cover and refrigerate for at least 1 hour. Serve in a lettuce-lined bowl if desired. **Yield:** 6 servings.

ZESTY CORN SALAD

Jennifer Sikes, Tyler, Texas

We discovered this recipe at a Fourth of July celebration years ago. It's been a favorite ever since.

 1 can (15-1/4 ounces) whole kernel corn, drained
 1 can (15-1/4 ounces) white *or* shoepeg corn, drained
 2 celery ribs with leaves, chopped
1/2 cup green pepper, chopped
1/2 cup sweet red pepper, chopped
 4 green onions, sliced
 1 jalapeno pepper, seeded and chopped
1/2 cup Italian salad dressing
1/2 teaspoon ground cumin

In a large bowl, combine the first seven ingredients. Combine salad dressing and cumin; pour over corn mixture and toss to coat. Cover and refrigerate for 1 hour or until chilled. **Yield:** 5 servings.

Editor's Note: When cutting or seeding hot peppers, use rubber or plastic gloves to protect your hands. Avoid touching your face.

BACON POTATO CHOWDER

(Pictured above right)

Bob Wedemeyer, Lynnwood, Washington

This is a hearty, stick-to-your-ribs soup. In place of the bacon, you can substitute cubed cooked ham.

12 bacon strips, diced
 2 medium onions, chopped
 6 celery ribs, sliced
12 medium potatoes, peeled and cubed
2/3 cup butter
 1 cup all-purpose flour
 2 quarts milk
 2 medium carrots, shredded
 1 tablespoon salt
 1 teaspoon pepper

In a large skillet, cook bacon over medium heat until crisp. Remove with a slotted spoon to paper towels. Saute onions and celery in the drippings until tender; drain.

Place potatoes in a Dutch oven and cover with water. Bring to a boil. Reduce heat; cover and cook for 20 minutes or until tender. Drain; set potatoes aside.

In the same pan, melt butter. Stir in flour until smooth; gradually stir in milk. Bring to a boil over medium heat; cook and stir for 2 minutes or until thickened.

Reduce heat; add onion mixture, potatoes, carrots, salt and pepper. Cook for 10 minutes or until heated through. Sprinkle with bacon. **Yield:** 12-14 servings.

CUCUMBER TOMATO SALAD

Maxine Foreman, Columbus, Nebraska

This recipe comes from my husband's great-grandmother. It's especially good with ripe tomatoes from the garden, but drained canned tomatoes may also be used.

 2 medium tomatoes, chopped
 1 medium green pepper, chopped
 1 medium cucumber, peeled and thinly sliced
1/2 cup chopped green onions
 3 tablespoons sugar
1/2 cup water
1/2 cup cider vinegar
1/2 teaspoon salt
1/4 teaspoon pepper

In a serving bowl, combine the tomatoes, green pepper, cucumber and onions. Sprinkle with sugar; toss to coat. Let stand for 15 minutes.

Stir in water, vinegar, salt and pepper. Cover and refrigerate for 2 hours. Stir; serve with a slotted spoon. **Yield:** 6-8 servings.

Hawaiian Chicken Salad
(Pictured below)

Lynn Schwarz, Sanford, Florida

A friend shared this recipe with me. It's great for brunch or a summer supper.

2-1/2 cups diced cooked chicken
    1 can (20 ounces) pineapple tidbits, drained
    1 cup seedless red grapes, halved
    3/4 cup sliced celery
    3/4 cup mayonnaise
    1/2 teaspoon salt
    1/4 teaspoon pepper
    1 cup navel orange segments
    3/4 cup sliced firm bananas
    1/3 cup salted peanuts

In a bowl, combine the first seven ingredients. Fold in oranges. Cover and refrigerate until chilled. Just before serving, fold in bananas and sprinkle with peanuts. **Yield:** 8 servings.

Turkey Cabbage Soup

Marlene Schieferstein, Decatur, Indiana

I learned to cook from my mother, who comes from Germany. I added the turkey to this soup, which she frequently made when I was growing up.

    1 pound lean ground turkey
    2 medium onions, chopped
    1 tablespoon canola oil
    3 pounds potatoes, peeled and cut into 1-inch pieces
    3 medium carrots, sliced
    1 small head cabbage, chopped
    1 can (49-1/2 ounces) reduced-sodium chicken broth
    1 tablespoon prepared Dijon mustard
1-1/2 teaspoons prepared horseradish
    3/4 teaspoon salt
    1/2 teaspoon pepper
    2 teaspoons cornstarch
    1 tablespoon cold water

In a Dutch oven, cook turkey and onions in oil over medium heat until turkey is no longer pink; drain. Add the next eight ingredients; bring to a boil. Reduce heat; cover and simmer for 15-20 minutes or until potatoes are tender, stirring occasionally.

Combine cornstarch and cold water until smooth; stir into soup. Bring to a boil; cook and stir for 2 minutes or until slightly thickened. **Yield:** 10 servings (about 3-1/2 quarts).

Nutritional Analysis: One serving (1-1/2 cups) equals 242 calories, 6 g fat (1 g saturated fat), 36 mg cholesterol, 661 mg sodium, 36 g carbohydrate, 6 g fiber, 14 g protein. **Diabetic Exchanges:** 2 vegetable, 1-1/2 starch, 1 lean meat, 1/2 fat.

Corn Bread Salad

Pam Holloway, Marion, Louisiana

Despite my hectic schedule, I enjoy cooking for family and friends. This recipe is one of my favorites.

    1 package (8-1/2 ounces) corn bread/muffin mix
    2 cans (11 ounces *each*) Mexicorn, drained, *divided*
    3 medium tomatoes, diced
    3/4 cup chopped green pepper
    1 medium onion, chopped
    1 cup mayonnaise
    4 bacon strips, cooked and crumbled

Prepare corn bread according to package directions; stir in one can of Mexicorn. Bake according to package directions. Cool and crumble.

In a large bowl, combine the crumbled corn bread, tomatoes, green pepper, onion and remaining corn. Add mayonnaise; toss to coat. Sprinkle with bacon. Serve or refrigerate. **Yield:** 10-12 servings.

Salads are the meal of choice when our Texas temperatures hover in the 90s. In this one, I use locally grown strawberries, fresh greens and chicken strips.

DRESSING:
- 1/2 cup honey
- 1/2 cup red wine vinegar
- 4 teaspoons soy sauce
- 1 garlic clove, minced
- 1/2 teaspoon ground ginger
- 1/4 teaspoon salt

Dash pepper

SALAD:
- 1 pound boneless skinless chicken breasts, cut into strips
- 1 tablespoon vegetable oil
- 1 teaspoon butter
- 8 cups torn mixed salad greens
- 1 pint fresh strawberries, sliced
- 1/4 cup chopped walnuts

Additional whole strawberries, optional

In a small bowl, combine the dressing ingredients. In a large skillet, cook and stir chicken in oil and butter until no longer pink; drain. Add 1/2 cup salad dressing; cook 1 minute longer.

Place the salad greens in a serving bowl. Top with chicken, sliced strawberries and walnuts. Garnish with whole strawberries if desired. Serve with remaining dressing. **Yield:** 4 servings.

CRANBERRY WALDORF GELATIN

(Pictured above)

Debbie Short, Carlisle, Iowa

We enjoy this easy-to-make salad in the fall when fresh cranberries and apples are in season.

- 1 envelope unflavored gelatin
- 1 cup cold water, *divided*
- 1 package (3 ounces) cranberry gelatin
- 2 cups boiling water
- 1 can (16 ounces) whole-berry cranberry sauce
- 1/2 to 1 teaspoon ground cinnamon
- 1/4 teaspoon ground ginger
- 1/8 to 1/4 teaspoon salt
- 2 medium tart apples, peeled and diced
- 1 cup chopped walnuts

Sprinkle unflavored gelatin over 1/4 cup cold water; let stand for 5 minutes. In a bowl, dissolve softened gelatin and cranberry gelatin in boiling water. Stir in cranberry sauce until blended. Add cinnamon, ginger, salt and remaining cold water.

Cover and refrigerate until almost set. Fold in apples and nuts. Pour into an ungreased 2-1/2-qt. serving bowl. Refrigerate until firm. **Yield:** 10-12 servings.

STRAWBERRY CHICKEN SALAD

(Pictured at right)

Lorna Dressler, Universal City, Texas

▀▀▀▀▀▀▀▀▀▀▀▀

MUSHROOM PIZZA BURGERS

Harriet Stichter, Milford, Indiana

There is nothing better than a good, grilled burger for a picnic. This one fills the bill, and it is especially good with its zesty pizza touch.

✓ **Uses less fat, sugar or salt. Includes Nutritional Analysis and Diabetic Exchanges.**

> 1/2 cup sliced fresh mushrooms
> 1/4 cup chopped onion
> 1 garlic clove, minced
> 1/2 teaspoon dried oregano
> 1 cup crushed tomatoes, undrained

BURGERS:

> 1-1/2 cups finely chopped fresh mushrooms
> 1/3 cup minced fresh basil
> 1 egg white, beaten
> 2 tablespoons grated Parmesan cheese
> 2 tablespoons dry bread crumbs
> 1/2 teaspoon salt
> 1/8 teaspoon pepper
> 1 pound lean ground beef
> 6 slices part-skim mozzarella cheese
>   (3 ounces)
> 6 hamburger buns, split and toasted

In a small skillet coated with nonstick cooking spray, saute mushrooms and onion for 3 minutes. Add garlic and oregano; saute 1-2 minutes longer or until onion is tender. Stir in tomatoes. Cook, uncovered, over medium-low heat for 5 minutes, stirring occasionally. Set aside; keep warm.

In a large bowl, combine the mushrooms, basil, egg white, Parmesan cheese, bread crumbs, salt and pepper. Crumble beef over mixture; mix well. Shape into six patties.

Coat grill rack with nonstick cooking spray before starting the grill. Grill patties, covered, over medium-hot heat for 4-5 minutes on each side or until meat is no longer pink. Top patties with cheese and tomato sauce. Serve on buns. **Yield:** 6 servings.

Nutritional Analysis: One serving (1 burger) equals 333 calories, 12 g fat (5 g saturated fat), 36 mg cholesterol, 757 mg sodium, 28 g carbohydrate, 3 g fiber, 25 g protein. **Diabetic Exchanges:** 3 lean meat, 2 starch.

CREAMY CORN CRAB SOUP

(Pictured above)

Carol Ropchan, Willingdon, Alberta

This creamy soup is fast, easy and very tasty. Corn really stars in this delectable recipe, and crabmeat makes it a little more special. It will get high marks from both busy cooks and lovers of flavorful home-made food.

> 1 medium onion, chopped
> 2 tablespoons butter
> 3 cups chicken broth
> 3 cups frozen corn
> 3 medium potatoes, peeled and diced
> 1 can (6 ounces) crabmeat, drained,
>   flaked and cartilage removed *or* 1 cup
>   flaked imitation crabmeat
> 1 cup milk
> 1/2 teaspoon salt
> 1/4 teaspoon pepper

In a large saucepan, saute onion in butter until tender. Add the broth, corn and potatoes; bring to a boil. Reduce heat; cover and simmer for 15 minutes.

Remove from the heat; cool slightly. In a blender or food processor, puree half of the corn mixture. Return to the pan. Stir in the crab, milk, salt and pepper; cook over low heat until heated through (do not boil). **Yield:** 7 servings.

TOSSED SALAD WITH ARTICHOKES

(Pictured at right)

Karen Kay Brondel, Centertown, Missouri

This is a wonderful salad recipe that I acquired from a friend. It's quick and easy to prepare, and it is always a hit with my family and guests.

1 medium head iceberg lettuce, torn
1 bunch romaine, torn
1 cup thinly sliced red onion
1 jar (6-1/2 ounces) marinated artichoke
   hearts, drained
1/2 cup shredded Parmesan cheese
1/2 cup olive oil
1/3 cup red wine vinegar

In a large bowl, combine the lettuces, onion, artichoke hearts and Parmesan cheese. In a small bowl, whisk the oil and vinegar; drizzle over salad and toss to coat. **Yield:** 8-10 servings.

WILD RICE TURKEY SALAD

(Pictured at right)

Gay Woodgate, Bloomington, Minnesota

I tasted a wonderful wild rice and chicken salad at a restaurant during a stay at our cabin, so I developed this recipe using turkey when I returned home.

3 cups cooked wild rice
3 cups cubed cooked turkey
1/3 cup chopped green onions
1/3 cup chopped celery
1 can (8 ounces) sliced water chestnuts,
   drained and halved

2/3 cup mayonnaise
2/3 cup sour cream
1 teaspoon salt
1/2 teaspoon white pepper
1/2 teaspoon dill weed
1 cup cashews, *divided*
1 cup halved seedless red grapes

In a large bowl, combine the rice, turkey, onions, celery and water chestnuts. Combine the mayonnaise, sour cream, salt, pepper and dill; pour over salad and gently stir to coat. Cover and refrigerate for at least 2 hours.

Coarsely chop 3/4 cup cashews. Just before serving, stir the grapes and chopped cashews into salad. Garnish with remaining cashews. **Yield:** 6-7 servings.

SECOND-DAY SALAD TIPS

• Use leftover meat as the base for a main course salad the next day. Add salad greens or chopped fresh vegetables, and you'll have a meal in minutes.
• Speed up salad making by washing, cutting and drying all ingredients as soon as you buy them. Store in a plastic bag. At mealtime, just pull out the bag and make the salad.

TANGY BEAN SOUP

(Pictured below)

Joan Hallford, North Richland Hills, Texas

This soup has a great southwestern flavor. I love it because I can have the soup cooking in my slow cooker, and when I get home from work, I can quickly make the dumplings and fix dinner in a jiffy.

    2 cans (14-1/2 ounces *each*) chicken
      broth
    1 package (16 ounces) frozen mixed
      vegetables
    1 can (15 ounces) black beans, rinsed
      and drained
    1 can (15 ounces) pinto beans, rinsed
      and drained
    1 can (14-1/2 ounces) diced tomatoes,
      undrained
    1 medium onion, chopped
    1 tablespoon chili powder
    1 tablespoon minced fresh cilantro
    4 garlic cloves, minced
  1/4 teaspoon pepper
CORNMEAL DUMPLINGS:
  1/2 cup all-purpose flour
  1/2 cup shredded sharp cheddar cheese
  1/3 cup cornmeal
    1 tablespoon sugar
    1 teaspoon baking powder
    1 egg
    2 tablespoons milk
    2 teaspoons vegetable oil

In a slow cooker, combine the broth, vegetables, beans, tomatoes, onion, chili powder, cilantro, garlic and pepper. Cover and cook on high for 4-5 hours.

For dumplings, combine the flour, cheese, cornmeal, sugar and baking powder in a bowl. In another bowl, combine the egg, milk and oil; add to dry ingredients just until moistened (batter will be stiff). Drop by heaping tablespoons onto soup.

Cover and cook on high 30 minutes longer (without lifting cover) or until a toothpick inserted in a dumpling comes out clean. **Yield:** 6 servings.

PEPPERONI CAESAR PASTA SALAD

(Pictured above)

Barbara Nowakowski, North Tonawanda, New York

This salad is a flavorful and attractive dish to take to picnics and other summertime gatherings.

1-1/2 cups uncooked medium pasta shells
    1 cup cubed mozzarella cheese
    1 package (3-1/2 ounces) sliced
      pepperoni, quartered
    1 cup fresh broccoli florets
  1/2 cup prepared Caesar salad dressing

Cook pasta according to package directions. In a large bowl, combine the cheese, pepperoni and broccoli. Drain pasta and rinse in cold water; add to pepperoni mixture. Drizzle with salad dressing; toss to combine. Refrigerate until serving. **Yield:** 4 servings.

SLOPPY JOES

Anna Adams, Chatsworth, California

I adjusted three different recipes to come up with this one. Kids like the tangy taste and request the sandwiches for birthday parties.

  1 pound ground beef
  1 cup finely chopped onion
3/4 cup finely chopped sweet red pepper
1/4 cup finely chopped celery
1/2 cup ketchup
  1 tablespoon white vinegar
  2 teaspoons chili powder
1-1/2 teaspoons Worcestershire sauce
  1 teaspoon sugar
  1 teaspoon salt
  6 hamburger buns, split

In a large skillet, cook beef, onion, pepper and celery over medium heat until meat is no longer pink and vegetables are crisp-tender; drain.

In a small bowl, combine the ketchup, vinegar, chili powder, Worcestershire sauce, sugar and salt; stir into beef mixture. Simmer, uncovered, for 10 minutes, stirring occasionally. Serve on buns. **Yield:** 6 servings.

CABBAGE-CUCUMBER GELATIN CUPS

DeEtta Rasmussen, Fort Madison, Iowa

When we have fresh cabbage and cucumbers from the garden, this is one of my favorite salads to make for Sunday dinner. But with fresh produce available year-round, it's good anytime.

  1 package (3 ounces) lime gelatin
  1 cup boiling water
1/2 cup mayonnaise
  1 cup shredded cabbage
1/2 cup chopped cucumber
  2 tablespoons chopped green pepper

In a bowl, dissolve gelatin in boiling water. Whisk in the mayonnaise until smooth. Stir in the cabbage, cucumber and green pepper. Pour into four custard cups. Cover and refrigerate until firm. **Yield:** 4 servings.

Editor's Note: Reduced-fat or fat-free mayonnaise may not be substituted for regular mayonnaise in this recipe.

MACARONI SALAD

(Pictured below)

Betty Malone, Humboldt, Tennessee

I live in an area that's hot and humid, so I'm always experimenting with new recipes to find a dish that is tasty and nutritious. I like that I can make this salad without turning on my oven.

  2 cups cooked elbow macaroni
  1 can (15 ounces) garbanzo beans or chickpeas, rinsed and drained
  2 hard-cooked eggs, chopped
1/2 cup chopped dill pickles
1/2 cup mayonnaise
1/2 cup applesauce
  3 tablespoons chopped onion
  3 tablespoons minced fresh parsley
  3 tablespoons sliced ripe olives
  1 tablespoon mustard seed
  1 tablespoon pickle juice
1/2 teaspoon salt
1/4 teaspoon pepper
Pinch garlic powder
Lettuce leaves
Paprika

In a large bowl, combine macaroni, beans, eggs, pickles, mayonnaise, applesauce, onion, parsley, olives, mustard seed, pickle juice, salt, pepper and garlic powder; toss to coat. Cover and refrigerate for 1-2 hours. Serve in a lettuce-lined bowl; sprinkle with paprika. **Yield:** 8 servings.

Artichoke Spinach Salad
(Pictured above)

Nancy Lee Jennings, Fairfax, Virginia

The fresh spinach makes this a bright green salad, and the dressing adds just the right flavor.

- 12 cups torn fresh spinach
- 8 green onions, chopped
- 6 hard-cooked eggs, sliced
- 1/2 pound fresh mushrooms, sliced
- 1 can (8 ounces) sliced water chestnuts, drained
- 1 jar (6-1/2 ounces) marinated artichokes, drained and quartered
- 8 bacon strips, cooked and crumbled

DRESSING:
- 1/2 cup cider vinegar
- 1/2 cup sugar
- 1/2 teaspoon salt
- 1/2 teaspoon ground mustard
- 1 teaspoon grated onion
- 1 cup vegetable oil

In a large bowl, combine the first seven ingredients. For dressing, combine the vinegar, sugar, salt, mustard and onion in a blender; cover and process until smooth. While processing, gradually add oil in a steady stream. Drizzle over salad; gently toss to coat. Refrigerate any leftover dressing. **Yield:** 10-12 servings.

Slow Cooker Chili
(Pictured at right)

Sandra McKenzie, Braham, Minnesota

I like to use home-canned tomatoes and pizza sauce to give this chili my own unique flavor.

- 2 pounds ground beef
- 4 cans (16 ounces *each*) kidney beans, rinsed and drained
- 1 can (28 ounces) stewed tomatoes, undrained
- 1 can (15 ounces) pizza sauce
- 1 can (4 ounces) chopped green chilies
- 1/4 cup chopped onion
- 4 to 5 teaspoons chili powder
- 2 garlic cloves, minced
- 1 teaspoon dried basil
- 1/2 teaspoon salt
- 1/8 teaspoon pepper

In a large skillet, cook beef over medium heat until no longer pink; drain. Transfer to a 5-qt. slow cooker. Stir in the remaining ingredients. Cover and cook on low for 6 hours. **Yield:** 12 servings.

Shaker Pork Sandwiches

Jenni Oyler, Poughkeepsie, New York

The first time Dad tasted this pork, he said it was better than Mom's cooking! So Mom requested the recipe and later served the pork as sandwiches.

- 1 teaspoon rubbed sage
- 1/2 teaspoon salt
- 1/4 teaspoon pepper
- 1 garlic clove, minced
- 1 boneless pork loin roast (4 to 5 pounds)
- 3/4 cup sugar
- 2 tablespoons cornstarch
- 3/4 cup water

1/2 cup cider vinegar
1/4 cup soy sauce
12 to 16 hamburger buns, split

Combine the sage, salt, pepper and garlic; rub over roast. Place on a rack in a shallow roasting pan. Cover and bake at 350° for 1-3/4 to 2-1/4 hours or until tender. Remove meat and shred with a fork.

In a large saucepan, combine the sugar and cornstarch; add water, vinegar and soy sauce until smooth. Bring to a boil; cook and stir for 2 minutes or until thickened. Add shredded pork; stir until meat is coated and heated through. Serve on buns. **Yield:** 12-16 servings.

TOSSED CHICKEN SALAD

Gabriela Cappelli, Rock Springs, Wyoming

My mom came up with the recipe for this delicious chicken salad. It's great as a side dish or as a meal.

☑ Uses less fat, sugar or salt. Includes Nutritional Analysis and Diabetic Exchanges.

     6 cups torn lettuce
1-1/2 cups cubed cooked chicken breast
1-1/2 cups chopped fresh broccoli
     1 can (15 ounces) garbanzo beans *or* chickpeas, rinsed and drained
     2 medium tomatoes, cut into wedges
     1 cup grated carrot
   1/2 cup minced fresh cilantro
   1/2 cup reduced-fat ranch salad dressing *or* reduced-fat salad dressing of your choice

In a large bowl, combine the first seven ingredients. Drizzle with salad dressing and toss to coat. **Yield:** 6 servings.

Nutritional Analysis: One serving (2 cups) equals 199 calories, 7 g fat (1 g saturated fat), 35 mg cholesterol, 463 mg sodium, 18 g carbohydrate, 5 g fiber, 16 g protein. **Diabetic Exchanges:** 2 very lean meat, 2 vegetable, 1 fat, 1/2 starch.

HEARTY RICE SALAD

(Pictured above right)

Robin Bernard, Greeneville, Tennessee

I first tried this salad at a party and asked my friend who catered the event for the recipe. I modified it a little, and it's received rave reviews from my family.

     2 cups cooked rice
     1 medium carrot, chopped

     1 small zucchini, chopped
     1 celery rib, thinly sliced
   1/2 cup cubed cooked chicken
   1/2 cup cubed fully cooked ham
   1/2 cup cubed Swiss cheese
     2 hard-cooked eggs, chopped
     2 tablespoons chopped onion
     2 tablespoons mayonnaise
     1 tablespoon minced fresh parsley
     1 tablespoon lemon juice
     1 tablespoon olive oil
   1/2 teaspoon salt
   1/8 teaspoon pepper

In a large bowl, combine all ingredients. Cover and refrigerate for 4 hours or overnight. **Yield:** 6-8 servings.

CHICKEN SALAD SAVERS

- When simmering chicken to be used in a salad, make it extra-special by adding salt, dried rosemary and onion powder to the water.
- Chicken cooked in the microwave will be moist and juicy if it is covered and cooked for the proper amount of time. Estimate 7 minutes per pound for a whole chicken and 5 minutes per pound if cut up.

ITALIAN BEEF PATTIES

(Pictured below)

Mary Lutz, Arnold, Missouri

I love to cook, but I don't have time to spend all day in the kitchen. This recipe is fairly quick to make as well as very tasty.

> 1-1/2 pounds ground beef
> 1/2 teaspoon salt
> Dash pepper
> 1/4 cup all-purpose flour
> 2 eggs, beaten
> 1 cup dry bread crumbs
> 3 tablespoons vegetable oil
> 6 slices mozzarella cheese
> 1 cup sliced fresh mushrooms
> 1 jar (14 ounces) spaghetti sauce
> 3 tablespoons grated Parmesan cheese
> Toasted sandwich rolls *or* hot cooked spaghetti

In a bowl, combine the beef, salt and pepper; mix well. Shape into six patties. Place the flour, eggs and crumbs in three separate shallow bowls. Dredge beef patties in flour; dip into eggs, then coat with bread crumbs.

In a large skillet, cook patties in oil over medium heat until meat is no longer pink. Arrange in a single layer in a greased 13-in. x 9-in. x 2-in. baking dish. Top each patty with mozzarella cheese, mushrooms, spaghetti sauce and Parmesan cheese. Bake, uncovered, at 400° for 25 minutes or until hot and bubbly. Serve on rolls or over spaghetti. **Yield:** 6 servings.

EGG SALAD TUNA WRAPS

Francine Wingate
New Smyrna Beach, Florida

I like this combination of egg salad and tuna salad, rolled together in flour tortillas. Whether I eat them right away or in a day or two, they retain their flavor.

> 12 hard-cooked eggs, chopped
> 2 cans (6 ounces *each*) tuna, drained and flaked
> 2 celery ribs, chopped
> 1/2 cup sweet pickle relish
> 1/2 cup mayonnaise
> 3 tablespoons dry onion soup mix
> 1 tablespoon minced fresh parsley
> 1/2 teaspoon pepper
> Lettuce leaves, optional
> 6 flour tortillas (10 inches)

In a bowl, combine the first eight ingredients; mix well. Place lettuce leaves on tortillas if desired. Top each with about 3/4 cup egg mixture; roll up tightly. Serve immediately or wrap in plastic wrap and refrigerate. **Yield:** 6 servings.

GAZPACHO SALAD

Ruby Williams, Bogalusa, Louisiana

This is a colorful, refreshing salad that features a nice blend of flavors. It's a great way to enjoy your garden bounty.

> ✓ Uses less fat, sugar or salt. Includes Nutritional Analysis and Diabetic Exchanges.

> 4 large tomatoes, cubed
> 1 large cucumber, chopped
> 1 cup chopped red onion
> 1 cup chopped green pepper
> 1/3 cup minced fresh basil *or* parsley
> **DRESSING:**
> 1/3 cup cider vinegar
> 1 tablespoon canola oil
> 2 garlic cloves, minced
> 1/2 teaspoon salt
> 1/2 teaspoon pepper
> 1/2 teaspoon sugar

In a large bowl, combine the first five ingredients. In a small bowl, whisk the dressing ingredients. Pour over vegetables and toss to coat. Cover and chill for at least 1 hour. **Yield:** 12 servings.

Nutritional Analysis: One serving (3/4 cup) equals 28 calories, 1 g fat (trace saturated fat), 0 cholesterol, 102 mg sodium, 4 g carbohydrate, 1 g fiber, 1 g protein. **Diabetic Exchange:** 1 vegetable.

POTATO ROAST BEEF SALAD
(Pictured below)

Eva Kryzanowski, Beaumont, Alberta

I love to collect old cookbooks and found this wonderful recipe in one of them.

    1 pound thinly sliced deli roast beef
    3 medium red potatoes, cooked and thinly
      sliced
    1 small onion, thinly sliced and separated
      into rings
    1 small cucumber, diced
  1/2 cup sliced ripe olives
    2 teaspoons minced chives
    2 teaspoons minced fresh parsley
  1/2 teaspoon coarsely ground pepper,
      divided
  1/4 cup vegetable oil
    2 tablespoons red wine vinegar
  1/4 teaspoon dill weed
  1/4 teaspoon salt

On a large serving platter, arrange the roast beef, potatoes and onion. Sprinkle with the cucumber, olives, chives, parsley and 1/4 teaspoon pepper. Cover and refrigerate for 8 hours or overnight.

In a bowl, whisk the oil, vinegar, dill, salt and remaining pepper. Pour over salad just before serving. **Yield:** 6 servings.

CORN AND BLACK BEAN SALAD
(Pictured above)

Carrie Palmquist, Canova, South Dakota

I'm often asked to create "different" recipes for parties. This corn salad, cooked up for a barbecue, was an instant hit. Filled with vegetables and seasonings, it has great eye appeal and loads of flavor.

    1 can (15-1/4 ounces) whole kernel corn,
      drained
    1 can (15 ounces) black beans, rinsed
      and drained
    1 medium sweet red pepper, chopped
    1 medium tomato, seeded and chopped
    6 green onions, chopped
  1/2 cup chopped red onion
    1 jalapeno pepper, seeded and finely
      chopped, optional
    1 garlic clove, minced
  3/4 cup Italian salad dressing
    1 tablespoon minced fresh cilantro
    1 tablespoon lime *or* lemon juice
  3/4 teaspoon hot pepper sauce
  1/2 teaspoon chili powder

In a large bowl, combine the first eight ingredients. In a small bowl, combine the salad dressing, cilantro, lime juice, hot pepper sauce and chili powder.

Pour over corn mixture and toss to coat. Cover and refrigerate for at least 6 hours or overnight. Serve with a slotted spoon. **Yield:** 6-8 servings.

In a large bowl, layer the cabbage, bananas and tangerines. Drain pineapple, reserving 2 tablespoons juice. Place pineapple over tangerines.

In a small bowl, combine mayonnaise and reserved pineapple juice until smooth; drizzle over salad. Cover and refrigerate for at least 2 hours. Toss just before serving. **Yield:** 10-12 servings.

FRENCH POTATO SALAD

(Pictured at right)

Joan Custer, Huntington Beach, California

My family enjoys this unique blend so much that they can hardly wait until my green beans and red potatoes are ready to harvest.

      3 medium red potatoes
  1/2 pound fresh green beans, cut
          into 1-inch pieces
      8 bacon strips, cooked and crumbled
DRESSING:
  1/4 cup olive oil
  1/4 cup chopped green onions
      3 tablespoons white wine vinegar
      2 tablespoons minced fresh parsley
      1 garlic clove, minced
  1/2 teaspoon salt
  1/2 teaspoon ground mustard
  1/4 teaspoon dried basil
  1/4 teaspoon dried tarragon
Pepper to taste

Place potatoes in a saucepan and cover with water. Bring to a boil. Reduce heat; cover and cook

MARINATED VEGGIE SALAD

(Pictured above)

Lynn Grate, South Bend, Indiana

This is my favorite potluck salad. I get compliments every time I make it. It's also an ideal make-ahead dish since it needs to marinate overnight.

      1 pint cherry tomatoes, halved
      1 medium zucchini, cubed
      1 medium yellow summer squash, cubed
      1 medium cucumber, cubed
      1 *each* medium sweet yellow, red and
          green pepper, cut into 1-inch pieces
      1 can (6 ounces) pitted ripe olives,
          drained
      1 small red onion, chopped
  1/2 to 3/4 cup Italian salad dressing

In a serving bowl, combine all ingredients. Cover and refrigerate overnight. **Yield:** 12 servings.

FRUITED CABBAGE SALAD

(Pictured at right)

Rita Rial, Rochester, New Hampshire

This refreshing salad is always a hit when I take it to picnics, family get-togethers and church suppers.

      4 cups shredded cabbage
      2 medium firm bananas, sliced
      2 medium tangerines, peeled, sectioned
          and seeded
      1 can (20 ounces) pineapple tidbits
      3 tablespoons mayonnaise

Soups, Salads & Sandwiches

for 15-20 minutes or until tender. Place beans in a saucepan and cover with water. Bring to a boil. Cook, uncovered, for 8-10 minutes or until crisp-tender; drain. Drain and slice potatoes.

In a large bowl, combine the potatoes, beans and bacon. In a jar with a tight-fitting lid, combine the dressing ingredients; shake well.

Pour over the potato mixture and toss to coat. Serve the salad at room temperature or cover and refrigerate for 2-3 hours. **Yield:** 8-10 servings.

ZESTY BUTTERMILK SALAD DRESSING

Cassandra Corridon, Frederick, Maryland

This homemade dressing is wonderful over a variety of greens and vegetables. Plus, you can feel good knowing it's a little lighter than regular dressing.

✓ Uses less fat, sugar or salt. Includes Nutritional Analysis and Diabetic Exchanges.

    2/3 cup fat-free plain yogurt
    1/2 cup 1% buttermilk
    1/4 cup reduced-fat mayonnaise
      1 tablespoon minced fresh parsley
1-1/2 teaspoons minced fresh basil *or* 1/2
        teaspoon dried basil
      1 teaspoon sugar
      1 teaspoon minced fresh oregano *or* 1/4
        teaspoon dried oregano
    1/2 teaspoon minced fresh garlic
    1/8 teaspoon salt

In a food processor or blender, combine the yogurt, buttermilk and mayonnaise; cover and process un-

til smooth. Add remaining ingredients; cover and process until blended. Cover and refrigerate at least 1 hour before serving. **Yield:** 1-1/3 cups.

Nutritional Analysis: One serving (2 tablespoons) equals 35 calories, 2 g fat (trace saturated fat), 3 mg cholesterol, 99 mg sodium, 3 g carbohydrate, trace fiber, 1 g protein. **Diabetic Exchange:** 1/2 fat.

TACO SOUP

(Pictured below)

Sue Burton, Frankfort, Kansas

This is a quick-and-easy recipe to make, and it's one of our favorite meals for cold winter nights.

1-1/2 pounds ground beef
      1 large onion, chopped
      1 can (15 ounces) pinto beans, rinsed
        and drained
      1 can (14-1/2 ounces) stewed tomatoes
      1 can (10 ounces) diced tomatoes and
        green chilies
      1 can (10 ounces) chili without beans
      1 pound process cheese (Velveeta), cubed
Salt, pepper and garlic powder to taste
      2 cups (16 ounces) sour cream, *divided*

In a Dutch oven or soup kettle, cook beef and onion over medium heat until meat is no longer pink; drain. Add the beans, tomatoes, chili, cheese and seasonings. Reduce heat to low; cook and stir until cheese is melted. Stir in 1 cup sour cream; heat through (do not boil). Garnish with remaining sour cream. **Yield:** 3-1/4 quarts.

TAKING SIDES *to determine your family's favorite side dish will be difficult with all the selections shared in this chapter.*

VEGGIE VARIETY. From top: Nutty Brussels Sprouts, Scalloped Corn and Cranberry Sweet Potato Bake (all recipes on p. 81).

SCALLOPED CORN

(Pictured at left)

Ellen Burnside, Piqua, Ohio

My sister-in-law gave me this recipe many years ago, and it's become a favorite of my family. I'm always asked to bring it to reunions and picnics.

- 2 cans (14-3/4 ounces *each*) cream-style corn
- 2 eggs, beaten
- 1 cup crushed butter-flavored crackers (about 20 crackers)
- 1 cup diced fresh *or* jarred mango *or* 1 cup diced fresh *or* frozen peaches
- 1/2 cup diced onion
- 1/2 teaspoon sugar
- 1/2 teaspoon salt
- 1/8 teaspoon pepper
- 1 tablespoon minced fresh parsley

In a bowl, combine first eight ingredients. Transfer to a greased shallow 2-qt. baking dish. Sprinkle with parsley. Bake, uncovered, at 350° for 40-45 minutes or until golden. **Yield:** 6 servings.

NUTTY BRUSSELS SPROUTS

(Pictured at left)

Laura Hamrick, Buena Park, California

Even my son will eat brussels sprouts when I make this English recipe, which is traditionally made with chestnuts.

- 1 pound fresh *or* frozen brussels sprouts, thawed and halved
- 1 cup water
- 1/2 teaspoon salt
- 1/4 teaspoon pepper
- 3 tablespoons butter
- 1/4 cup chopped pecans

In a saucepan, bring brussels sprouts, water and salt to a boil. Reduce heat. Cover and simmer for 6-8 minutes or until crisp-tender; drain. Sprinkle with pepper; keep warm.

In a skillet, heat butter over medium heat until golden brown. Add pecans; cook for 1-2 minutes or until lightly browned. Add to brussels sprouts; toss to coat. **Yield:** 4-6 servings.

CRANBERRY SWEET POTATO BAKE

(Pictured at left)

Martha Nadelhoffer, Eau Claire, Wisconsin

This recipe is a different and tasty way to serve sweet potatoes. It goes well with ham, turkey or chicken.

- 2 cans (15 ounces *each*) cut sweet potatoes, drained
- 1 cup fresh *or* frozen cranberries
- 1/4 cup coarsely chopped pecans
- 1/2 cup orange marmalade, warmed

Place the sweet potatoes in a greased 11-in. x 7-in. x 2-in. baking dish. Sprinkle with the cranberries and pecans; spoon the marmalade over top.

Cover and bake at 350° for 25-30 minutes or until heated through. **Yield:** 4-6 servings.

ITALIAN-STYLE PEAS

Kathleen Valle, Philadelphia, Pennsylvania

This side dish is a big hit on any occasion. I've been making it for at least 35 years, and it was made by my mother before me.

☑ Uses less fat, sugar or salt. Includes Nutritional Analysis and Diabetic Exchanges.

- 1 small onion, diced
- 4 ounces diced fully cooked lean ham
- 4 teaspoons canola oil
- 1 package (16 ounces) frozen peas
- 1/2 teaspoon salt
- 1/4 teaspoon dried oregano
- 1/4 teaspoon pepper

In a nonstick skillet, saute onion and ham in oil until onion is tender. Add the remaining ingredients. Reduce heat; cover and cook until peas are tender. **Yield:** 4 servings.

Nutritional Analysis: One serving (3/4 cup) equals 148 calories, 5 g fat (1 g saturated fat), 5 mg cholesterol, 390 mg sodium, 17 g carbohydrate, 6 g fiber, 8 g protein. **Diabetic Exchanges:** 1 starch, 1 very lean meat, 1 fat.

CHRISTMAS PICKLES
(Pictured below)

Patricia Martin, Shelbyville, Tennessee

My recipe was adapted from one a dear family friend shared. These morsels are delicious anytime, but the green, red and white hues of the pickles, cherries and onions make them ideal for Christmas gift-giving.

       1 gallon whole dill pickles
11-1/4 cups sugar
       1 cup white vinegar
       1 tablespoon mustard seed
       1 tablespoon whole cloves
       3 to 4 jalapeno peppers, chopped
       4 to 5 garlic cloves, minced
       5 to 6 whole cinnamon sticks
       1 pound whole candied cherries
       3 jars (15 ounces *each*) pearl onions,
         drained
       1 teaspoon olive oil

Remove pickles from juice; set juice aside. Cut pickles into 1/2-in. slices; set aside. In a Dutch oven or large kettle, combine the sugar, vinegar, mustard seed, cloves, peppers, garlic, cinnamon sticks and pickle juice.

Cook over medium heat for 10 minutes or until sugar is dissolved, stirring occasionally. Bring to a boil. Reduce heat; simmer, uncovered, for 10 minutes. Remove from the heat; cool slightly. Discard cinnamon sticks.

In a large bowl, combine cherries, onions and pickle slices. Pour liquid over pickle mixture. Stir in oil. Cover and refrigerate for 48 hours, stirring occasionally. Divide mixture among jars.

BROWN RICE VEGETABLE CASSEROLE
(Pictured above)

Gloria De Berardinis, Greentown, Pennsylvania

One taste of this crowd-pleasing casserole brings compliments and requests for my recipe. The blend of tender vegetables and rice is perfect for holiday meals and dish-to-pass affairs.

       3 cups chicken broth
  1-1/2 cups uncooked brown rice
       2 cups chopped onions, *divided*
       3 tablespoons soy sauce
       2 tablespoons butter, melted
   1/2 teaspoon dried thyme
       4 cups cauliflowerets
       4 cups broccoli florets
       2 medium sweet red peppers, julienned
       2 garlic cloves, minced
       3 tablespoons olive oil
       1 cup salted cashew halves
       2 cups (8 ounces) shredded cheddar
         cheese, optional

In a greased 3-qt. baking dish, combine the broth, rice, 1 cup onion, soy sauce, butter and thyme. Cover and bake at 350° for 65-70 minutes or until rice is tender.

Meanwhile, in a large skillet, saute the cauliflower, broccoli, peppers, garlic and remaining onion in oil until crisp-tender; spoon over rice mixture. Cover and bake for 10 minutes.

Uncover and sprinkle with cashews and cheese if desired. Bake 5-7 minutes longer or until cheese is melted. **Yield:** 8-10 servings.

Cover and store in the refrigerator for up to 1 month. **Yield:** 6-1/2 quarts.

Editor's Note: When cutting or seeding hot peppers, use rubber or plastic gloves to protect your hands. Avoid touching your face.

CREAMY VEGGIE VERMICELLI
(Pictured above)

Robyn Thompson, Culver City, California

When I first met my husband, he didn't like any green vegetables. Now, this is his favorite dish!

    2 cups broccoli florets
    2 cups cut fresh asparagus (1-inch pieces)
  1/4 cup butter
    8 ounces uncooked vermicelli
    2 packages (3 ounces *each*) cream cheese,
      cubed
    1 cup milk
  3/4 cup grated Parmesan cheese
  1/4 teaspoon salt
  1/4 teaspoon pepper
    1 tablespoon grated lemon peel

In a large skillet, saute the broccoli and asparagus in butter for 8-10 minutes or until crisp-tender. Meanwhile, cook vermicelli according to package directions.

In a saucepan, cook and stir the cream cheese and milk over medium heat until smooth and blended. Add Parmesan cheese, salt and pepper; cook 2 minutes longer or until blended. Remove from heat. Stir lemon peel into vegetables. Drain vermicelli; place in a serving bowl. Add vegetables and cheese sauce; toss to coat. Serve immediately. **Yield:** 4-6 servings.

MUSHROOM WILD RICE BAKE
(Pictured below)

Jann Marie Foster, Minneapolis, Minnesota

The wild rice adds a wonderful flavor to this casserole. I like to serve it on special occasions.

      1 cup uncooked wild rice
      2 cups boiling water
      1 pound sliced fresh mushrooms
      1 medium onion, chopped
      2 tablespoons butter
    3/4 cup uncooked long grain rice
    1/2 cup sliced almonds
      3 cups chicken broth
  1-1/2 cups heavy whipping cream
      1 teaspoon salt
    1/8 teaspoon pepper
      3 tablespoons grated Parmesan cheese

Place wild rice in a bowl and cover with boiling water; soak for 1 hour. Drain and set aside. In a large skillet, saute mushrooms and onion in butter until tender. In a large bowl, combine the mushroom mixture, wild rice, long grain rice, almonds, broth, cream, salt and pepper.

Transfer to a greased 2-1/2-qt. baking dish. Cover and bake at 350° for 75 minutes. Uncover; sprinkle with Parmesan cheese. Bake 10 minutes longer or until rice is tender. **Yield:** 8-10 servings.

TURNIP CASSEROLE

Doris Hubert, East Killingly, Connecticut

No holiday meal in our home is complete without this dish handed down by my Finnish grandmother.

- 4 medium turnips, peeled and cubed
- 1 cup water
- 1 egg, beaten
- 1/3 cup sugar
- 3 tablespoons butter
- 1/2 teaspoon salt
- 1/4 teaspoon ground cinnamon

In a saucepan, cook turnips in water for 15-20 minutes or until tender. Drain and mash. Add the egg, sugar, butter and salt; mix well. Transfer to a greased 1-qt. baking dish; sprinkle with cinnamon. Cover and bake at 350° for 20-25 minutes or until heated through. **Yield:** 4-6 servings.

COCONUT CARROT CASSEROLE

(Pictured below)

Mary Beth Keim, Crawfordsville, Indiana

I can about 30 pounds of carrots every fall, so I'm always looking for new ways to prepare them. This recipe is one that my family really likes.

- 1/4 cup butter, softened
- 1/2 cup sugar
- 2 eggs
- 1/3 cup milk
- 1 teaspoon vanilla extract

- 3 cans (16 ounces *each*) sliced carrots, drained and mashed
- 1/2 cup flaked coconut

TOPPING:
- 1/2 cup packed brown sugar
- 1/2 cup chopped pecans
- 1/4 cup all-purpose flour
- 2 tablespoons butter, melted

In a mixing bowl, cream butter and sugar. Add eggs, milk, vanilla and carrots; mix well. Stir in coconut. Pour into a greased 2-qt. baking dish. Combine topping ingredients; sprinkle over the top. Bake, uncovered, at 350° for 35-40 minutes or until golden brown and bubbly. **Yield:** 6-8 servings.

SWEET POTATO CRANBERRY BAKE

Jill Doyle, Kingston, Massachusetts

In October, my husband helps harvest cranberries at a friend's bogs, so I have access to the very freshest ingredients. Their bold autumn flavor pairs up with sweet potatoes to make this seasonal side dish.

- 4 large sweet potatoes
- 2 cups fresh or frozen cranberries
- 1/2 cup packed brown sugar
- 2 tablespoons butter, melted
- 1/2 cup orange juice

TOPPING:
- 1/2 cup chopped walnuts
- 1/4 cup packed brown sugar
- 1/2 teaspoon ground cinnamon
- 3 tablespoons cold butter

Place sweet potatoes in a Dutch oven; cover with water. Bring to a boil. Reduce heat; cover and simmer for 40-50 minutes or until tender. Drain.

When cool enough to handle, peel potatoes and cut into 1/4-in. slices. Place half in a greased 2-1/2-qt. baking dish. Top with half of the cranberries, sugar and butter. Repeat layers. Pour orange juice over top. Cover and bake at 350° for 30 minutes. In a bowl, combine nuts, sugar and cinnamon; cut in butter. Sprinkle over sweet potato mixture. Bake, uncovered, 10 minutes longer or until topping is golden brown. **Yield:** 6-8 servings.

DOUBLE-CRUST POTATO PIE

(Pictured above right)

Josephine Schuemaker, York, Pennsylvania

Before my husband and I were married, my future sister-in-law made this Pennsylvania Dutch recipe for me. It's become one of my favorite dishes.

4 cups sliced peeled potatoes (1/4 inch
  thick)
1 cup chicken broth
1 medium onion, diced
1 tablespoon butter
3/4 teaspoon salt
1/4 teaspoon pepper
Pastry for double-crust pie (9 inches)
1 teaspoon milk

In a large saucepan, combine the potatoes, broth, onion, butter, salt and pepper. Cook, uncovered, over low heat until potatoes are crisp-tender and broth is absorbed, about 20 minutes; drain.

Line a 9-in. pie plate with the bottom pastry. Spoon potato mixture into the crust. Roll out remaining pastry to fit top of pie. Trim, seal and flute edges; cut vents in top. Brush with milk. Bake at 425° for 30-35 minutes or until golden brown. Serve warm. **Yield:** 6-8 servings.

▪▪▪▪▪▪▪▪▪▪▪▪▪▪

OVEN POTATOES

Ronda Thompson, Wellsville, Utah

As executive director for a living history site, I've learned the basics of milking cows, making candles and cooking hearty fare like potatoes. This dish has the right combination of cheeses, seasonings and potatoes.

5 large potatoes, peeled and thinly sliced
1 medium onion, thinly sliced
1/3 cup butter, melted
1 teaspoon salt
1/4 to 1/2 teaspoon pepper
1/2 teaspoon garlic powder

1/3 cup grated Parmesan cheese
1 cup (4 ounces) shredded cheddar
  cheese

In a greased 13-in. x 9-in. x 2-in. baking dish, layer the potatoes and onion. In a small bowl, combine the butter, salt, pepper and garlic powder; drizzle over potatoes and onion. Sprinkle with Parmesan cheese; stir gently to combine.

Cover and bake at 400° for 45 minutes or until the potatoes are tender. Uncover; sprinkle with the cheddar cheese. Bake 5-10 minutes longer or until the cheese is melted. **Yield:** 6 servings.

▪▪▪▪▪▪▪▪▪▪▪▪▪▪

CARROT MUSHROOM MEDLEY
(Pictured below)

Jeanie Beers, Montgomery, New York

The carrots make this side dish both colorful and tasty. It's great to serve to family and friends.

1 pound carrots, cut into 2-inch julienned
  strips
1 small onion, finely chopped
5 fresh mushrooms, sliced
1 teaspoon minced fresh rosemary *or* 1/4
  teaspoon dried rosemary, crushed
1/4 teaspoon ground cardamom
1/8 teaspoon garlic salt
1/8 teaspoon pepper
2 tablespoons butter

In a large skillet, saute vegetables and seasonings in butter until vegetables are crisp-tender, about 10 minutes. Serve immediately. **Yield:** 4 servings.

1/2 to 1 teaspoon vanilla extract
1/2 teaspoon salt
1/8 teaspoon cayenne pepper
  1 can (15-1/4 ounces) whole kernel corn, drained
  1 can (14-3/4 ounces) cream-style corn
  4 bacon strips, cooked and crumbled
  4 green onions, chopped
1/2 cup shredded cheddar cheese
Maple syrup, optional

In a large mixing bowl, beat the first seven ingredients until smooth. Stir in the corn, cream-style corn, bacon and onions. Pour into a greased 1-1/2-qt. baking dish. Sprinkle with cheese.

Bake, uncovered, at 350° for 35-40 minutes or until a knife inserted near the center comes out clean. Let stand for 5-10 minutes before serving. Serve with syrup if desired. **Yield:** 8 servings.

Editor's Note: This corn pudding has a soft texture and may be served with a spoon, or it can be cut after standing for a bit.

HEARTY CORN PUDDING
(Pictured above)

Linda Hutmacher, Teutopolis, Illinois

Corn is a staple around our house in summer—and so is this comforting dish. Every year, we grow corn in our garden. I keep packages of our corn in the freezer so I can make recipes like this in any season.

  4 eggs
1/2 cup heavy whipping cream
  3 tablespoons sugar
  3 tablespoons cornstarch

SUNDAY BEST CORN

Cathy Steinkuhler, Burr, Nebraska

A friend of mine shared this recipe with me a number of years ago. It's a favorite with my brother, who is a big fan of corn.

A Basketful of Corn Tips

• To cook corn on the cob in the microwave, wrap a husked ear in waxed paper and twist the ends. Cook for 2 to 2-1/2 minutes. For two ears, wrap separately and cook for 4 to 5 minutes.
—*Sharon Crouse, Ogden, Iowa*

• For the best flavor and quality, always be sure to pick and husk your corn early in the morning.
—*Violet Gertsch, Darlington, Wisconsin*

• Wipe a dampened terry cloth towel or paper towel over ears of corn to help remove strands of silk.
—*Martha Polasek, Markham, Texas*

• When storing ears of corn in the refrigerator, wrap them in a damp dish towel and place in a plastic bag.
—*Kathy Rhoads, Circleville, Ohio*

• I've found that you can stop worms from infesting corn by pouring a tablespoon of vegetable oil on the tassels when they appear.
—*Joanne Doucet, Weymouth, Nova Scotia*

• Plant corn in a square in your garden instead of in long rows. This will help the plants pollinate better.
—*Violet Klause, Onoway, Alberta*

• To freeze corn, I first husk the ears and place them in boiling water for 10 minutes. Next, I place them in cold water, then ice water. Finally, I drain the ears and wrap each individually in foil before putting them in the freezer. To serve, I simply unwrap the frozen ears and cook in boiling water for 10 minutes.
—*Janice Bell Monticello, Kentucky*

6 bacon strips, diced
1 cup sliced fresh mushrooms
1/4 cup chopped onion
2 packages (10 ounces *each*) frozen corn, thawed
1 cup (8 ounces) process cheese sauce

In a skillet, cook bacon over medium heat until crisp. Remove to paper towels. Drain, reserving 1 tablespoon drippings.

Saute mushrooms and onion in the drippings until tender. Stir in corn, process cheese and bacon. Cook and stir for 2-4 minutes or until cheese is melted. **Yield:** 6-8 servings.

CORN PUDDING STUFFED TOMATOES

(Pictured below)

Jean Smalls, Cooper City, Florida

I use tomatoes and sweet corn harvested fresh from my garden to make this tasty and attractive side dish.

8 medium tomatoes
1 teaspoon salt, *divided*
1/2 teaspoon pepper, *divided*
2 tablespoons all-purpose flour
2 tablespoons sugar
1/2 teaspoon baking powder
2 eggs, lightly beaten
1 cup half-and-half cream
1 cup whole kernel corn
2 tablespoons butter, melted
Minced fresh parsley

Cut a thin slice off the top of each tomato; scoop out and discard pulp. Sprinkle inside of tomatoes with half of the salt and pepper. Invert on paper

towels to drain.

In a large bowl, combine the flour, sugar, baking powder and remaining salt and pepper. Combine the eggs, cream, corn and butter; stir into dry ingredients. Spoon into tomatoes.

Place in a shallow baking dish. Bake, uncovered, at 350° for 38-40 minutes or until a knife inserted near center comes out clean. Sprinkle with parsley. **Yield:** 8 servings.

CORNY RICE

(Pictured above)

Mrs. Zannie Rasberry, Zwolle, Louisiana

When I pick fresh corn, I freeze it right with the shucks on. It stays good all winter.

1/4 cup chopped sweet red pepper
1/4 cup chopped onion
2 tablespoons finely chopped jalapeno pepper
3 garlic cloves, minced
1 tablespoon olive oil
2 cups cooked rice
1 cup frozen corn
1/2 teaspoon salt
1/4 teaspoon pepper
3 green onions, chopped
Soy sauce, optional

In a large skillet, saute red pepper, onion, jalapeno and garlic in oil until tender. Add rice, corn, salt and pepper; cook and stir until heated through. Sprinkle with green onions. Serve with soy sauce if desired. **Yield:** 4 servings.

Editor's Note: When cutting or seeding hot peppers, use rubber or plastic gloves to protect your hands. Avoid touching your face.

MAPLE-APPLE BAKED BEANS

(Pictured below)

Vicky Heise, South Porcupine, Ontario

This is an old French-Canadian recipe. We use pure maple syrup, but it's the apple slices that make this my favorite recipe for baked beans.

>   4 cups dried navy beans
>   10 cups water
>   1 pound sliced bacon, quartered
>   1 large onion, chopped
>   2 teaspoons salt
>   1 teaspoon ground mustard
>   1 cup maple syrup
>   3 medium tart apples, sliced
>   1/2 cup butter, softened
>   1 cup packed brown *or* maple sugar

Place beans in a soup kettle or Dutch oven; add water to cover by 2 in. Bring to a boil; boil for 2 minutes. Remove from the heat; cover and let stand for 1 hour.

Drain and rinse beans; discard liquid. Return beans to the pan; add 10 cups water. Bring to a boil. Reduce heat; cover and simmer for 30 minutes. Drain, reserving 1/2 cup liquid.

Line the bottom of a 4-qt. baking dish with bacon. In a bowl, combine the beans, onion, salt and mustard. Spoon over bacon. Pour syrup over the top. Cover and bake at 350° for 3 hours, gently stirring occasionally and adding reserved bean liquid if needed.

Arrange sliced apples over the top. In a small mixing bowl, cream butter and brown sugar; spread over apples. Cover and bake 1 hour longer or until beans are tender. **Yield:** 12-14 servings.

SAVORY GREEN BEANS

(Pictured above and on front cover)

Devon Brown, San Jose, California

When we have family get-togethers, this is the dish I'm always asked to bring.

>   1 pound fresh green beans, trimmed
> 1-1/2 cups sliced fresh mushrooms
>   2 tablespoons chopped green onion
>   2 tablespoons butter
>   2 tablespoons minced fresh savory *or* 2 teaspoons dried savory
>   2 tablespoons minced fresh parsley
>   1 tablespoon lemon juice
>   1 tablespoon cider vinegar
>   1 tablespoon vegetable oil
>   1 teaspoon sugar
>   1 teaspoon salt
>   1/8 teaspoon pepper
>   4 bacon strips, cooked and crumbled

Place the beans in a steamer basket; place in a saucepan over 1 in. of water. Bring to a boil; cover and steam for 7-9 minutes or until crisp-tender.

Meanwhile, in a large skillet, saute mushrooms and onion in butter until tender. Remove from heat; stir in savory, parsley, lemon juice, vinegar, oil, sugar, salt and pepper. Add beans; toss to coat. Sprinkle with bacon. **Yield:** 4 servings.

CREAMY POTATOES 'N' PEAS

(Pictured at right)

Debbie Jones, California, Maryland

This recipe has great eye as well as stomach appeal. I like to serve it in a pretty glass bowl.

- 1 pound small unpeeled red potatoes, cut into wedges
- 1 package (10 ounces) frozen peas
- 2 tablespoons chopped onion
- 2 tablespoons butter
- 2 tablespoons all-purpose flour
- 3/4 teaspoon salt
- 1/4 teaspoon pepper
- 1-1/2 cups milk
- 1/2 teaspoon dill weed

Place potatoes in a large saucepan and cover with water; cook until tender. Cook peas according to package directions.

Meanwhile, in a small saucepan, saute onion in butter until tender. Stir in flour, salt and pepper until blended. Gradually stir in milk. Bring to a boil over medium heat; cook and stir for 2 minutes or until thickened. Add dill.

Drain potatoes and peas; place in a serving bowl. Top with sauce and stir to coat. Serve immediately. **Yield:** 6-8 servings.

HOT CURRIED FRUIT SAUCE
(Pictured above right)

Jean Houston, Kelowna, British Columbia

This mouth-watering zesty fruit sauce truly works magic on old-fashioned baked ham. In fact, it turns it into instant party food. Since the sauce relies on canned fruit, it's handy to use year-round.

- 1/2 cup butter
- 1 cup packed brown sugar
- 2 to 3 teaspoons curry powder
- 1/4 teaspoon salt
- 1 can (20 ounces) pineapple tidbits, drained
- 1 can (15 ounces) mandarin oranges, drained
- 1 can (8-1/2 ounces) sliced peaches, drained and chopped
- 1 can (8-1/2 ounces) sliced pears, drained and chopped
- 12 maraschino cherries, halved

In a small saucepan, melt butter. Stir in the brown sugar, curry powder and salt. Bring to a boil. Reduce heat; simmer, uncovered, for 5 minutes.

In a lightly greased 2-qt. baking dish, combine the fruit; mix well. Pour sauce over the mixed fruit. Bake, uncovered, at 300° for 30 minutes or until heated through. **Yield:** 5 cups.

GLAZED TO PERFECTION

Looking for an easy glaze to keep on hand? Small amounts of jelly left in jars can be combined, melted and used as glaze for ham. For another twist on your next ham, make dressing as you would for chicken or turkey—but without seasoning. Bake with your ham, letting the juices flavor the dressing.

COOKIE BAKING *comes easy when you have taste-tempting treats galore to choose from in this chapter.*

SWEETHEART SWEETS. From top: Chunky Peanut Brittle and Linzer Heart Cookies (recipes on p. 91).

Cookies, Bars & Candies

LINZER HEART COOKIES

(Pictured at left)

Jane Pearcy, Verona, Wisconsin

I bake these tender jam-filled hearts when I need something fancy to serve for special occasions.

- 1-1/4 cups butter, softened
- 1 cup sugar
- 1/2 teaspoon salt
- 2 eggs
- 2 cups ground almonds
- 1 tablespoon baking cocoa
- 1/4 teaspoon ground cinnamon
- 1/4 teaspoon ground nutmeg
- 1/8 teaspoon ground cloves
- 3 cups all-purpose flour

Raspberry jam
Confectioners' sugar

In a mixing bowl, cream the butter, sugar and salt. Add eggs, one at a time, beating well after each addition. Add the almonds, cocoa, cinnamon, nutmeg and cloves; mix well. Add flour; mix well. Refrigerate 1 hour or until easy to handle.

On a lightly floured surface, roll dough to 1/8-in. thick. Cut with a 3-in. heart-shaped cookie cutter. Cut a 1-1/2-in. heart from center of half of cookies. Place on ungreased baking sheets. Bake at 350° for 10-12 minutes or until edges are golden brown. Remove to wire racks to cool.

Spread 1/2 teaspoon jam over the bottom of the solid cookies; place cutout cookies over jam. Sprinkle with confectioners' sugar. **Yield:** 3 dozen.

CHUNKY PEANUT BRITTLE

(Pictured at left)

Janet Gomola, East McKeesport, Pennsylvania

As a farm girl, I often made Christmas goodies with my mother for our family of eight candy-loving kids. Now, my own children and grandkids say the season wouldn't be the same without this peanut brittle.

- 1-1/2 teaspoons plus 1-1/2 cups butter, *divided*
- 2 cups peanut butter chips, *divided*
- 1-3/4 cups sugar
- 3 tablespoons light corn syrup
- 3 tablespoons water
- 1-1/2 cups salted peanuts, coarsely chopped
- 1/2 cup semisweet chocolate chips

Butter the bottom and sides of a 15-in. x 10-in. x 1-in. baking pan with 1-1/2 teaspoons of butter. Sprinkle with 1 cup peanut butter chips; set aside.

In a heavy saucepan, bring sugar, corn syrup, water and remaining butter to a boil over medium heat, stirring constantly. Cook and stir until butter is melted. Cook, without stirring, until a candy thermometer reads 300° (hard-crack stage).

Remove from heat; stir in peanuts. Quickly pour onto prepared baking pan; sprinkle with chocolate chips and remaining peanut butter chips. With a knife, gently swirl softened chips over top of brittle. Cool before breaking into pieces. Store in an airtight container. **Yield:** 2-1/2 pounds.

Editor's Note: We recommend that you test your candy thermometer before each use by bringing water to a boil; the thermometer should read 212°. Adjust your recipe temperature up or down based on your test.

SPICED SPRITZ COOKIES

These crisp confections from our Test Kitchen have a tantalizing twist—pumpkin pie spice!

- 1 cup butter, softened
- 1/2 cup sugar
- 1 egg
- 1 teaspoon vanilla extract
- 2-1/3 cups all-purpose flour
- 1 teaspoon baking powder
- 1 teaspoon pumpkin pie spice

Red and green colored sugar

In a small mixing bowl, cream butter and sugar. Add egg and vanilla; mix well. Combine flour, baking powder and pumpkin pie spice; gradually add to the creamed mixture.

Using a cookie press fitted with the disk of your choice, press dough 2 in. apart onto ungreased baking sheets. Sprinkle with colored sugar. Bake at 375° for 8-10 minutes or until edges begin to brown. Remove to wire racks to cool. **Yield:** about 5 dozen.

CARAMEL NUT MARSHMALLOWS

(Pictured above)

Berdine See, Independence, Iowa

These are a different kind of treat for the holiday candy plate. I had this recipe long before microwaves, but now preparation is much easier.

1-1/2 cups finely chopped pecans
   36 caramels
    2 tablespoons hot water
   20 large marshmallows

Line a baking sheet with waxed paper; set aside. Place nuts in a shallow dish. In a large microwave-safe bowl, combine caramels and water. Microwave, uncovered, on high for 1-2 minutes or until melted, stirring twice.

Dip each marshmallow into melted caramel, then roll in pecans. Place on prepared baking sheet. Let stand until set. **Yield:** 20 servings.

Editor's Note: This recipe was tested in an 850-watt microwave.

FUDGY WALNUT BROWNIES

(Pictured at right)

Diane Truver, Valencia, Pennsylvania

We have lots of great cooks in our clan, so adding to our collection of family recipes is a tradition. I came up with these moist nut-covered brownies while doing my Christmas baking. Now everyone requests them.

3/4 cup butter
    4 squares (1 ounce *each*) unsweetened chocolate
    4 eggs
    2 cups sugar
    1 teaspoon vanilla extract
    1 cup all-purpose flour
WALNUT CRUNCH TOPPING:
  3/4 cup packed brown sugar
  1/4 cup butter, cubed
    2 eggs, lightly beaten
    2 tablespoons all-purpose flour
    1 teaspoon vanilla extract
    4 cups chopped walnuts

In a microwave or heavy saucepan, melt butter and chocolate; stir until smooth. Cool slightly. In a bowl, beat eggs and sugar; stir in vanilla and chocolate mixture. Stir in flour until well blended. Pour into a greased 13-in. x 9-in. x 2-in. baking pan; set aside.

For topping, in a saucepan, combine brown sugar and butter. Cook and stir over low heat until butter is melted. Stir in the eggs, flour and vanilla until well blended. Stir in nuts. Spread evenly over brownie batter.

Bake at 350° for 40-45 minutes or until a toothpick inserted near the center comes out with moist crumbs (do not overbake). Cool completely on a wire rack. **Yield:** 1-1/2 dozen.

PEANUT BUTTER CEREAL BARS

Brenda Alexander, Frankton, Indiana

I enjoy giving gifts that are simple and homemade. I cut these bars into squares and serve them on holiday trays as gifts.

1 tablespoon butter
6 cups Rice Chex cereal
1-1/2 cups salted peanuts
1 cup sugar
1 cup light corn syrup
1 cup peanut butter
1 teaspoon vanilla extract

Line a 13-in. x 9-in. x 2-in. baking pan with foil and grease the foil with butter; set aside. In a large bowl, combine the cereal and nuts; set aside. In a microwave-safe 1-qt. bowl, combine the sugar and corn syrup. Microwave, uncovered, on high for 30-60 seconds. Stir and cook 4-5 minutes longer or until sugar is dissolved.

Stir in peanut butter and vanilla until smooth. Pour sugar mixture over cereal and nuts; stir to coat. Press into the prepared pan. Refrigerate until set.

Using foil, lift out of pan. Discard foil; cut into bars. **Yield:** 3 dozen.

Editor's Note: This recipe was tested in an 850-watt microwave.

FROSTED CREAMS

Vivian Clarke, Milwaukee, Wisconsin

These tasty bars have wonderful flavor from the molasses, ginger and cinnamon. They remind me of old-fashioned goodness.

1/4 cup shortening
1/4 cup sugar
1/2 cup molasses
1 egg
2 cups all-purpose flour
1 teaspoon baking soda
1 to 2 teaspoons ground ginger
1 teaspoon ground cinnamon
1/2 teaspoon salt
3/4 cup water
GLAZE:
1-1/2 cups confectioners' sugar
2 tablespoons plus 1-1/2 teaspoons milk
1/4 teaspoon vanilla extract

In a mixing bowl, cream shortening and sugar. Add the molasses and egg; mix well. Combine the flour, baking soda, ginger, cinnamon and salt; add to the creamed mixture alternately with water. Pour into a greased 13-in. x 9-in. x 2-in. baking pan.

Bake at 400° for 13-15 minutes or until a toothpick inserted near the center comes out clean. Cool completely on a wire rack. In a small bowl, combine the glaze ingredients until smooth. Spread over cooled bars. **Yield:** 3 dozen.

OAT PECAN COOKIE MIX
(Pictured above)

Bev Woodcock, Kingston, Ontario

This mix is simple to prepare and the results are yummy. I give it as a gift for the holidays. I enjoy decorating the jar lids with fabric and a tag with baking instructions.

1 cup all-purpose flour
1/2 cup sugar
1/2 teaspoon baking soda
1/2 teaspoon baking powder
1/2 cup packed brown sugar
3/4 cup old-fashioned oats
1/2 cup chopped pecans
1 cup crisp rice cereal
ADDITIONAL INGREDIENTS:
1/2 cup butter, softened
1 egg
1 teaspoon vanilla extract

In a bowl, combine the flour, sugar, baking soda and baking powder. In a 1-qt. glass container, layer the flour mixture, brown sugar, oats, pecans and rice cereal, packing well between each layer. Cover and store in a cool dry place up to 6 months. **Yield:** 1 batch (about 4 cups total).

To prepare cookies: In a mixing bowl, cream the butter. Beat in egg and vanilla. Add the cookie mix and mix well. Drop by rounded teaspoonfuls 2 in. apart onto greased baking sheets. Bake at 350° for 8-10 minutes or until golden brown. Cool for 2 minutes before removing from pans to wire racks. **Yield:** about 3 dozen.

BANANA NUT BARS
(Pictured below)

Susan Huckaby, Smiths, Alabama

My sister gave me this recipe, which is always in demand with family, friends and co-workers. It's amazing how fast these tempting bars vanish.

      1 cup butter, cubed
  1/2 cup water
      2 cups all-purpose flour
1-1/2 cups sugar
  1/2 cup packed brown sugar
      1 teaspoon baking soda
      2 eggs
      1 cup mashed ripe bananas
         (about 2 medium)
  1/2 cup buttermilk
      1 teaspoon vanilla extract
  1/2 cup chopped pecans *or* walnuts
FROSTING:
      1 package (8 ounces) cream cheese,
         softened
  1/2 cup butter, softened
      1 teaspoon vanilla extract
3-1/2 cups confectioners' sugar

In a saucepan, bring butter and water to a boil. Remove from heat; set aside. In a mixing bowl, combine flour, sugars, baking soda, eggs, bananas, buttermilk and vanilla. Beat until blended. Carefully add butter mixture; mix well. Stir in nuts.

Pour into a greased 15-in. x 10-in. x 1-in. baking pan. Bake at 350° for 18-22 minutes or until a toothpick comes out clean. Cool on a wire rack.

For frosting, in a mixing bowl, beat cream cheese and butter until light and fluffy. Beat in vanilla. Gradually add the confectioners' sugar. Spread over bars. Store bars in the refrigerator. **Yield:** 3 dozen.

FRUIT 'N' NUT SPICE BARS
(Pictured above)

Loretta Dunn, Lyons, Oregon

I'm always looking for new dessert recipes, and this one combines several of my favorite flavors.

  3/4 cup chopped maraschino cherries
2-1/4 cups all-purpose flour, *divided*
      1 package (8 ounces) cream cheese,
         softened
  1/2 cup butter, softened
1-1/2 cups packed brown sugar
      1 egg
  1/4 cup honey
1-1/2 teaspoons baking powder
      1 teaspoon salt
      1 teaspoon ground cinnamon
      1 teaspoon ground nutmeg
      1 cup chopped walnuts
  3/4 cup miniature chocolate chips
1-1/3 cups confectioners' sugar
      2 tablespoons milk
  1/4 teaspoon vanilla extract

In a small bowl, toss cherries with 1/4 cup flour; set aside. In a mixing bowl, beat cream cheese, butter and brown sugar until smooth. Add egg and honey; mix well. Combine the baking powder, salt, cinnamon, nutmeg and remaining flour; add to creamed mixture. Stir in nuts, chocolate chips and reserved cherries.

Spread into a greased 15-in. x 10-in. x 1-in. baking pan. Bake at 350° for 30-35 minutes or until golden brown. In a small bowl, combine the confectioners' sugar, milk and vanilla until smooth; drizzle over warm bars. Cool on a wire rack for 1 hour. **Yield:** 4 dozen.

CHERRY CHOCOLATE CHIP COOKIES

Pamela Alexander Auld, Prosser, Washington

We run a cherry orchard, so I'm always dreaming up new cherry recipes. These cookies are among of my family's favorites.

        1 cup dried cherries, chopped
      1/3 cup hot water
        6 tablespoons shortening
        6 tablespoons butter, softened
    1-1/2 cups packed brown sugar
      1/2 cup sugar
        2 eggs
        3 teaspoons grated orange peel
    1-1/2 teaspoons vanilla extract
        3 cups quick-cooking oats
    1-3/4 cups all-purpose flour
      3/4 teaspoon baking soda
      3/4 teaspoon ground cinnamon
      1/2 teaspoon salt
        1 cup (6 ounces) semisweet chocolate chips

In a small bowl, soak cherries in hot water for at least 10 minutes. In a mixing bowl, cream the shortening, butter and sugars until fluffy. Beat in the eggs, orange peel and vanilla.

Combine the oats, flour, baking soda, cinnamon and salt; gradually add to creamed mixture, beating until combined. Stir in the chocolate chips and cherries with liquid.

Drop by rounded tablespoonfuls 2 in. apart onto ungreased baking sheets. Bake at 350° for 12-14 minutes or until edges are lightly browned. Cool for 1 minute before removing from pans to wire racks. **Yield:** about 3-1/2 dozen.

PEACHES 'N' CREAM BARS
(Pictured at right)
Hubert Scott, Cockeysville, Maryland

If you like peach pie, you'll love these easy-to-make bars with a crunchy almond topping.

        1 tube (8 ounces) refrigerated crescent
           rolls
        1 package (8 ounces) cream cheese,
           softened
      1/2 cup sugar
      1/4 teaspoon almond extract
        1 can (21 ounces) peach pie filling
      1/2 cup all-purpose flour
      1/4 cup packed brown sugar
        3 tablespoons cold butter
      1/2 cup sliced almonds

Unroll crescent dough into one long rectangle. Press onto the bottom and slightly up the sides of a greased 13-in. x 9-in. x 2-in. baking pan; seal perforations. Bake at 375° for 5 minutes. Cool completely on a wire rack.

In a mixing bowl, beat the cream cheese, sugar and extract until smooth. Spread over the crust. Spoon the peach pie filling over cream cheese layer.

In a bowl, combine the flour and brown sugar. Cut in butter until the mixture resembles coarse crumbs. Stir in nuts; sprinkle over peach pie filling.

Bake at 375° for 25-28 minutes or until edges are golden brown. Cool for 1 hour on a wire rack. Store bars in the refrigerator. **Yield:** about 2 dozen.

1 package (12 ounces) semisweet
   chocolate chips
1 package (11 ounces) butterscotch
   chips
1 package (10 ounces) peanut butter
   chips
1 cup coarsely crushed cornflakes
1/2 cup chopped peanuts, optional

In a large heavy saucepan, melt the chocolate chips, butterscotch chips and peanut butter chips over low heat. Remove from the heat; stir in the cornflakes. Add the peanuts if desired.

Let stand for 10-15 minutes or until slightly cooled. Drop by teaspoonfuls into petit four cups placed on a 15-in. x 10-in. x 1-in. baking sheet. Refrigerate until the cups are firm. **Yield:** about 5 dozen.

CARROT COOKIES

(Pictured above)

Kay Sciglino, Halleck, Nevada

These cookies are both flavorful and colorful. The shredded carrots add nice bright flecks of orange color and a nice flavor.

  1 cup shortening
3/4 cup sugar
  2 eggs
  1 cup shredded carrots
  2 cups all-purpose flour
  2 teaspoons baking powder
1/2 teaspoon salt

In a mixing bowl, cream shortening and sugar. Add eggs; mix well. Stir in carrots. Combine the flour, baking powder and salt; gradually add to carrot mixture. Drop by rounded teaspoonfuls 2 in. apart onto ungreased baking sheets.

Bake at 400° for 8-10 minutes or until lightly browned. Remove to wire racks to cool. **Yield:** 4-1/2 dozen.

CRUNCHY CHOCOLATE CUPS

Elizabeth Prestie, Preeceville, Saskatchewan

These chocolates are easy to make, look pretty and taste great! I make them every Christmas for gifts.

CREAM CHEESE CUTOUTS

Julie Dawson, Galena, Ohio

Decorating Christmas cookies always puts me in the holiday spirit. Cookies from this recipe don't rise a lot or lose their shape.

    1 cup butter, softened
    1 cup sugar
    1 package (3 ounces) cream cheese,
       softened
    1 egg
    1 teaspoon vanilla extract
2-1/2 cups all-purpose flour
  1/4 teaspoon salt
FROSTING:
    3 cups confectioners' sugar
  1/3 cup butter, softened
    2 tablespoons milk
1-1/2 teaspoons vanilla extract
Food coloring, optional

In a mixing bowl, cream butter and sugar. Add cream cheese and beat until smooth. Beat in egg and vanilla; mix well. Combine flour and salt; gradually add to creamed mixture and mix well. Cover and refrigerate for 1-2 hours or until easy to handle.

On lightly floured surface, roll dough to 1/8-in. thickness. Cut with Christmas cookie cutters dipped in flour. Place 1 in. apart on ungreased baking sheets.

Bake at 375° for 7-8 minutes or until edges are lightly browned. Cool for 1 minute before removing to wire racks.

In a mixing bowl, beat frosting ingredients until smooth. Add food coloring if desired. Frost the cookies. **Yield:** about 7 dozen cookies.

BLUEBERRY BARS

(Pictured below)

Sue Neilson, Lansdale, Pennsylvania

Our three sons like these bars so much that each of my daughters-in-law asked for the recipe.

>   1 cup butter, softened
> 1-3/4 cups sugar
>   4 eggs
>   1 teaspoon vanilla extract
>   3 cups all-purpose flour
> 1-1/2 teaspoons baking powder
>   1/2 teaspoon salt
>   1 can (21 ounces) blueberry pie filling
>   1/8 teaspoon ground nutmeg
> GLAZE:
> 1-1/4 cups confectioners' sugar
>   2 tablespoons lemon juice
>   1 tablespoon butter, melted

In a large mixing bowl, cream butter and sugar. Add eggs, one at a time, beating well after each addition. Beat in vanilla. Combine the flour, baking powder and salt; add to creamed mixture just until combined.

Spread half of the batter into a greased 15-in. x 10-in. x 1-in. baking pan. Spread with pie filling; sprinkle with nutmeg. Drop remaining batter by teaspoonfuls over the top.

Bake at 350° for 40-45 minutes or until golden brown. In a small bowl, combine the glaze ingredients until smooth. Drizzle over warm bars. **Yield:** 4 dozen.

PINEAPPLE CHOCOLATE CHIP COOKIES

(Pictured above)

Karen Bontrager, Macon, Mississippi

These cookies are always popular at bake sales. I sometimes use 1 cup of coconut instead of the chopped walnuts.

>   1 cup shortening
>   1 cup sugar
>   1 cup packed brown sugar
>   2 eggs
>   2 cans (8 ounces *each*) crushed
>   pineapple, drained
>   2 teaspoons vanilla extract
>   4 cups all-purpose flour
>   2 teaspoons baking soda
>   2 teaspoons baking powder
>   1/2 teaspoon salt
>   1 cup (6 ounces) semisweet chocolate
>   chips
>   1 cup chopped walnuts, optional

In a mixing bowl, cream shortening and sugars. Add eggs, one at a time, beating well after each addition. Beat in pineapple and vanilla. Combine the flour, baking soda, baking powder and salt; gradually add to creamed mixture. Stir in chocolate chips and walnuts if desired.

Drop by rounded tablespoonfuls 2 in. apart onto greased baking sheets. Press down lightly. Bake at 375° for 10-12 minutes or until lightly browned. Remove to wire racks to cool. **Yield:** about 4-1/2 dozen.

WANT PROOF *that good things come in small packages? Cupcakes make it evident that you can pack a lot of taste into dozens of tiny treats!*

CUP'S OVERFLOWING. Clockwise from top: Shoofly Cupcakes (p. 100), Heavenly Surprise Cupcakes (p. 99) and Cream-Filled Pumpkin Cupcakes (p. 99).

Cakes, Pies & Desserts

HEAVENLY SURPRISE CUPCAKES

Judie Heiderscheit, Holy Cross, Iowa

The recipe for these filled and frosted cupcakes was handed down by my mother-in-law, who taught this fledgling cook what to do in the kitchen. She's no longer with us—but baking these treats reminds me of our good times together.

> 2 eggs
> 1-1/4 cups sugar
> 1 cup buttermilk
> 2/3 cup vegetable oil
> 1 teaspoon vanilla extract
> 1-1/2 cups all-purpose flour
> 1/2 cup baking cocoa
> 1-1/4 teaspoons baking soda
> 1 teaspoon salt

FROSTING:

> 2/3 cup butter-flavored shortening
> 2/3 cup butter, softened
> 1 cup sugar
> 1 can (5 ounces) evaporated milk
> 1 tablespoon water
> 1/2 teaspoon vanilla extract
> 2 cups confectioners' sugar

In a mixing bowl, beat the eggs, sugar, buttermilk, oil and vanilla. Combine the flour, cocoa, baking soda and salt; gradually add to the egg mixture. Fill paper-lined muffin cups two-thirds full.

Bake at 350° for 20-22 minutes or until a toothpick comes out clean. Cool the cupcakes for 10 minutes before removing from pans to wire racks to cool completely.

For frosting, in a mixing bowl, cream the shortening, butter and sugar. Stir in the milk, water and vanilla. Gradually beat in confectioners' sugar.

Cut a small hole in the corner of a pastry or resealable plastic bag; insert a small star tip. Fill bag with frosting.

Push tip 1 in. into the center of each cupcake and fill with frosting just until top of cake begins to crack. Pipe the frosting in a spiral pattern over the top, beginning near the edge of the cupcake. **Yield:** 1-1/2 dozen.

Editor's Note: The texture of this frosting is typical of one made with granulated sugar.

CREAM-FILLED PUMPKIN CUPCAKES

Ali Johnson, Petersburg, Pennsylvania

Here's a deliciously different use for pumpkin. Bursting with flavor and plenty of eye-catching appeal, these sweet and spicy filled cupcakes are bound to dazzle your family any time of the year.

> 4 eggs
> 2 cups sugar
> 3/4 cup vegetable oil
> 1 can (15 ounces) solid-pack pumpkin
> 2 cups all-purpose flour
> 2 teaspoons baking soda
> 1 teaspoon salt
> 1 teaspoon baking powder
> 1 teaspoon ground cinnamon

FILLING:

> 1 tablespoon cornstarch
> 1 cup milk
> 1/2 cup shortening
> 1/4 cup butter, softened
> 2 cups confectioners' sugar
> 1/2 teaspoon vanilla extract, optional

In a mixing bowl, combine the eggs, sugar, oil and pumpkin. Combine the flour, baking soda, salt, baking powder and cinnamon; add to pumpkin mixture and beat until well mixed. Fill paper-lined muffin cups two-thirds full.

Bake at 350° for 18-22 minutes or until a toothpick inserted near the center comes out clean. Cool for 10 minutes before removing from pans to wire racks to cool completely.

For filling, combine cornstarch and milk in a small saucepan until smooth. Bring to a boil, stirring constantly. Remove from the heat; cool to room temperature.

In a mixing bowl, cream shortening, butter and confectioners' sugar. Beat in vanilla if desired. Gradually add the cornstarch mixture, beating until light and fluffy.

Using a sharp knife, cut a 1-in. circle 1 in. deep in the top of each cupcake. Carefully remove tops and set aside. Spoon or pipe filling into cupcakes. Replace tops. **Yield:** about 1-3/4 dozen.

These moist old-fashioned molasses cupcakes were my grandmother's specialty. To keep them from disappearing too quickly, she used to store them out of sight. Somehow, we always figured out her hiding places!

- 4 cups all-purpose flour
- 2 cups packed brown sugar
- 1/4 teaspoon salt
- 1 cup cold butter
- 2 teaspoons baking soda
- 2 cups boiling water
- 1 cup molasses

In a large bowl, combine flour, brown sugar and salt. Cut in butter until crumbly. Set aside 1 cup for topping. Add baking soda to remaining crumb mixture. Stir in water and molasses. Fill paper-lined muffin cups two-thirds full. Sprinkle with reserved crumb mixture.

Bake at 350° for 20-25 minutes or until a toothpick comes out clean. Cool for 10 minutes before removing from pans to wire racks to cool. **Yield:** 2 dozen.

Editor's Note: This recipe uses no eggs.

PEANUT BUTTER BANANA PUDDING
(Pictured above)

Laura McGinnis, Colorado Springs, Colorado

If there's anything I like better than bananas, it's bananas paired with peanut butter. That's how I came up with this pudding.

- 4 cups milk
- 1 package (3 ounces) vanilla cook-and-serve pudding mix
- 1 package (3-1/2 ounces) butterscotch cook-and-serve pudding mix
- 1-1/2 cups peanut butter, *divided*
- 1 cup graham cracker crumbs
- 1 cup confectioners' sugar
- 4 medium firm bananas, sliced

In a large saucepan, combine milk and pudding mixes until blended. Bring to a boil over medium heat, stirring constantly. Remove from the heat; stir in 1/2 cup peanut butter until blended. Refrigerate until chilled.

Meanwhile, in a small bowl, combine the cracker crumbs and confectioners' sugar; cut in remaining peanut butter until crumbly. In individual dessert bowls, layer half of the pudding, half of the crumb mixture and half of the bananas. Repeat layers. **Yield:** 12 servings.

Editor's Note: This dessert may also be prepared in one large serving bowl.

LEMON SPARKLE CUPCAKES
(Pictured on page 102)

Janice Porter, Platte, South Dakota

Bursting with lemony zing, these cupcakes don't require frosting. A dear friend shared the recipe with me, and it has long been in demand at our house.

- 2/3 cup shortening
- 1 cup sugar
- 3 eggs
- 1-2/3 cups all-purpose flour
- 2-1/2 teaspoons baking powder
- 1/2 teaspoon salt
- 2/3 cup milk
- 1 tablespoon grated lemon peel

TOPPING:
- 1/4 cup sugar
- 1 tablespoon grated lemon peel
- 1/8 teaspoon ground nutmeg

In a mixing bowl, cream shortening and sugar. Add eggs, one at a time, beating well after each addition. Combine the flour, baking powder and salt; add to the creamed mixture alternately with milk. Stir in lemon peel. Fill paper-lined muffin cups two-thirds full. Combine the topping ingredients; sprinkle a rounded 1/2 teaspoonful over each cupcake.

Bake at 350° for 20-24 minutes or until a toothpick comes out clean. Cool for 10 minutes before removing from pans to wire racks to cool completely. **Yield:** about 1-1/4 dozen.

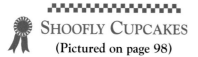

SHOOFLY CUPCAKES
(Pictured on page 98)
Beth Adams, Jacksonville, Florida

CHOCOLATE ORANGE CUPCAKES

(Pictured on page 103)

Shirley Brazel, Coos Bay, Oregon

Chocolate and orange are perfect together in these fudgy morsels. To give them a moist brownie-like texture, I add mayonnaise. The cupcakes taste even better when served with a scoop of homemade ice cream.

1-1/2 cups all-purpose flour
  1/2 cup sugar
  1/4 cup baking cocoa
    1 teaspoon baking soda
  1/4 teaspoon salt
  1/2 cup mayonnaise
    1 teaspoon grated orange peel
    1 teaspoon vanilla extract
  1/2 cup orange juice
  1/2 cup semisweet chocolate chips
Confectioners' sugar

In a bowl, combine the flour, sugar, cocoa, baking soda and salt. In another bowl, combine the mayonnaise, orange peel and vanilla; gradually add orange juice until blended. Stir into dry ingredients just until combined. Stir in chocolate chips (batter will be thick). Fill paper-lined muffin cups two-thirds full.

Bake at 350° for 18-23 minutes or until a toothpick comes out clean. Cool for 10 minutes before removing from pan to a wire rack to cool completely. Dust with confectioners' sugar. **Yield:** 9 cupcakes.

Editor's Note: Reduced-fat or fat-free mayonnaise may not be substituted for regular mayonnaise in this recipe.

A Host of Cupcake Hints

• To make cupcake-filled ice-cream cones look like the real thing, swirl whipped cream around the top of the cone to resemble ice cream, then cover with sprinkles. —*Leslie McGill, Longmont, Colorado*

• I often top cupcakes with a boiled frosting that needs to be stirred while it cools. To help the topping lose heat more quickly, I place the pan of frosting in a container filled with an inch of cold water. —*Darla Stegman, Kinsley, Kansas*

• When making cupcakes for bake sales, I cut a cone-shaped wedge out of the center of each cake after it has cooled. Then I place frosting in a pastry bag fitted with a large tip and fill the centers. This way, I don't have to deal with sticky frosting on top of the treats. —*Sharon Hostetter, Lititz, Pennsylvania*

• I sprinkle a topping of nuts, sugar and cinnamon over my banana cupcakes before baking. Since there is no frosting, they are easy to pack for lunches. For those with a sweet tooth, cut the cupcakes in half, then spread with frosting and close—that way, they're still easy to pack for lunches. —*Mary Wilhelm, Sparta, Wisconsin*

• Use a liquid measuring cup with a spout to fill cupcake pans with batter. It helps keep messes to a minimum! —*Marla Keady, Redmond, Oregon*

• Here's a festive dessert: Prepare two cake mixes, one yellow and one chocolate, in separate bowls. Spoon both batters into ice-cream cones and swirl the batters to marbleize. For a party theme, the baked cones can be decorated as animal faces. —*Dianne Conway, London, Ontario*

• We love cupcakes made with cream cheese and chocolate chips. To lighten them up, I substitute fat-free cream cheese for the regular kind. The flavor stays nice and rich. —*Darlene Phillips, West Fargo, North Dakota*

• For a quick icing, place a small candy bar on top of each cupcake right after removing the pan from the oven. The heat will melt the chocolate, which then can be spread easily over the top. —*Geneva McKenzie, South Bend, Indiana*

• To make heart-shaped cupcakes, place a glass marble between the cupcake liner and the pan before baking. —*Mary Kemps, Menasha, Wisconsin*

TAKES THE CAKES (cupcakes, that is). Clockwise from top left: Lemon Sparkle Cupcakes (p. 100), Cream Cheese Chocolate Cupcakes (p. 104), Chocolate Orange Cupcakes (p. 101), Orange Applesauce Cupcakes (p. 104) and Chocolate Banana Split Cupcakes (p. 105).

PEAR CRUNCH PIE

(Pictured above)

Marian Platt, Sequim, Washington

This pie recipe is one of my favorites. The pecan topping gives it a nice crunch.

- 1 cup all-purpose flour
- 1/2 cup packed brown sugar
- 1/2 teaspoon ground nutmeg, *divided*
- 1/4 teaspoon ground cinnamon
- 1/2 cup plus 1 tablespoon cold butter, *divided*
- 1/2 cup chopped pecans
- 2 cans (15-1/4 ounces *each*) pear halves in syrup
- 1/4 cup sugar
- 2 tablespoons cornstarch
- 1/4 teaspoon salt
- 1 tablespoon lemon juice
- 1 teaspoon grated lemon peel
- 1 unbaked pastry shell (9 inches)

In a bowl, combine the flour, brown sugar, 1/4 teaspoon of the nutmeg and cinnamon. Cut in 1/2 cup butter until mixture resembles coarse crumbs; stir in nuts. Set aside.

Drain the pears, reserving 1 cup juice. In a saucepan, combine the sugar, cornstarch, salt, remaining nutmeg and reserved juice until smooth. Bring to a boil; cook and stir for 2 minutes or until thickened. Remove from the heat; stir in the lemon juice and peel and remaining butter.

Cut pears in half; arrange in pastry shell. Pour sauce over pears; sprinkle with reserved nut topping. Bake at 375° for 50-55 minutes or until golden brown. **Yield:** 6-8 servings.

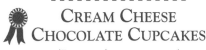

CREAM CHEESE CHOCOLATE CUPCAKES

(Pictured on page 102)

Shirley Dunbar, Mojave, California

Smooth cream cheese inside makes these cupcakes so rich. The classic combination of peanut butter and chocolate chips comes through in every yummy bite.

- 1 package (8 ounces) cream cheese, softened
- 1/3 cup sugar
- 1 egg
- 1/8 teaspoon salt
- 1 cup semisweet chocolate chips
- 1 cup peanut butter chips

CUPCAKES:
- 1-1/2 cups all-purpose flour
- 1 cup sugar
- 1/4 cup baking cocoa
- 1 teaspoon baking soda
- 1/2 teaspoon salt
- 1 cup water
- 1/3 cup vegetable oil
- 1 tablespoon white vinegar
- 1 teaspoon vanilla extract

In a bowl, beat the cream cheese until smooth. Add the sugar, egg and salt; mix well. Fold in the chocolate and peanut butter chips; set aside. For cupcakes, in a bowl, combine the flour, sugar, cocoa, baking soda and salt. Add the water, oil, vinegar and vanilla; mix well.

Fill paper-lined muffin cups half full with batter. Top each with about 2 tablespoons of the cream cheese mixture. Bake at 350° for 25-30 minutes or until toothpick inserted into cupcake comes out clean. Cool for 10 minutes before removing from pans to wire racks to cool completely. **Yield:** 1-1/2 dozen.

Editor's Note: The filling will partially cover the top of the cupcakes.

ORANGE APPLESAUCE CUPCAKES

(Pictured on page 103)

Janis Plourde, Smooth Rock Falls, Ontario

Kids of all ages rave about these fruity cupcakes. I've been making them for 25 years.

- 6 tablespoons butter, softened
- 1 cup packed brown sugar
- 1 egg
- 1/2 cup unsweetened applesauce
- 1 teaspoon vanilla extract
- 1 teaspoon grated orange peel

1 cup all-purpose flour
1 teaspoon baking powder
1/2 teaspoon salt
1/4 teaspoon baking soda
1/2 cup chopped pecans
FROSTING:
1/4 cup butter, softened
2 cups confectioners' sugar
1-1/2 teaspoons grated orange peel
2 to 4 teaspoons orange juice

In a mixing bowl, cream the butter and brown sugar. Add egg; beat well. Beat in applesauce, vanilla and orange peel. Combine the flour, baking powder, salt and baking soda; add to creamed mixture. Stir in pecans.

Fill paper-lined muffin cups half full. Bake at 350° for 20-25 minutes or until a toothpick comes out clean. Cool for 10 minutes before removing from pan to a wire rack to cool completely.

For frosting, in a small mixing bowl, cream butter and confectioners' sugar. Add orange peel and enough orange juice to achieve spreading consistency. Frost cupcakes. **Yield:** 1 dozen.

BANANA SUNDAE SAUCE

(Pictured below)

Kathy Rairigh, Milford, Indiana

Try this luscious banana-based topping at your next ice-cream social. I guarantee you'll be asked to bring it again. Luckily, it's quick and easy to make.

1/2 cup butter
1-1/2 cups confectioners' sugar
1 tablespoon water
1 teaspoon lemon juice

1 teaspoon vanilla extract
1/4 teaspoon ground cinnamon
2 cups sliced firm bananas (about 2 large)
Vanilla ice cream

In a small saucepan, melt the butter. Whisk in the confectioners' sugar, water and lemon juice until smooth. Cook over medium-low heat for 3-5 minutes, stirring occasionally. Remove from the heat; stir in vanilla and cinnamon. Fold in bananas. Serve warm over ice cream. **Yield:** 2 cups.

CHOCOLATE BANANA SPLIT CUPCAKES

(Pictured on page 102)

Lorelie Miller, Benito, Manitoba

My mom often made these cute cupcakes when I was young. They go over just as well now when I bake them for our three children.

1-1/4 cups all-purpose flour
1/2 cup sugar
1/4 teaspoon baking soda
1/4 teaspoon salt
1/2 cup mashed banana (about 1 medium)
1/2 cup butter, melted
1/4 cup buttermilk
1 egg, lightly beaten
1/2 teaspoon vanilla extract
1/2 cup chopped walnuts
2 milk chocolate bars (1.55 ounces *each*), broken into squares, *divided*
FROSTING:
1 tablespoon butter, melted
1/2 teaspoon vanilla extract
1-1/2 cups confectioners' sugar
1 to 2 tablespoons milk
12 maraschino cherries with stems

In a bowl, combine the flour, sugar, baking soda and salt. In another bowl, combine the banana, butter, buttermilk, egg and vanilla. Add to the dry ingredients; mix just until combined. Fold in the nuts. Spoon 1 tablespoon of batter into each paper-lined muffin cup. Top each with one candy bar square. Fill the remainder of the cup two-thirds full with batter.

Bake at 350° for 20-25 minutes or until a toothpick inserted in the cupcake comes out clean. Cool for 10 minutes before removing from pan to a wire rack to cool completely.

In a bowl, combine the butter, vanilla, confectioners' sugar and enough milk to achieve spreading consistency. Frost cupcakes. In a microwave, melt the remaining candy bar squares; drizzle over frosting. Top each with a cherry. **Yield:** 1 dozen.

Pour into two greased and floured 9-in. round baking pans. Bake at 350° for 30-35 minutes or until a toothpick inserted near the center comes out clean. Cool for 10 minutes before removing from pans to wire racks to cool completely.

For frosting, in a small mixing bowl, beat the melted chips, cream cheese, vanilla and salt until light and fluffy. Add confectioners' sugar alternately with enough milk to achieve spreading consistency. Spread frosting between layers and over top and sides of cake. **Yield:** 12-14 servings.

PEANUT BUTTER LAYER CAKE
(Pictured above)

Carolyn Hylton, Covington, Virginia

My husband loves peanut butter, so this cake is his favorite. Sometimes I switch frosting recipes and use a chocolate frosting garnished with peanuts.

      1/2 cup butter, softened
  1-1/4 cups sugar
      1/2 cup peanut butter chips, melted
        2 eggs
        1 teaspoon vanilla extract
        2 cups all-purpose flour
        1 teaspoon baking soda
      1/2 teaspoon baking powder
      1/4 teaspoon salt
  1-1/2 cups milk
PEANUT BUTTER FROSTING:
        1 cup peanut butter chips, melted
        1 package (8 ounces) cream cheese, softened
        1 teaspoon vanilla extract
      1/8 teaspoon salt
        3 cups confectioners' sugar
        2 to 3 tablespoons milk

In a large mixing bowl, cream butter and sugar until light and fluffy. Add melted peanut butter chips; mix well. Add eggs, one at a time, beating well after each addition. Beat in vanilla. Combine the flour, baking soda, baking powder and salt; add to creamed mixture alternately with milk.

GRANDMA'S CHOCOLATE CAKE
(Pictured below)

Dorothy Eagen, Allentown, Pennsylvania

My grandma made this delicious cake for me throughout the years on my birthday. It's wonderful for chocolate lovers!

      1/2 cup shortening
  1-1/2 cups sugar
        2 eggs
        2 cups all-purpose flour
      1/2 cup baking cocoa
        1 teaspoon baking soda
        1 teaspoon baking powder
      1/2 teaspoon salt
        1 cup buttermilk
      1/2 cup hot water
CHOCOLATE FUDGE FROSTING:
        2 squares (1 ounce *each*) unsweetened chocolate

1 tablespoon butter
1-1/2 cups sugar
1/2 cup water
1/4 teaspoon cream of tartar
1 teaspoon vanilla extract
1 to 2 tablespoons half-and-half cream

In a mixing bowl, cream shortening and sugar. Add eggs, one at a time, beating well after each addition. Combine flour, cocoa, baking soda, baking powder and salt. Add to creamed mixture alternately with buttermilk and hot water; mix well.

Pour into a greased 13-in. x 9-in. x 2-in. baking pan. Bake at 350° for 40-45 minutes or until a toothpick inserted near the center comes out clean. Cool on a wire rack.

For frosting, melt chocolate and butter in a saucepan. Add the sugar, water and cream of tartar. Bring to a boil, stirring constantly. Cook and stir until a candy thermometer reads 240° (softball stage). Remove from the heat. Cool completely, without stirring, about 1 hour. Add vanilla; beat until thickened. Add cream; beat until smooth. Frost cake. **Yield:** 12-16 servings.

Editor's Note: We recommend that you test your candy thermometer before each use by bringing water to a boil; the thermometer should read 212°. Adjust your recipe temperature up or down based on your test.

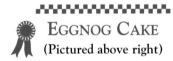

EGGNOG CAKE
(Pictured above right)

Debra Frappolli, Wayne, New Jersey

This wonderful cake is full of eggnog flavor. I especially like to serve it around the holidays.

1/2 cup butter, softened
1-1/4 cups sugar
3 eggs
1/2 teaspoon vanilla extract
1/2 teaspoon rum extract
2 cups all-purpose flour
2 teaspoons baking powder
1 teaspoon salt
1 cup eggnog
FROSTING:
1/4 cup all-purpose flour
1/4 teaspoon salt
1-1/2 cups eggnog
1 cup butter, softened
1-1/2 cups sugar
1-1/2 teaspoons vanilla extract
Red and green gel food coloring, optional

In a large mixing bowl, cream butter and sugar. Add eggs, one at a time, beating well after each

addition. Add extracts; mix well. Combine the flour, baking powder and salt; add to creamed mixture alternately with eggnog.

Pour into two 9-in. round baking pans coated with nonstick cooking spray. Bake at 350° for 30-35 minutes or until a toothpick inserted near the center comes out clean. Cool for 10 minutes before removing from pans to wire racks.

For frosting, combine flour and salt in a saucepan. Gradually stir in eggnog until smooth. Bring to a boil over medium heat; cook and stir for 2 minutes or until thickened. Remove from the heat; cool to room temperature.

In a large mixing bowl, cream butter and sugar. Add eggnog mixture and vanilla; beat on high until fluffy. Remove 1/4 cup frosting for decorating if desired; tint 3 tablespoons green and 1 tablespoon red.

Spread plain frosting between layers and over top and sides of cake. Use green and red frosting to pipe leaves and berries on cake. Store in the refrigerator. **Yield:** 12 servings.

Editor's Note: This recipe was tested with commercially prepared eggnog.

TASTY TOAST
During the holiday season, make French toast with eggnog instead of the usual egg mixture. It uses up extra eggnog and tastes great!

1/3 cup chopped pecans
1/4 teaspoon salt
1/2 cup butter, melted
Vanilla ice cream

In a bowl, combine the apples, cranberries and sugar. Transfer to a greased 13-in. x 9-in. x 2-in. baking dish. In a bowl, combine the oats, brown sugar, flour, pecans and salt; stir in butter. Sprinkle over apple mixture. Bake, uncovered, at 350° for 45-50 minutes or until apples are tender. Serve warm with ice cream. **Yield:** 12-14 servings.

CRUSTLESS PUMPKIN PIE
(Pictured above)

Linda McClung, Robbinsville, North Carolina

Baked in a water bath, this pie has a texture that's more like a custard than a traditional pumpkin pie.

1-1/4 cups sugar
   3 tablespoons all-purpose flour
   3 eggs
   2 cups canned pumpkin
3/4 cup evaporated milk
1-1/2 teaspoons vanilla extract
1/4 teaspoon ground cinnamon, optional

In a mixing bowl, combine the sugar and flour. Add eggs; mix well. Stir in the pumpkin, milk, vanilla and cinnamon if desired; mix until well blended. Pour into a greased 9-in. pie plate. Place pie plate in a 15-in. x 10-in. x 1-in. baking pan; add 1/2 in. of hot water to pan.

Bake at 350° for 50-55 minutes or until a knife inserted near the center comes out clean. **Yield:** 6-8 servings.

CRANBERRY APPLE CRISP
(Pictured at right)

Sherry Golightly, Paducah, Kentucky

I first tasted this recipe at a potluck dinner. It's become one of the desserts I like to serve at Thanksgiving.

7-1/2 cups chopped peeled tart apples
   5 cups fresh *or* frozen cranberries
2/3 cup sugar
1-1/2 cups quick-cooking oats
1/2 cup packed brown sugar
1/3 cup all-purpose flour

SANDRA'S APPLE-RHUBARB PIE

Sandra Gonzales, Klamath Falls, Oregon

Apple trees line our driveway, so it's easy to find the ingredients for this tasty pie.

Pastry for double-crust pie (9 inches)
   2 eggs, lightly beaten
1/4 cup sour cream
   3 tablespoons butter, melted
3/4 teaspoon grated orange peel
1/4 teaspoon salt
1-1/2 cups fresh *or* frozen chopped rhubarb
   2 medium baking apples, peeled and sliced
1-1/4 cups sugar
   1 tablespoon all-purpose flour

Line a 9-in. pie plate with bottom pastry; trim even with edge of plate. In a bowl, combine the eggs, sour cream, butter, orange peel and salt. Stir in the rhubarb and apples. Add the sugar and flour; toss to coat. Pour into prepared crust.

Roll out remaining pastry to fit top of pie; place over filling. Trim, seal and flute edges. Cut slits in

pastry. Cover edges loosely with foil. Bake at 425° for 15 minutes. Reduce heat to 350°; remove foil. Bake 40-45 minutes longer or until crust is golden brown. Cool on a wire rack. **Yield:** 6-8 servings.

Mini Brownie Treats

(Pictured above)

Pam Kokes, North Loup, Nebraska

I like to take these quick-and-easy treats to potlucks and family gatherings. They disappear quickly!

1 package fudge brownie mix
   (13-inch x 9-inch pan size)
48 striped chocolate kisses

Prepare brownie mix according to package directions for fudge-like brownies. Fill paper-lined miniature muffin cups two-thirds full. Bake at 350° for 18-21 minutes or until a toothpick comes out clean.

Immediately top each with a chocolate kiss. Cool for 10 minutes before removing from pans to wire racks to cool completely. **Yield:** 4 dozen.

Hawaiian Cheesecake

(Pictured at right)

A taste of the tropics is as close as your kitchen thanks to our Test Kitchen cooks.

1-3/4 cups flaked coconut
   2 tablespoons butter, melted
FILLING:
   3 packages (8 ounces *each*) cream cheese,
      softened

1 cup sugar
2 tablespoons all-purpose flour
1 cup (8 ounces) sour cream
1 teaspoon vanilla extract
3 eggs
PINEAPPLE SAUCE:
   1 tablespoon sugar
   1 tablespoon cornstarch
   2 cans (8 ounces *each*) crushed pineapple,
      undrained
   1 drop yellow food coloring
Fresh mint and edible orchids for garnish,
   optional

In a bowl, combine the coconut and butter; mix well. Press onto the bottom of a greased 9-in. springform pan. Bake at 350° for 10 minutes. Cool on a wire rack.

In a large mixing bowl, combine cream cheese, sugar and flour until smooth. Beat in sour cream and vanilla until blended. Add eggs; beat on low speed just until combined. Pour into crust. Place pan on a baking sheet. Bake at 350° for 45-50 minutes or until center is almost set (top of cheesecake may crack). Cool on a wire rack for 10 minutes. Carefully run a knife around edge of pan to loosen; cool 1 hour longer. Refrigerate overnight.

For sauce, combine sugar and cornstarch in a large saucepan. Stir in pineapple. Bring to a boil; cook and stir for 2 minutes or until thickened. Add food coloring if desired. Cover and refrigerate overnight. Remove sides of springform pan. Spread pineapple sauce over cheesecake. Garnish with mint and orchids if desired. **Yield:** 10-12 servings.

Editor's Note: Be sure to use edible orchids. They can be found in many specialty food stores.

Appealing Banana Tips

• Miniature marshmallows make a nice addition to banana salad and can help stretch the dish.
—*Pam Hooley, Goshen, Indiana*

• I like to make open-faced sandwiches from toast and peanut butter, then top them off with banana slices.
—*Rhee Wirtz*
Great Falls, Montana

• I cut bananas in half, insert a Popsicle stick in each half and put them in the freezer. After they're frozen, I place chocolate syrup (the kind that hardens into a shell) in a narrow plastic container and dip the frozen bananas into the syrup and refreeze.
—*Jeanette Greve*
Sibley, Iowa

• I dress up bananas for fruit salad by fluting the edges. To flute a peeled banana, run the tines of a fork lengthwise down the banana until all sides are scored, then cut widthwise into slices.

And to prevent discoloration, I dip banana slices into grapefruit, pineapple, lemon or orange juice.
—*Ruth Hayward*
Lake Charles, Louisiana

• If bananas ripen too fast, or it looks like we won't eat them all up, I just pop them—peel and all—right into the freezer.
When I need the fruit, I thaw it in the refrigerator or defrost it in the microwave. Then I snip the end off with kitchen shears and squeeze the pulp into a bowl.
—*Lisa Boychuk*
Beaumont, Alberta

• For extra-refreshing banana shakes, I add frozen bananas. I peel and cut the ripe fruit into pieces, put them in a freezer bag and pop the bag into the freezer. This way I'm always ready to make a delicious beverage.
—*Marilyn Machia*
South Burlington, Vermont

TRIPLE-LAYER BANANA CAKE

(Pictured at left)

Patty Roberts, Athens, Ohio

A year-round family favorite, the recipe for this moist layer cake was passed on to me by my mother. My grandchildren can't keep their fingers out of the tasty icing, which tastes just like peanut butter fudge.

      3/4 cup butter, softened
        2 cups sugar
        3 eggs
    1-1/2 cups mashed bananas (about 3 medium)
    1-1/2 teaspoons vanilla extract
        3 cups all-purpose flour
    1-1/2 teaspoons baking powder
    1-1/2 teaspoons baking soda
      3/4 teaspoon salt
        1 cup buttermilk
FROSTING:
        6 tablespoons peanut butter
        3 tablespoons butter, softened
    5-1/4 cups confectioners' sugar
     8 to 10 tablespoons milk
Peanut halves, optional

In a large mixing bowl, cream butter and sugar. Add eggs, one at a time, beating well after each addition. Beat in bananas and vanilla. Combine the flour, baking powder, baking soda and salt; add to creamed mixture alternately with buttermilk.

Pour into three greased and floured 9-in. round baking pans. Bake at 350° for 25-30 minutes or until a toothpick inserted near the center comes out clean. Cool for 10 minutes before removing from pans to wire racks to cool completely.

For frosting, in a mixing bowl, beat the peanut butter and butter until smooth. Beat in confectioners' sugar and enough milk to achieve spreading consistency. Frost between layers and over top and sides of cake. Garnish with peanuts if desired. **Yield:** 12-14 servings.

CHOCOLATE CHIP BANANA CREAM PIE

(Pictured at right)

Taylor Carroll, Parkesburg, Pennsylvania

This rich treat is a hit every time I serve it. The chilled filling, brimming with bananas, is refreshing, and the cookie crust provides a chocolaty crunch.

    1 tube (18 ounces) refrigerated chocolate
      chip cookie dough
1/3 cup sugar
1/4 cup cornstarch
1/8 teaspoon salt
2-1/3 cups milk
    5 egg yolks, lightly beaten
    2 tablespoons butter
    2 teaspoons vanilla extract, *divided*
    3 medium firm bananas
1-1/2 cups heavy whipping cream
    3 tablespoons confectioners' sugar

Cut cookie dough in half widthwise. Let one portion stand at room temperature for 5-10 minutes to soften (return the other half to the refrigerator for another use). Press dough onto the bottom and up the sides of an ungreased 9-in. pie plate. Bake at 375° for 11-12 minutes or until lightly browned. Cool on a wire rack.

In a saucepan, combine the sugar, cornstarch and salt. Stir in milk until smooth. Cook and stir over medium-high heat until thickened and bubbly. Reduce heat; cook and stir 2 minutes longer. Remove from the heat. Stir a small amount of hot filling into egg yolks; return all to the pan, stirring constantly. Bring to a gentle boil; cook and stir 2 minutes longer. Remove from the heat; stir in butter and 1 teaspoon vanilla.

Spread 1 cup filling into prepared crust. Slice ba-nanas; arrange over filling. Pour remaining filling over bananas. Refrigerate for 2 hours or until set.

In a chilled mixing bowl, beat cream until it begins to thicken. Add confectioners' sugar and remaining vanilla; beat until stiff peaks form. Spread over pie. Refrigerate for 1 hour or until chilled. Refrigerate leftovers. **Yield:** 6-8 servings.

BANANA UPSIDE-DOWN CAKE

Lois Schlickau, Haven, Kansas

Because this starts with a cake mix, this is a fast and easy dessert to make. Plus, it uses up your ripe bananas and tastes great!

1/4 cup butter
1/2 cup packed brown sugar
    3 medium firm bananas, cut into 1/2-inch
      slices
    1 package (9 ounces) yellow cake mix
Whipped cream

Place butter in a 9-in. square baking pan. Heat at 350° for 4-5 minutes or until melted; sprinkle with brown sugar. Arrange bananas in pan; set aside. Prepare cake mix according to package directions; pour over bananas.

Bake at 350° for 30-35 minutes or until a toothpick inserted near the center comes out clean. Immediately invert cake onto a serving platter. Let stand for 5 minutes; remove pan. Serve warm with whipped cream. **Yield:** 9 servings.

Editor's Note: This recipe was tested with Jiffy cake mix.

HAWAIIAN CREAM PIE
(Pictured below)

Jane Wilsdorf, Holliday, Missouri

When it comes to pie, coconut cream is my favorite, while my husband is a banana cream fan. I decided to make us both happy and combine them in this dessert. Pineapple accents the tropical flavor.

- 2/3 cup sugar
- 1/4 cup cornstarch
- 1/2 teaspoon salt
- 2 cups milk
- 3 egg yolks, lightly beaten
- 2 tablespoons butter
- 1 teaspoon vanilla extract
- 1/2 cup crushed pineapple, drained
- 1/4 cup flaked coconut
- 1 to 2 large firm bananas, sliced
- 1 pastry shell (9 inches), baked

MERINGUE:
- 3 egg whites
- 1/4 teaspoon cream of tartar
- 6 tablespoons sugar
- 1/4 cup flaked coconut

In a saucepan, combine the sugar, cornstarch and salt. Stir in milk until smooth. Cook and stir over medium-high heat for 2 minutes or until thickened and bubbly. Reduce heat; cook and stir 2 minutes longer. Remove from the heat.

Stir a small amount of hot filling into egg yolks; return all to pan, stirring constantly. Bring to a gentle boil; cook and stir 2 minutes more. Remove from the heat; stir in butter and vanilla. Fold in pineapple and coconut. Place sliced bananas into pastry shell; set aside.

In a mixing bowl, beat egg whites and cream of tartar on medium speed until soft peaks form. Gradually beat in sugar, 1 tablespoon at a time, on high until stiff glossy peaks form and sugar is dissolved. Pour hot filling over bananas. Spread meringue evenly over hot filling, sealing edges to crust. Sprinkle with coconut.

Bake at 350° for 15 minutes or until the meringue is golden. Cool on a wire rack for 1 hour. Refrigerate for at least 3 hours before serving. Store leftovers in the refrigerator. **Yield:** 6-8 servings.

CUPCAKE CONES

Betty Anderson, Sturgeon Bay, Wisconsin

I experimented with these cupcakes when my girls were young. Now, I'm a grandmother of nine, and these are still our favorites. They're a great treat for kids to bring to school.

- 1 package (18-1/4 ounces) chocolate cake mix
- 1 package (8 ounces) cream cheese, softened
- 1/3 cup sugar
- 1 egg
- 1/2 teaspoon vanilla extract
- 1 cup miniature semisweet chocolate chips
- 36 ice-cream cake cones (about 3 inches tall)

FROSTING:
- 1/2 cup shortening
- 3-3/4 cups confectioners' sugar
- 1 teaspoon vanilla extract
- 4 to 5 tablespoons milk

Prepare cake mix according to package directions; set aside. In a mixing bowl, beat the cream cheese, sugar, egg and vanilla until smooth; stir in the chocolate chips.

Place ice-cream cones in muffin cups. Spoon about 1 tablespoon of cake batter into each cone; top with a rounded teaspoon of cream cheese mixture. Fill with remaining batter to within 3/4 in. of top. Bake at 350° for 25-30 minutes or until a toothpick comes out clean.

In a mixing bowl, beat the shortening, confectioners' sugar and vanilla. Add enough milk to achieve spreading consistency. Frost tops of cooled cones. **Yield:** about 3 dozen.

Editor's Note: These cupcakes are best served the day they are made.

Cakes, Pies & Desserts

CARAMEL PEAR CAKE

(Pictured below)

Darlene Markel, Sublimity, Oregon

I love making this upside-down cake when fresh pears are in season.

    3 medium ripe pears, peeled and sliced
   28 caramels
1-1/2 cups water, *divided*
    2 tablespoons butter
    1 package (18-1/4 ounces) yellow cake
      mix
  1/3 cup vegetable oil
    3 eggs
Whipped cream

Arrange pear slices in rows in a greased 13-in. x 9-in. x 2-in. baking dish; set aside. In a saucepan, melt the caramels with 1/2 cup water; stir in butter until smooth. Pour over pears. In a mixing bowl, combine the cake mix, oil, eggs and remaining water. Beat on medium speed for 2 minutes. Pour over the caramel layer.

Bake at 350° for 45-50 minutes or until a toothpick inserted near the center of cake comes out clean. Cool for 5 minutes before inverting onto a serving platter. Serve with whipped cream. **Yield:** 12-16 servings.

CHILLED CRANBERRY CHEESECAKE

(Pictured above)

An Tonucci, Sault Ste. Marie, Ontario

Whenever I'm invited to an outing involving food, so is my cheesecake. Light in texture, it has a deliciously rich flavor. With its cranberry-pink color, it looks too pretty to cut...but don't let that stop you.

1-1/2 cups graham cracker crumbs (about 24
      squares)
    2 tablespoons sugar
    2 teaspoons grated orange peel, *divided*
  1/3 cup butter, melted
    1 envelope unflavored gelatin
  1/4 cup orange juice
    1 package (8 ounces) cream cheese,
      softened
    1 can (16 ounces) whole-berry
      cranberry sauce
1-1/2 cups heavy whipping cream

In a bowl, combine the cracker crumbs, sugar and 1 teaspoon orange peel; stir in butter. Press onto the bottom of a greased 9-in. springform pan. Bake at 350° for 10 minutes. Cool completely.

In a small saucepan, sprinkle gelatin over orange juice and let stand for 1 minute. Cook over low heat, stirring until gelatin is completely dissolved; cool slightly. Meanwhile, in a bowl, beat cream cheese and remaining orange peel until blended. Beat in cranberry sauce until smooth. Beat in cooled gelatin mixture; mix well.

In a mixing bowl, beat cream until stiff peaks form. Fold into cream cheese mixture. Pour over crust. Refrigerate for 3-4 hours before serving. Carefully run a knife around the edge of pan to loosen. Remove sides of pan. Refrigerate leftovers. **Yield:** 12 servings.

PECAN COCONUT PIE

(Pictured below)

Dorothy Genovese, Chandler, Arizona

Someone brought this pie to my nephew's wedding, and I had to get the recipe. It's the best I ever tasted.

3 eggs
1 cup sugar
1/2 cup light corn syrup
3 tablespoons butter, melted
3 teaspoons vanilla extract
Pinch salt
1-1/2 cups pecan halves
1-1/2 cups shredded coconut
1 unbaked pastry shell (9 inches)

In a mixing bowl, beat eggs. Add the sugar, corn syrup, butter, vanilla and salt; mix well. Stir in pecans and coconut. Pour into pastry shell. Make a domed cover with foil. Bake at 350° for 35 minutes. Uncover; bake 10-15 minutes longer or until a knife inserted near the center comes out clean. Cool on a wire rack. **Yield:** 6-8 servings.

FROZEN CHOCOLATE CRUNCH

(Pictured above)

Flo Burtnett, Gage, Oklahoma

An original recipe of mine, this cool and crunchy concoction has won prizes in a couple of contests. Everyone agrees the fun mix of chocolate, cookies, cream and nuts makes a tempting alternative to ice cream.

8 squares (1 ounce *each*) German sweet chocolate, chopped
2/3 cup light corn syrup
2 cups heavy whipping cream, *divided*
1-1/2 cups coarsely crushed cream-filled chocolate sandwich cookies (about 12 cookies)
1 cup chopped walnuts
Additional chopped walnuts and crushed cream-filled chocolate sandwich cookies, optional

In a heavy saucepan or microwave-safe bowl, melt chocolate with corn syrup; stir until smooth. Stir in 1/2 cup of the cream. Refrigerate for 1 hour or until cool.

Stir in crushed cookies and walnuts. In a mixing bowl, beat remaining cream until stiff peaks form; fold into chocolate mixture. Spread into a 9-in. square dish.

Cover and freeze for 4-6 hours or until firm. Sprinkle with additional walnuts and crushed cookies if desired. **Yield:** 12-16 servings.

PINEAPPLE BREAD PUDDING

Margie Behnke, Neenah, Wisconsin

Pineapple puts a different twist on this moist and flavorful bread pudding. This festive pudding couldn't be easier to make or more delicious to dish up.

10 slices white bread
3/4 cup butter, melted

5 eggs
1 can (20 ounces) crushed pineapple,
  drained
1/4 cup dried currants *or* raisins
1 cup sugar
1-1/2 teaspoons vanilla extract
3/4 teaspoon ground cinnamon
Whipped cream, optional

Place bread on a baking sheet. Bake at 375° for 4 minutes; turn over and bake 4 minutes longer or until very light brown. Cut toasted bread into 1-in. cubes. Toss with melted butter; set aside.

In a bowl, beat the eggs until thick and lemon-colored. Add the pineapple, currants, sugar and vanilla; mix well. Fold in the bread cubes.

Pour into a greased 2-1/2-qt. baking dish. Sprinkle with cinnamon. Cover and bake at 350° for 30-35 minutes or until bubbly and golden brown. Serve warm with whipped cream if desired. **Yield:** 8-10 servings.

RASPBERRY SWIRL CUPCAKES

Christine Sohm, Newton, Ontario

I'm a teeanage farm girl who likes cooking and baking. These cupcakes are a favorite of mine.

1 package (18-1/4 ounces) white cake
  mix
1/4 cup raspberry pie filling
1/2 cup shortening
1/3 cup milk
1 teaspoon vanilla extract
1/4 teaspoon salt
3 cups confectioners' sugar
Fresh raspberries and mint, optional

Prepare cake mix according to package directions. Fill paper-lined muffin cups two-thirds full. Drop 1/2 teaspoon of pie filling in the center of each; swirl with a knife.

Bake at 350° for 20-25 minutes or until a toothpick inserted into cupcake comes out clean. Cool for 10 minutes before removing from pans to wire racks to cool completely.

In a mixing bowl, cream shortening. Add milk, vanilla, salt and confectioners' sugar; beat until fluffy. Frost cupcakes. Garnish with raspberries and mint if desired. **Yield:** about 1-1/2 dozen.

PINEAPPLE-CHERRY NUT CAKE

(Pictured above right)

Wanda Jones, Ridgedale, Missouri

A good friend shared her mother's fruitcake recipe with me. It's simply the best I've ever eaten.

1 package (8 ounces) candied cherries,
  halved
1 package (8 ounces) chopped candied
  pineapple
1 cup chopped pecans
4 cups all-purpose flour, *divided*
1-1/2 cups butter, softened
2-1/4 cups packed brown sugar
6 eggs
1 teaspoon vanilla extract
1 teaspoon lemon extract
2 teaspoons baking powder
GLAZE:
1 cup confectioners' sugar
1 tablespoon milk
1/2 teaspoon vanilla extract

In a bowl, toss the cherries, pineapple and pecans with 1/2 cup flour; set aside. In a mixing bowl, cream butter and brown sugar. Add eggs, one at a time, beating well after each addition. Beat in extracts. Combine baking powder and remaining flour; add to creamed mixture. Beat on low speed until well mixed. Fold in cherry mixture until moistened. Pour into a greased and floured 10-in. fluted tube pan.

Bake at 300° for 2 hours or until a toothpick inserted near the center comes out clean. Cool for 10 minutes before removing from pan to a wire rack to cool completely. Combine glaze ingredients; drizzle over cooled cake. **Yield:** 16 servings.

BUTTERMILK LEMON PIE

(Pictured below and on front cover)

Gail Prather, Bethel, Minnesota

Our family tradition is to have a variety of cream pies for dessert at Easter dinner. This old-fashioned recipe is always a hit.

Pastry for single-crust pie (9 inches)
- 1 cup sugar
- 3 tablespoons all-purpose flour
- 1/2 teaspoon salt
- 2 cups buttermilk
- 4 eggs
- 1/4 cup butter, melted
- 1/3 cup lemon juice
- 1 tablespoon grated lemon peel
- 1 teaspoon vanilla extract
- 1/4 teaspoon ground nutmeg

Line a 9-in. pie plate with pastry. Trim, seal and flute edges; set aside. In a large bowl, combine the sugar, flour and salt. In a large mixing bowl, beat the buttermilk, eggs, butter, lemon juice, lemon peel and vanilla. Add to the sugar mixture; mix well. Pour into crust. Sprinkle with nutmeg.

Bake at 400° for 10 minutes. Reduce temperature to 325°; bake 40-45 minutes longer or until a knife inserted near the center comes out clean. Cool on a wire rack. Store in the refrigerator. **Yield:** 6-8 servings.

CHOCOLATE BANANA CREAM PIE

(Pictured above)

Lynn McAllister, Mt. Ulla, North Carolina

I have three daughters, and this is their favorite pie to help make and to eat. Most of the time, we make two pies so there's enough for seconds.

- 1-1/4 cups sugar
- 1/3 cup cornstarch
- 1/3 cup baking cocoa
- 1/4 teaspoon salt
- 3 cups milk
- 3 tablespoons butter
- 1-1/2 teaspoons vanilla extract
- 1 pastry shell (9 inches), baked
- 2 medium firm bananas, sliced
- 1 cup whipped topping

Chocolate curls and additional sliced bananas, optional

In a large saucepan, combine the sugar, cornstarch, cocoa, salt and milk until smooth. Bring to a boil; cook and stir for 2 minutes or until thickened. Remove from the heat; stir in butter and vanilla.

Pour half of the filling into pastry shell. Top with sliced bananas and remaining filling. Refrigerate for 3-4 hours. Garnish with whipped topping. Decorate with chocolate curls and additional bananas if desired. **Yield:** 6-8 servings.

Cakes, Pies & Desserts

PECAN CHESS PIE

Martha Fautheree, Midway, Texas

My favorite hobby is old-fashioned country cooking, but my job sometimes limits my kitchen time. This pie is one enjoyed by my husband and me.

- 1/3 cup shortening
- 3 tablespoons hot water
- 1 cup all-purpose flour
- 1/4 teaspoon salt

FILLING:
- 1/2 cup butter, softened
- 2 cups sugar
- 4-1/2 teaspoons all-purpose flour
- 1/2 teaspoon salt
- 3 eggs
- 1/2 cup evaporated milk
- 1 tablespoon vanilla extract
- 1-1/2 cups finely chopped pecans
- Whipped cream

In a mixing bowl, beat the shortening and water until combined. Add flour and salt; beat until crumbly. Shape into a ball. Roll out pastry to fit a 9-in. pie plate. Transfer pastry to pie plate. Trim pastry to 1/2 in. beyond edge of pie plate; flute edges. Line unpricked pastry shell with a double thickness of heavy-duty foil. Bake at 450° for 8 minutes. Remove foil; bake 5 minutes longer. Remove to a wire rack; reduce heat to 350°.

In another mixing bowl, cream the butter, sugar, flour and salt. Add the eggs, milk and vanilla; beat well. Stir in the pecans. Pour into prepared crust. Bake at 350° for 40-45 minutes or until a knife inserted near the center comes out clean. Cool on a wire rack for 1 hour. Refrigerate for at least 1 hour. Serve with whipped cream. **Yield:** 6-8 servings.

LEMON ICEBOX DESSERT

(Pictured at right)

Corene Thorsen, Oconomowoc, Wisconsin

This dessert has a nice light lemon flavor with a tender, flaky crust. It's perfect for serving during the warm summer months.

- 1-1/2 cups all-purpose flour
- 4-1/2 teaspoons sugar
- 3/4 cup cold butter

FILLING:
- 8 eggs, *separated*
- 2 cups sugar, *divided*
- 2/3 cup lemon juice
- 3 tablespoons grated lemon peel
- 1 tablespoon unflavored gelatin
- 1/2 cup plus 2 tablespoons cold water, *divided*
- 1/2 teaspoon cream of tartar

TOPPING:
- 1 cup heavy whipping cream
- 1 tablespoon confectioners' sugar
- 1 cup flaked coconut
- 1 tablespoon grated orange peel

In a bowl, combine flour and sugar. Cut in butter until crumbly. Press into a greased 13-in. x 9-in. x 2-in. baking dish. Bake at 350° for 18-22 minutes or until lightly browned. Cool on a wire rack.

In a heavy saucepan, combine egg yolks, 1 cup sugar, lemon juice and peel. Sprinkle gelatin over 1/2 cup cold water; let stand for 1 minute. Add to the egg yolk mixture. Cook and stir over medium heat until mixture reaches 160° and coats the back of a metal spoon. Remove from the heat; cool completely.

In another saucepan, combine egg whites, cream of tartar, and remaining sugar and water. Cook over low heat, beating with a hand mixer on low speed until mixture reaches 160°. Pour into a large mixing bowl; beat on high until soft peaks form. Gently fold into yolk mixture. Spread over crust.

In a mixing bowl, beat the cream and confectioners' sugar until soft peaks form; spread over filling. Combine coconut and orange peel; sprinkle over top. Cover and chill for 4 hours or overnight. Refrigerate leftovers. **Yield:** 12-16 servings.

Remove from the heat; stir in vanilla. Cool. In a small mixing bowl, cream butter. Gradually beat in cooled chocolate mixture until smooth.

To assemble, place one cake layer on a serving plate; spread with half of the mocha filling. Top with another cake layer; spread with raspberry jam. Place remaining cake on top; spread with the remaining mocha filling. Refrigerate for 3 hours. Garnish with raspberries and mint if desired. **Yield:** 8-10 servings.

RASPBERRY MOCHA TORTE
(Pictured above)

Adrene Schmidt, Waldersee, Manitoba

I combined three of my favorite things to make this dessert...raspberries, chocolate and coffee.

>   6 eggs, *separated*
> 3/4 cup sugar, *divided*
>   1 cup all-purpose flour
> FILLING:
>   1/3 cup sugar
>   3 eggs
>   2 egg yolks
>   1 teaspoon instant coffee granules
>   2 squares (1 ounce *each*) semisweet
>   chocolate, melted
>   1 teaspoon vanilla extract
>   1 cup butter, softened
>   1/2 cup raspberry jam
> **Fresh raspberries and mint, optional**

In a large mixing bowl, beat egg yolks and 1/2 cup sugar until thick and lemon-colored. In a small mixing bowl, beat the egg whites on medium speed until soft peaks form. Gradually beat in remaining sugar, 1 tablespoon at a time, on high until stiff peaks form. Gently fold into egg yolk mixture along with the flour.

Divide batter between three waxed paper-lined ungreased 9-in. round baking pans. Bake at 350° for 15-20 minutes or until golden. Cool 10 minutes before removing from pans to wire racks.

In a small saucepan, whisk sugar, eggs, yolks and coffee granules. Add chocolate. Cook over medium heat, stirring constantly, until mixture reaches 160° and coats the back of a metal spoon.

CARAMEL CHOCOLATE CAKE
(Pictured below)

Esther Wise, Longmont, Colorado

A creamy caramel frosting lends old-fashioned flavor to this moist chocolate cake.

>   3 squares (1 ounce *each*) unsweetened
>   chocolate
>   1 cup water
>   1 teaspoon red food coloring, optional
>   1/2 cup shortening
>   2 cups sugar
>   3 eggs
> 2-1/2 cups all-purpose flour
> 1-1/2 teaspoons baking soda
>   1/2 teaspoon salt
>   1 cup (8 ounces) sour cream
> CARAMEL FROSTING:
>   2 cups packed brown sugar
>   2/3 cup milk
>   1/4 cup butter
>   1/4 teaspoon salt
>   1 cup confectioners' sugar
>   2 tablespoons heavy whipping cream

2 teaspoons vanilla extract
15 pecan halves

In a saucepan, melt chocolate in water. Stir in food coloring if desired; set aside. In a mixing bowl, cream shortening and sugar. Add eggs, one at a time, beating well after each. Combine the flour, baking soda and salt; add to the creamed mixture alternately with sour cream. Add chocolate mixture; beat on medium speed for 1 minute.

Pour into a greased 13-in. x 9-in. x 2-in. baking dish. Bake at 350° for 35-40 minutes or until a toothpick inserted near the center comes out clean. Cool on a wire rack.

For frosting, combine the brown sugar, milk, butter and salt in a heavy saucepan. Bring to a boil over medium heat, stirring constantly. Cook and stir until a candy thermometer reads 234° (softball stage). Remove from the heat; cool to lukewarm. Transfer to a mixing bowl; beat in confectioners' sugar, cream and vanilla until mixture achieves spreading consistency. Frost cake. Garnish with pecans. **Yield:** 15 servings.

Editor's Note: We recommend that you test your candy thermometer before each use by bringing water to a boil; the thermometer should read 212°. Adjust your recipe temperature up or down based on your test.

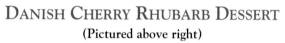

DANISH CHERRY RHUBARB DESSERT
(Pictured above right)

Joan Kallhoff, O'Neill, Nebraska

"Can I have the recipe?" is the question I'm always asked whenever I serve this delicious dessert. Rhubarb is generally ready the first thing in spring, and these bars are a great way to welcome the season.

2-1/2 cups all-purpose flour
   1 teaspoon salt
   1 cup cold butter
  1/2 cup milk
   1 egg, *separated*
   1 cup cornflakes
   4 to 5 cups diced fresh *or* frozen rhubarb, thawed
1-1/2 cups plus 1 tablespoon sugar, *divided*
   1 can (21 ounces) cherry pie filling
   1 teaspoon vanilla extract
GLAZE:
  1/2 cup confectioners' sugar
  1/4 teaspoon vanilla extract
1-1/2 to 2 teaspoons milk

In a bowl, combine the flour and salt; cut in butter until crumbly. Add the milk and egg yolk; mix well. Divide in half. On a lightly floured sur-

face, roll each portion into a 13-in. x 9-in. rectangle. Place one rectangle in a greased 13-in. x 9-in. x 2-in. baking dish. Sprinkle with cornflakes.

In a bowl, combine the rhubarb and 1-1/2 cups sugar. Stir in the pie filling and vanilla; spread over cornflakes. Top with the remaining pastry. Cut slits in the top. Beat egg white; brush over pastry. Sprinkle with remaining sugar. Bake at 350° for 50-55 minutes or until crust is golden brown. Cool on a wire rack.

In a bowl, combine glaze ingredients; drizzle over bars. Store in the refrigerator. **Yield:** 12-16 servings.

PEANUT BUTTER CUPCAKES

Alyce Wyman, Pembina, North Dakota

My family just loves these cupcakes, especially the subtle taste of peanut butter in the frosting. Chocolate frosting is equally delicious on top.

   1 package (18-1/4 ounces) white cake mix
  18 miniature peanut butter cups
1-1/3 cups prepared vanilla frosting
   2 tablespoons creamy peanut butter

Prepare cake mix according to package directions. Spoon about 2 tablespoons of batter into each paper-lined muffin cup. Place a peanut butter cup in each; fill two-thirds full with remaining batter.

Bake at 350° for 20-25 minutes or until lightly browned and a toothpick inserted into cupcake comes out clean. Cool for 10 minutes before removing to wire racks to cool completely.

In a bowl, stir together the frosting and peanut butter until smooth. Frost cupcakes. **Yield:** 1-1/2 dozen.

The Proof Is Definitely In the Pudding!

▪▴▪▴▪▴▪▴▪▴▪▴▪▴▪

CRANBERRY BREAD PUDDING

Margery Richmond, Fort Collins, Colorado

This down-home dessert takes on a touch of elegance when I serve it warm and drizzled with a thin orange custard sauce.

16 slices bread, crusts removed and cubed
1-1/2 cups fresh *or* frozen cranberries, thawed
1 tablespoon grated orange peel
1/4 cup butter, melted

6 eggs
4 cups milk
3/4 cup plus 1 tablespoon sugar, *divided*
1 teaspoon vanilla extract
ORANGE CUSTARD SAUCE:
3 egg yolks
1/4 cup sugar
1 cup heavy whipping cream
1 orange peel strip (1/4 inch)
1/2 teaspoon orange extract

In a greased 13-in. x 9-in. x 2-in. baking dish, layer half of the bread cubes, cranberries and orange peel. Repeat layers. Drizzle with butter. In a large mixing bowl, beat the eggs, milk, 3/4 cup sugar and vanilla; pour over bread mixture. Let stand for 15-30 minutes. Sprinkle with remaining sugar.

Bake, uncovered, at 375° for 65-75 minutes or until a knife comes out clean.

PUDDING APLENTY. Clockwise from top right: Cranberry Bread Pudding, Raspberry Rice Pudding, Baked Lemon Pudding and Old-Fashioned Cocoa Pudding.

For sauce, in a heavy saucepan, beat egg yolks and sugar. Stir in cream and orange peel. Cook and stir over low heat for 20-25 minutes or until mixture reaches 160° and coats the back of a metal spoon. Remove from the heat; discard orange peel. Stir in extract. Cover; refrigerate until chilled. Serve with bread pudding. **Yield:** 12 servings.

▟▟▟▟▟▟▟▟▟▟
BAKED LEMON PUDDING

Aida Von Babbel, Coquitlam, British Columbia

Looking for a light and lemony delicate delight of a dessert? This is an old-fashioned family favorite. It is cake-like on top with a custard texture on the bottom.

- 2/3 cup sugar, *divided*
- 5 tablespoons all-purpose flour
- 1/4 teaspoon baking powder
- 1/8 teaspoon salt
- 2 eggs, *separated*
- 1 cup milk
- 3 tablespoons lemon juice
- 2 tablespoons butter, melted
- 1-1/2 teaspoons grated lemon peel
- Confectioners' sugar, optional

In a mixing bowl, combine 1/3 cup sugar, flour, baking powder and salt. In another mixing bowl, beat egg yolks; add milk, lemon juice, butter and lemon peel. Add to dry ingredients; mix well.

Beat egg whites until soft peaks form; gradually add remaining sugar, beating until stiff peaks form. Fold into lemon mixture.

Pour into a lightly greased 1-1/2-qt. baking dish. Place in a large baking pan. Add 1 in. of hot water to larger pan.

Bake, uncovered, at 350° for 45-50 minutes or until lightly browned. Serve warm or chilled. Dust with confectioners' sugar if desired. **Yield:** 4 servings.

▟▟▟▟▟▟▟▟▟▟
OLD-FASHIONED COCOA PUDDING

Sue Knapp, Camden, Michigan

My husband's favorite pudding is this one, which my mother used to make. It gets so many compliments that I also use it as a pie filling on special occasions!

- 1 cup sugar
- 1/3 cup baking cocoa
- 1/4 cup all-purpose flour
- 1/4 teaspoon salt
- 1-1/2 cups water
- 2 egg yolks
- 1 tablespoon butter
- 1 teaspoon vanilla extract
- Whipped topping and chocolate curls

In a saucepan, combine the sugar, cocoa, flour and salt. Gradually whisk in water and egg yolks. Cook over medium heat until mixture comes to a boil, stirring constantly. Cook and stir for 2 minutes or until thickened.

Remove from the heat; stir in butter and vanilla until blended. Pour into individual dishes. Refrigerate until set. Garnish with whipped topping and chocolate curls. **Yield:** 4 servings.

▟▟▟▟▟▟▟▟▟▟
RASPBERRY RICE PUDDING

Shirley Privratsky, Dickinson, North Dakota

This is one of my family's all-time favorites. It's so festive looking—especially when served in a clear glass bowl or topped with raspberries like a sundae.

- 2 cups water
- 1 cup long grain rice
- 3 cups milk
- 3/4 to 1 cup sugar
- 1 carton (8 ounces) frozen whipped topping, thawed
- 2 packages (10 ounces *each*) frozen raspberries, thawed
- 2 tablespoons cornstarch

In a large saucepan, bring water to a boil. Stir in rice. Reduce heat; cover and simmer for 10 minutes, stirring occasionally. Stir in milk and sugar. Cook 20-30 minutes longer or until rice is tender and mixture is thick and creamy. Remove from heat; cool. Fold in whipped topping. Refrigerate.

Drain berries, reserving juice. In a small saucepan, combine cornstarch and reserved juice until smooth. Bring to a boil; cook and stir for 2 minutes or until thickened. Stir in berries. Remove from heat; cool.

Spoon the rice pudding into individual dishes; top with the berry mixture. Cover and refrigerate until serving. **Yield:** 10-12 servings.

 ## WALNUT GLORY CAKE

(Pictured above)

Marjorie Yoder, Epworth, Georgia

I've served this sponge cake at church dinners, re-unions and other occasions for 40 years. It's always on the table when any of our four children, three granddaughters and great-granddaughter visit.

> 9 eggs, *separated*
> 1-1/2 cups sugar, *divided*
> 2 teaspoons vanilla extract
> 3/4 cup all-purpose flour
> 2 teaspoons ground cinnamon
> 1 teaspoon salt
> 2 cups finely chopped walnuts
> 2 cups confectioners' sugar
> 2 to 3 tablespoons milk

In a mixing bowl, beat egg yolks until slightly thickened. Gradually add 3/4 cup sugar, beating until thick and lemon-colored. Beat in vanilla. Combine the flour, cinnamon and salt; add to batter and beat until smooth.

In another mixing bowl, beat egg whites on medium speed until soft peaks form. Add the re-maining sugar, 1 tablespoon at a time, beating on high until stiff peaks form. Fold a fourth of the egg whites into batter; fold in remaining egg whites. Fold in walnuts.

Spoon into an ungreased 10-in. tube pan (pan will be full). Bake at 350° for 45-50 minutes or un-til cake springs back when lightly touched. Im-mediately invert pan; cool completely. Run a knife around side of cake and remove from pan.

In a small bowl, combine confectioners' sugar and enough milk to achieve drizzling consistency; drizzle over cake. **Yield:** 10-12 servings.

PEACH ICE CREAM

(Pictured below)

Linda Wallace, Hartsville, South Carolina

South Carolina is one of the leading producers of peaches. Luckily, we live only 3 miles from a large peach orchard. This ice cream is one of my most popular uses for the luscious fruit. We can hardly wait for the harvest so we can enjoy it.

> 1 tablespoon unflavored gelatin
> 2 tablespoons cold water
> 1-1/2 cups milk
> 1 cup half-and half cream
> 1/2 cup evaporated milk
> 2 cups sliced peeled ripe peaches
> 1-3/4 cups sugar, *divided*
> 1 teaspoon vanilla extract
> 1/4 teaspoon almond extract
> 1/8 teaspoon salt

In a small microwave-safe bowl, sprinkle gelatin over cold water; let stand for 1 minute. Microwave on high for 20 seconds; stir. Let stand until gelatin is completely dissolved. In a large bowl, combine the gelatin, milk, cream and evaporated milk.

In another bowl, mash the peaches with 1 cup sugar. Add the peach mixture, extracts, salt and remaining sugar to the cream mixture; stir until sugar is dissolved. Fill cylinder of ice cream freez-er two-thirds full; freeze according to manufac-turer's directions. Allow to ripen in ice cream freezer or firm up in the refrigerator freezer for 2-4 hours before serving. **Yield:** about 1 quart.

COCONUT CUSTARD PUDDING

Wilma Lincoln, Montezuma, Iowa

Here's an easy dessert that my whole family loves. I use an artificial sweetener when I make it for diabetic dinner guests and pretty it up with nutmeg.

      6 eggs
   2/3 cup sugar
   1/8 teaspoon salt
4-1/2 cups milk
   1/2 teaspoon vanilla extract
   1/2 teaspoon coconut extract
Dash ground nutmeg

In a bowl, whisk the eggs, sugar and salt until the eggs are just blended. In a saucepan, heat milk just to simmering. Gradually whisk into egg mixture. Stir in extracts. Pour into ten 8-oz. custard cups. Sprinkle with nutmeg.

Place cups in two 13-in. x 9-in. x 2-in. baking pans. Add 1 in. of hot water to the pans. Bake, uncovered, at 350° for 45-50 minutes or until a knife inserted near the center comes out clean.

Remove cups to a wire rack; cool for 1 hour. Store in the refrigerator. **Yield:** 10 servings.

CAPPUCCINO CUPCAKES

Carol Forcum, Marion, Illinois

A dusting of cocoa powder deliciously tops off these pretty cupcakes. They're so scrumptious, no one ever guesses how easy they are to make.

      2 cups all-purpose flour
1-1/2 cups sugar
   1/2 cup baking cocoa
      1 teaspoon baking soda
   1/2 teaspoon salt
   1/4 cup instant coffee granules
   1/2 cup hot water
      2 eggs
   1/2 cup prune baby food
   1/4 cup vegetable oil
      2 teaspoons vanilla extract
1-1/2 cups whipped topping
Additional baking cocoa

In a bowl, combine the flour, sugar, cocoa, baking soda and salt. Dissolve coffee granules in hot water. In another bowl, whisk the eggs, baby food, oil, vanilla and coffee mixture. Stir into dry ingredients just until moistened. Fill paper-lined muffin cups two-thirds full.

Bake at 350° for 18-20 minutes or until a toothpick comes out clean. Cool for 10 minutes before removing from pans to wire racks to cool completely.

Just before serving, frost the cupcakes with whipped topping and sprinkle with cocoa. **Yield:** 17 cupcakes.

 ## CHOCOLATE CHIPPER PIE MIX

(Pictured above)

Carole Martin, Coffeeville, Mississippi

Your friends will love the sweet surprise of finding a chocolate pecan pie under their Christmas tree. I enjoy giving this unique gift mix because it's a little bit different from traditional holiday fare.

      1 cup sugar
   1/2 cup all-purpose flour
      1 cup (6 ounces) semisweet chocolate
         chips
   1/2 cup flaked coconut
   1/2 cup chopped pecans
ADDITIONAL INGREDIENTS:
      2 eggs, lightly beaten
   1/4 cup butter, melted
      1 unbaked pastry shell (9 inches)

In a bowl, combine sugar and flour; place in a resealable plastic bag and label "Dry Ingredients." Place chips, coconut and pecans in another resealable plastic bag and label "Chocolate Filling Ingredients." Place both bags in a gift basket along with directions for preparing Chocolate Chipper Pie. **Yield:** 1 batch.

To prepare pie: In large bowl, combine the eggs, butter and contents of "Dry Ingredients" packet; mix well. Stir in the contents of the "Chocolate Filling Ingredients" packet. Spoon into pie shell. Bake at 350° for 30-35 minutes or until filling is set and crust is golden. Cool on a wire rack. **Yield:** 1 pie (6-8 servings).

APPLE PEAR PIE
(Pictured below)

Grace Camp, Owingsville, Kentucky

This fruit pie, brimming with apples and pears, really says "fall." What a yummy way to use your backyard bounty or pickings from local orchards! I've made plenty of pies, and this is a real standout.

Pastry for double-crust pie (9 inches)
    3 medium ripe pears, peeled and thinly sliced
    3 medium tart apples, peeled and thinly sliced
    1 cup plus 1 teaspoon sugar, *divided*
    1 teaspoon lemon juice
    1 teaspoon ground cinnamon
  1/4 teaspoon ground nutmeg
    3 tablespoons butter
    1 teaspoon milk

Line a 9-in. pie plate with bottom pastry; trim to 1 in. beyond edge of plate. In a large bowl, combine the pears, apples, 1 cup sugar, lemon juice, cinnamon and nutmeg. Transfer mixture to crust; dot with butter.

Roll out remaining pastry to fit top of pie; cut slits or decorative cutouts in pastry. Place over filling; trim, seal and flute edges. Add decorative cutouts if desired. Brush with milk; sprinkle with remaining sugar. Cover edges loosely with foil.

Bake at 350° for 30 minutes. Remove foil; bake 30-35 minutes longer or until crust is golden brown. Cool on a wire rack. **Yield:** 6-8 servings.

BANANA CUPCAKES

Arloia Lutz, Sebewaing, Michigan

I got this recipe from my mother-in-law more than 40 years ago. They taste as good today as they did back then!

✓ Uses less fat, sugar or salt. Includes Nutritional Analysis and Diabetic Exchanges.

  1/3 cup shortening
  2/3 cup sugar
    1 egg
    1 teaspoon vanilla extract
  3/4 cup mashed ripe bananas (about 2 small bananas)
1-1/3 cups cake flour
    1 teaspoon baking powder
  1/2 teaspoon salt
  1/2 teaspoon baking soda
  1/2 teaspoon ground cinnamon
  1/2 teaspoon ground cloves
  1/4 teaspoon ground nutmeg
    1 tablespoon confectioners' sugar

In a mixing bowl, cream shortening and sugar. Add egg, vanilla and bananas; mix well. Combine flour, baking powder, salt, baking soda, cinnamon, cloves and nutmeg; add to creamed mixture just until combined. Fill paper-lined muffin cups two-thirds full.

Bake at 375° for 18-20 minutes or until a toothpick comes out clean. Cool for 10 minutes before removing from pan to a wire rack to cool completely. Dust with confectioners' sugar. **Yield:** 1 dozen.

Nutritional Analysis: One cupcake equals 154 calories, 6 g fat (2 g saturated fat), 18 mg cholesterol, 175 mg sodium, 24 g carbohydrate, 1 g fiber, 2 g protein. **Diabetic Exchanges:** 1-1/2 starch, 1 fat.

CARAMEL CHOCOLATE CHEESECAKE BITES
(Pictured above right)

Barbara Nowakowski
North Tonawanda, New York

The wheat germ makes getting these delicious bites a snap to get out of the pan. They're cute as can be and are always a favorite.

✓ Uses less fat, sugar or salt. Includes Nutritional Analysis and Diabetic Exchanges.

3/4 cup toasted wheat germ
2 packages (8 ounces *each*) reduced-fat cream cheese
3/4 cup sugar
1/3 cup baking cocoa
4 egg whites
1 teaspoon vanilla extract
36 pecan halves
3 tablespoons fat-free caramel ice cream topping

Coat 36 miniature muffin cups with nonstick cooking spray; generously coat each with wheat germ. Set aside. In a mixing bowl, beat cream cheese and sugar until smooth. Add cocoa; mix well. Beat in egg whites and vanilla just until combined. Spoon 4 teaspoons into each muffin cup.

Bake at 350° for 13-16 minutes or until set. Cool in pans for 10 minutes before removing to wire racks. Cool for 30 minutes and refrigerate. (Cheesecakes may sink in center upon cooling.) To serve, top each with a pecan half. Microwave caramel topping on high for 10 seconds or until soft. Spoon 1/4 teaspoon over each. **Yield:** 3 dozen.

Nutritional Analysis: One serving (two mini cheesecakes) equals 147 calories, 8 g fat (3 g saturated fat), 12 mg cholesterol, 136 mg sodium, 15 g carbohydrate, 1 g fiber, 5 g protein. **Diabetic Exchanges:** 1-1/2 fat, 1 starch.

WALNUT CARROT CAKE

(Pictured at right)

Darlene Markel, Sublimity, Oregon

This carrot cake is surprisingly moist and very flavorful. It also has a nice texture and cuts beautifully for serving to your guests.

1 cup butter, softened
1-2/3 cups sugar
4 eggs
1 teaspoon vanilla extract
1 teaspoon grated lemon peel
2-1/2 cups all-purpose flour
1 package (3.4 ounces) instant lemon pudding mix
1-1/2 teaspoons baking powder
1 teaspoon baking soda
1 teaspoon ground cinnamon
1/2 teaspoon salt
1 cup (8 ounces) plain yogurt
2-1/2 cups grated carrots
3/4 cup chopped walnuts
1 can (16 ounces) cream cheese frosting

In a large mixing bowl, cream butter and sugar. Add eggs, one at a time, beating well after each addition. Beat in the vanilla and lemon peel. Combine the flour, pudding mix, baking powder, baking soda, cinnamon and salt; add to creamed mixture alternately with yogurt. Stir in carrots and nuts.

Transfer to a greased and floured 10-in. fluted tube pan. Bake at 350° for 50-55 minutes or until a toothpick inserted near the center comes out clean. Cool for 10 minutes before removing from pan to a wire rack. Cool completely before frosting. Store in the refrigerator. **Yield:** 12-16 servings.

1-3/4 cups sugar
  1/2 cup vegetable oil
  1/4 cup butter, softened
    2 eggs
  1/2 cup buttermilk
    1 teaspoon vanilla extract
2-1/2 cups all-purpose flour
  1/4 cup baking cocoa
    1 teaspoon baking soda
  1/2 teaspoon baking powder
  1/2 teaspoon ground cinnamon
  1/4 teaspoon ground cloves
    2 cups finely shredded zucchini
  1/2 cup semisweet chocolate chips
  1/2 cup sliced almonds

CUSTARD SAUCE:

  1/2 cup sugar
    2 tablespoons all-purpose flour
    2 tablespoons cornstarch
    3 cups milk
    3 egg yolks
    3 tablespoons butter
  1/4 teaspoon almond extract

In a mixing bowl, beat sugar, oil and butter. Add eggs, buttermilk and vanilla; mix well. Combine flour, cocoa, baking soda, baking powder, cinnamon and cloves; gradually add to creamed mixture. Stir in zucchini, chips and almonds.

Pour into a greased and floured 10-in. tube or fluted tube pan. Bake at 325° for 55-60 minutes or until a toothpick comes out clean. Cool for 10 minutes before removing from pan to a wire rack.

For sauce, combine the sugar, flour and cornstarch in a saucepan. Stir in milk until smooth. Bring to a boil; cook and stir for 2 minutes or until thickened. Remove from the heat. Stir a small amount of hot mixture into egg yolks; return all to pan, stirring constantly. Bring to a gentle boil.

COCONUT PEACH PIE

(Pictured above)

Beatrice Crutchfield, Norcross, Georgia

A relative shared this recipe with me. I love peaches, and the wonderful meringue crust is tender and crispy.

    3 egg whites
Dash salt
  3/4 cup plus 2 tablespoons sugar, *divided*
1-1/4 cups flaked coconut, toasted, *divided*
  1/3 cup chopped almonds, toasted
3-1/2 cups sliced peeled peaches (about 6 medium)
    1 cup heavy whipping cream

In a mixing bowl, beat egg whites and salt on medium speed until foamy. Gradually add 3/4 cup sugar, 1 tablespoon at a time, beating on high until stiff peaks form. Fold in 1 cup coconut and almonds. Spread onto the bottom and up the sides of a greased 9-in. pie plate. Bake at 350° for 30 minutes or until light golden brown. Cool completely on a wire rack.

Arrange peaches in crust. In a chilled mixing bowl, beat cream with remaining sugar until stiff peaks form. Spread over peaches; sprinkle with remaining coconut. Refrigerate for 1 hour before slicing. **Yield:** 6-8 servings.

CHOCOLATE ZUCCHINI CAKE

(Pictured at right)

Peggy Linton, Cobourg, Ontario

The minute I can get my hands on zucchini, I start making this light and luscious cake. For years it was an often-ordered dessert at my sister's deli.

Reduce heat; cook and stir for 2 minutes. Remove from the heat; stir in butter and extract. Serve warm with cake. **Yield:** 12-16 servings.

★★★★★★★★★★★★★★★★
WALNUT OAT PIE

Marilyn Hanshaw and Connie Allen
Washington, Kansas

More than 20 years ago, we began baking pies in our home for auctions and a local pie delivery route. Now we sell 60 different varieties of pies to supermarkets, restaurants and customers in our retail shop!

> 3 eggs, lightly beaten
> 1 cup packed brown sugar
> 1/2 cup quick-cooking oats
> 1/2 cup chopped walnuts
> 1/2 cup evaporated milk
> 1/2 cup maple syrup
> 1/4 cup butter, melted
> 1 teaspoon vanilla extract
> 1/8 teaspoon salt
> 1 unbaked pie shell (9 inches)

In a large bowl, combine the first nine ingredients; mix well. Pour filling into pie shell. Bake at 350° for 30-35 minutes or until set. Cool on a wire rack. **Yield:** 8 servings.

There's No Trick to These Treats!

★★★★★★★★★★★★★
CREAM PUFF GHOSTS

Dixi Terry, Goreville, Illinois

Don't get spooked by these spirited Halloween characters. The cream puff ghosts aren't difficult to make. I form basic cream puff batter into cute little phantoms.

> 3/4 cup water
> 6 tablespoons butter
> 1 teaspoon sugar
> 1/4 teaspoon salt
> 1 cup all-purpose flour
> 4 eggs
> **PUMPKIN FILLING:**
> 2 envelopes unflavored gelatin
> 1/2 cup cold orange juice
> 1 cup milk

> 2/3 cup packed brown sugar
> 1 can (15 ounces) solid-pack pumpkin
> 1-1/2 teaspoons pumpkin pie spice
> 1 cup heavy whipping cream, whipped
> **Confectioners' sugar**
> **Miniature black jelly beans** *or* **chocolate chips**

In a saucepan, bring the water, butter, sugar and salt to a boil. Add flour all at once and stir until a smooth ball forms. Remove from the heat; let stand for 5 minutes. Add eggs, one at a time, beating well after each addition.

Continue beating until mixture is smooth and shiny. Drop by 1/3 cupfuls 3 in. apart onto ungreased baking sheets; spread into 4-in. x 3-in. ovals. Using a knife coated with nonstick cooking spray, make a wavy edge at the bottom of the ghost. Bake at 400° for 30-35 minutes or until golden brown. Remove to wire racks to cool.

Meanwhile, in a saucepan, sprinkle gelatin over orange juice; let stand for 1 minute. Stir in the milk and brown sugar; cook and stir over low heat until gelatin and sugar are completely dissolved. Stir in pumpkin and pumpkin pie spice. Cover and refrigerate for 45-60 minutes or until thickened. Fold in whipped cream.

Split cream puffs in half; remove dough from inside. Set aside 1 to 2 tablespoons of filling for eyes. Spoon remaining filling into cream puffs; replace tops. Dust with confectioners' sugar. Place two small dots of reserved filling on each ghost; top with jelly beans. Serve immediately. **Yield:** 9 cream puffs.

Cooking for Two

*Turn to this chapter for satisfying meals
that are perfectly portioned for two.*

RACK OF LAMB

Margery Bryan, Moses Lake, Washington

We've raised sheep for years, so lamb has been a staple entree in our house as well as a favorite to serve when company comes. We do our own butchering and can cut the meat any way, but we've found the rack yields a perfect amount of meat for the two of us.

  1 tablespoon olive oil
  2 garlic cloves, minced
  1 tablespoon minced fresh parsley
  1 teaspoon minced fresh rosemary *or* 1/4
    to 1/2 teaspoon dried rosemary, crushed
  1 teaspoon minced fresh thyme *or* 1/4
    to 1/2 teaspoon dried thyme
  1 French-style rack of lamb (8 chops),
    about 1 pound

In a bowl, combine the oil, garlic, parsley, rosemary and thyme. Rub oil mixture over lamb. Place meat side up on a rack in a greased 11-in. x 7-in. x 2-in. baking pan.

  Bake, uncovered, at 400° for 20-30 minutes or until meat reaches desired doneness (for rare, a meat thermometer should read 140°; medium, 160°; well-done, 170°). **Yield:** 2 servings.

FRUITED CRANBERRY RELISH

Ruth Collins, Blossvale, New York

This recipe came from my aunt, who for many years invited our family to her home for Christmas dinner. I took great delight in helping myself to this relish because she always served it in one of her fancy dishes, used only for the holidays.

  1 medium navel orange, peeled and
    sectioned
  1 medium tart apple, cored and sliced
  1 cup fresh *or* frozen cranberries
  1/3 cup sugar

In a food processor, combine all ingredients; cover and process until the fruit is chopped. **Yield:** 1-1/4 cups.

HONEY MUSTARD SALAD DRESSING

Patty Brewer, Kansas City, Missouri

From the first time I tasted this salad dressing, it has been a favorite at our house, served almost exclusively. It's quick to prepare, and it's easily made "light" by using fat-free or reduced-fat mayonnaise.

  6 tablespoons mayonnaise
  2 tablespoons Dijon mustard
  2 tablespoons honey
Assorted salad greens, tomatoes and croutons

In a bowl, combine the mayonnaise, mustard and honey; mix well. Store in refrigerator. Serve over salad. **Yield:** about 1/2 cup dressing.

MINTED PEARS

Mary Selner, Green Bay, Wisconsin

My grandmother would use food coloring to make red and green pears only at Christmastime, and I enjoy carrying on her tradition. When I prepare this for a salad, I fill the centers with fresh fruit, fruit cocktail or cottage cheese. As a dessert, there are more options...a dab of whipping cream with a cherry on top, a drizzle of chocolate on top of the whipped cream or a scoop of sherbet in a contrasting color.

  1 cup sugar
  1 cup water
  2 drops green food coloring
  1/8 to 1/4 teaspoon mint extract
  3 medium ripe pears, peeled, halved and
    cored
Fresh mint sprigs

In a skillet, bring the sugar and water to a boil. Reduce heat; add food coloring and mint extract. Carefully place pears in syrup. Simmer, uncovered, for 5 minutes or until tender.

  Place pears in a deep bowl; pour syrup over pears. Make sure pears are completely covered in the syrup to prevent browning. Refrigerate for at least 1 hour or until serving. Garnish with fresh mint. **Yield:** 2-3 servings.

cornstarch and water until smooth; stir into cooking juices. Bring to a boil; cook and stir for 1-2 minutes or until thickened. Pour over chicken. Sprinkle with cashews. **Yield:** 2 servings.

FRUITY CHICKEN SALAD

(Pictured below)

Eleanor Loughlin, Southport, North Carolina

This quick and easy dish features a nice combination of flavors, textures and colors. The recipe is adequate for two, but if you'd like to serve it as a luncheon entree, simply double or triple the ingredients.

> 1 medium ripe avocado
> 1 tablespoon lemon juice, *divided*
> 2 cups coarsely chopped Boston lettuce
> 1-1/3 cups cubed cooked chicken
> 1 can (8 ounces) pineapple chunks, drained
> 1 small apple, cut into 3/4-inch chunks
> 1/4 cup chopped pecans
> 1/3 to 1/2 cup mayonnaise
> Lettuce leaves

Peel avocado; cut in half lengthwise and remove pit. Slice half of the avocado; brush with half of the lemon juice. Chop the remaining avocado; toss with remaining lemon juice.

In a bowl, gently combine the lettuce, chopped avocado, chicken, pineapple, apple, pecans and mayonnaise. Serve on lettuce-lined plates; top with sliced avocado. **Yield:** 2-3 servings.

ORANGE-HONEY CASHEW CHICKEN

(Pictured above)

Raymonde Bourgeois, Swastika, Ontario

The sweet honey-citrus sauce turns ordinary poultry into something special. I like to serve it with rice or riced potatoes.

> 1-1/4 cups orange juice, *divided*
> 1 tablespoon lemon juice
> 1/4 teaspoon salt
> Dash pepper
> 2 boneless skinless chicken breast halves (about 5 ounces *each*)
> 1 to 2 teaspoons olive oil
> 1/3 cup chopped onion
> 1/4 cup honey
> 1 teaspoon minced fresh parsley
> Hot cooked rice
> 1 tablespoon cornstarch
> 2 tablespoons water
> 3 tablespoons chopped salted cashews

In a resealable plastic bag, combine 1/2 cup of orange juice, lemon juice, salt and pepper; add chicken. Seal bag and turn to coat; refrigerate for 4-8 hours or overnight.

Drain and discard marinade. In a skillet, cook chicken in oil for 2-3 minutes on each side or until browned. Remove and keep warm. In the drippings, saute onion until tender. Combine the honey, parsley and remaining orange juice; stir into skillet. Bring to a boil.

Return chicken to the pan. Reduce heat; cover and simmer for 8-10 minutes or until chicken juices run clear. Place chicken over rice. Combine

In a small heavy saucepan, melt chocolate chips with water over low heat; stir until smooth. Stir a small amount of hot chocolate mixture into egg yolk; return all to the pan, stirring constantly. Cook and stir for 2 minutes or until slightly thickened. Remove from the heat; stir in vanilla. Cool, stirring several times.

In a mixing bowl, beat whipping cream until it begins to thicken. Add sugar; beat until soft peaks form. Fold in cooled chocolate mixture. Cover and refrigerate for at least 2 hours. Garnish with whipped cream if desired. **Yield:** 2 servings.

BACON 'N' EGG GRAVY

(Pictured above)

Terry Bray, Winter Haven, Florida

My husband created this wonderful breakfast gravy. Sometimes we ladle the gravy over homemade biscuits. Served with fruit salad, it's a great breakfast.

      6 bacon strips, diced
      5 tablespoons all-purpose flour
  1-1/2 cups water
      1 can (12 ounces) evaporated milk
      3 hard-cooked eggs, sliced
  Salt and pepper to taste
      4 slices bread, toasted

In a skillet, cook bacon over medium heat until crisp; remove to paper towels. Stir flour into the drippings until blended; cook over medium heat until browned, stirring constantly.

Gradually add water and milk. Bring to a boil; cook and stir for 2 minutes or until thickened. Add bacon, eggs, salt and pepper. Serve over toast. **Yield:** 2 servings.

CHOCOLATE MOUSSE

Judy Spencer, San Diego, California

I love to cook and have tons of recipes, but this one is a favorite. Best of all, it's easy to make.

  1/4 cup semisweet chocolate chips
      1 tablespoon water
      1 egg yolk, lightly beaten
  1-1/2 teaspoons vanilla extract
  1/2 cup heavy whipping cream
      1 tablespoon sugar
  Whipped cream, optional

MINI GREEN BEAN CASSEROLE

(Pictured below)

Mrs. Bert Benson, Park Rapids, Minnesota

This green bean casserole is appealing because it's lighter than those with a cream sauce. The french-fried onions add a delicious crunch.

      2 cups frozen cut green beans
      1 can (4 ounces) mushroom stems and
        pieces, drained
      1 tablespoon cornstarch
  1/2 teaspoon ground mustard
  3/4 cup chicken broth
      1 tablespoon butter
  3/4 cup french-fried onions

In a greased 1-qt. baking dish, combine the beans and mushrooms. In a small bowl, combine cornstarch and mustard; gradually stir in broth until smooth.

Pour over the vegetables. Dot with the butter. Bake, uncovered, at 375° for 25-30 minutes. Sprinkle with onions. Bake 5 minutes longer. **Yield:** 2 servings.

PORK BARBECUE SANDWICHES

George Hascher, Phoenicia, New York

We were happy when there was pork roast on the menu at home because we were sure that within the next few days we'd be feasting on leftover pork in these tasty sandwiches.

- 2 celery ribs, finely chopped
- 1 medium onion, finely chopped
- 1 teaspoon vegetable oil
- 1 cup ketchup
- 1 to 1-1/2 teaspoons salt
- 1 teaspoon ground mustard
- 2 cups shredded cooked pork
- 2 to 3 kaiser rolls *or* hamburger buns, split

In a saucepan, saute the celery and onion in oil until tender. Stir in the ketchup, salt and mustard. Add the pork.

Bring to a boil. Reduce the heat. Cover and simmer for 20-30 minutes. Serve pork on rolls. **Yield:** 2-3 servings.

OLD-FASHIONED COLESLAW

Joyce LeMonds, Castle Rock, Washington

My sister-in-law gave me this recipe over 50 years ago, and it's still a hit at potluck and other special dinners. I made it for company once, and they came by the next day with a large head of cabbage, hoping to exchange it for the recipe.

- 2 cups shredded cabbage
- 2 tablespoons finely chopped green pepper
- 2 tablespoons finely chopped sweet red pepper
- 2 tablespoons finely chopped onion
- 1/4 cup mayonnaise
- 1 tablespoon sugar
- 1 tablespoon white wine vinegar
- 1 tablespoon evaporated milk
- 1/4 teaspoon salt
- 1/8 teaspoon dill weed
- 1/8 teaspoon paprika

Dash pepper

In a bowl, combine the cabbage, peppers and onion. In a small bowl, combine the mayonnaise, sugar, vinegar, milk, salt, dill, paprika and pepper.

Add to the cabbage mixture and toss to coat. Cover and refrigerate for at least 1 hour before serving. **Yield:** 2 servings.

DEVILED EGGS

Margaret Sanders, Indianapolis, Indiana

This recipe comes from the Durbin Inn, a well-known restaurant in Rushville, Indiana from the 1920s until it closed in the late '70s. The eggs are delicious, and it's easy to make more for larger gatherings.

- 3 hard-cooked eggs
- 1 tablespoon mayonnaise
- 1/2 teaspoon sugar
- 1/2 teaspoon white vinegar
- 1/2 teaspoon prepared mustard
- 1/4 teaspoon salt

Paprika

Slice eggs in half lengthwise; remove yolks and set whites aside. In a small bowl, mash the yolks with a fork.

Add the mayonnaise, sugar, vinegar, mustard and salt. Spoon into egg whites. Sprinkle with paprika. Refrigerate until serving. **Yield:** 2-3 servings.

HEDGEHOG COOKIES

Sandi Pichon, Slidell, Louisiana

These little treats are as cute as they can be and delicious, too. A lady from my garden club shared this recipe one Christmas, but they're good for any occasion. They're a hit with both kids and grown-ups.

- 1 cup finely chopped walnuts
- 1/2 cup finely chopped dates
- 1/2 cup packed brown sugar
- 1 cup flaked coconut, *divided*
- 1 egg, lightly beaten

In a bowl, combine the walnuts, dates and brown sugar. Add 1/2 cup coconut and the egg; mix well. Shape into 1-in. balls; roll in remaining coconut. Place on greased baking sheets.

Bake at 350° for 12-13 minutes or until lightly browned. Remove to wire racks to cool. **Yield:** about 1-1/2 dozen.

KEEPING CABBAGE CRISP

Cut cabbage heads paper-thin with a slicing knife or mechanical shredder. The resulting pieces have more form and the cabbage stays crunchier than if you grated it.

No-Bake Lasagna
(Pictured below)

Norma Montgomery, Groveland, California

You don't need to turn on the oven for this lasagna, so it's perfect for summer. The noodles and sauce are simply layered on a plate…even my husband can make it! This is a satisfying vegetarian entree.

　1/2　cup sliced fresh mushrooms
　1/4　cup chopped onion
　　1　teaspoon vegetable oil
　3/4　cup spaghetti sauce
　1/2　cup chopped fresh tomato
　1/4　teaspoon dried basil
　1/8　teaspoon pepper
　　4　lasagna noodles
　1/2　cup shredded mozzarella cheese
Shredded Parmesan cheese

In a skillet, saute the mushrooms and onion in oil until tender. Add spaghetti sauce, tomato, basil and pepper. Bring to a boil. Reduce heat; cover and simmer for 10 minutes, stirring occasionally. Meanwhile, cook lasagna noodles according to package directions.

　Add mozzarella cheese to the sauce; cook on low until cheese is melted. Drain noodles; cut into thirds. For each serving, on a plate, layer 2 tablespoons of sauce and two noodle pieces. Repeat layers twice. Top with 2 tablespoons sauce. Sprinkle with Parmesan cheese. **Yield:** 2 servings.

Pecan Cheddar Snacks
(Pictured above)

Nellie Webb, Athens, Tennessee

Once you take a bite of these crisp and chewy cheese balls, you'll surely want more. I make them for the holidays and other special occasions, and I keep some in the freezer so they're ready to serve anytime.

　1/2　cup all-purpose flour
　　1　tablespoon biscuit/baking mix
Pinch cayenne pepper
　1/4　cup butter, softened
　1/2　cup shredded cheddar cheese
　　1　egg, beaten
　　1　cup crisp rice cereal
　1/2　cup chopped pecans

In a bowl, combine the flour, biscuit mix and cayenne. Stir in butter until crumbly. Add cheese and egg; mix well. Stir in cereal and nuts. Shape into 1-1/2-in. balls; place on an ungreased baking sheet. Bake at 350° for 18-20 minutes or until lightly browned. Serve warm. **Yield:** 2-3 servings.

Warm Potato Salad
(Pictured at right)

Donna Mundt, Watertown, Wisconsin

Because it's so easy to make and includes basic ingredients I usually have on hand, this salad is one I prepare often to serve two.

1 cup cubed red potatoes
1 cup water
1 tablespoon finely chopped red onion
1-1/2 teaspoons chopped green onion
1 teaspoon white wine vinegar
1/2 teaspoon olive oil
1/8 teaspoon sugar
1/8 teaspoon salt
1/8 teaspoon pepper

Place potatoes and water in a small saucepan; bring to a boil. Reduce heat; cover and simmer for 10 minutes or until tender. Drain. Add red and green onion. In a small bowl, combine the remaining ingredients; mix well. Pour over potatoes and toss gently to coat. **Yield:** 2 servings.

CHOCOLATE CHIP PUDDING PARFAITS

(Pictured at right)

Pauline Piper, Egg Harbor Township, New Jersey

This was one of our children's favorite desserts. It's simple to put together, and I like varying the ingredients in the parfait layers.

1 package (3 ounces) cook-and-serve
   vanilla pudding mix
1/2 cup semisweet chocolate chips
1/2 cup flaked coconut, toasted

Prepare pudding according to package directions. In two parfait glasses, layer 2 tablespoons chocolate chips, a fourth of the warm pudding and

2 tablespoons coconut. Repeat layers. Serve or refrigerate. **Yield:** 2 servings

EGGPLANT WITH MUSHROOM STUFFING

Joyce Towles, Houston, Texas

We had an abundance of eggplant in our garden one year, so I was happy to find this recipe, especially since it was such a hit with my family. It's not hard to make, and the best part is it's perfect for two people.

1 small eggplant
Salt
1 small onion, chopped
1/4 cup butter
3/4 cup soft bread crumbs
1/2 cup chopped fresh mushrooms
1 tablespoon minced fresh parsley
Dash pepper
1/2 cup shredded Swiss cheese

Cut eggplant in half lengthwise; scoop out pulp, leaving a 1/4-in.-thick shell. Set shell aside. Chop pulp; place in a colander over a plate. Sprinkle with salt; let stand for 30 minutes. Blot moisture with a paper towel.

In a skillet, saute eggplant pulp and onion in butter until tender. Add the bread crumbs, mushrooms, parsley and pepper. Spoon into eggplant shells. Place in a greased 8-in. square baking dish. Bake, uncovered, at 350° for 15 minutes. Sprinkle with cheese; bake 5 minutes longer or until cheese is melted. **Yield:** 2 servings.

CRISPY SALMON STEAKS

Maxine Pheasant, Mt. Airy, Maryland

My husband and I had always enjoyed fish, but I could never make it quite right until I found this recipe.

        1/4 cup butter, melted
        1/2 teaspoon salt
    Pinch paprika
        1/2 cup crushed saltines
        1/2 cup crushed potato chips
          2 salmon steaks (1 inch thick)

In a shallow bowl, combine butter, salt and paprika. In another bowl, combine saltines and chips. Dip both sides of salmon steaks in butter mixture, then coat with crumbs. Broil 4-6 in. from the heat for 5-6 minutes on each side or until fish flakes easily with a fork. **Yield:** 2 servings.

CUBED PARMESEAN POTATOES

Sarah Reinsch, Geneva, Nebraska

I often cook according to what I have on hand. This dish is compatible with a variety of entrees.

          2 tablespoons butter, melted
          1 teaspoon lemon juice
          2 medium baking potatoes, peeled and
             cubed
        1/4 cup grated Parmesan cheese
        1/2 teaspoon seasoned salt
        1/4 teaspoon pepper
    Dried parsley flakes

In a 1-qt. microwave-safe dish, combine butter and lemon juice. Add potatoes; toss to coat. Sprinkle with Parmesan cheese, seasoned salt and pepper; toss to coat. Cover and microwave on high for 5-6 minutes or until tender, turning once. Let stand for 5 minutes. Sprinkle with parsley. **Yield:** 2 servings.

Editor's Note: This recipe was tested in an 850-watt microwave.

ASPARAGUS SALAD

Peggy Davies, Canon City, Colorodo

This attractive salad appears on our table often. Pickle juice gives the dressing a distinctive flavor.

        1/2 pound fresh asparagus, (1-inch pieces)
        1/4 cup water
          2 tablespoons chopped sweet pickle
          2 tablespoons olive oil
          1 tablespoon lemon juice

          1 tablespoon pickle juice
          1 teaspoon minced chives
    Salt and pepper to taste
    Lettuce leaves
          1 medium tomato, sliced
          1 hard-cooked egg, sliced

Place the asparagus and water in a microwave-safe dish. Cover and microwave on high for 2-3 minutes or until crisp-tender. Drain and rinse in cold water. Place in a bowl. Combine the next seven ingredients; pour over asparagus and toss to coat. Cover and refrigerate for 1 hour.

Use a slotted spoon to serve the asparagus on lettuce-lined plates. Top with tomato and egg slices; drizzle with dressing. **Yield:** 2 servings.

LIME COCONUT BARS

Mary Jane Jones, Williamstown, West Virginia

I found this dessert in my mother's recipe collection. I also garnish them with whipped cream and lime.

        3/4 cup finely crushed crisp sugar cookies
          3 tablespoons cold butter
      2-1/4 cups flaked coconut
    FILLING:
        1/4 cup butter
        3/4 cup sugar
        1/2 cup lime juice
      4-1/2 teaspoons yellow cornmeal
    Pinch salt
          4 egg yolks
          1 teaspoon grated lime peel
    Confectioners' sugar

Place the crushed cookies in a bowl. Cut in butter until mixture resembles coarse crumbs. Stir in coconut; set aside 1 cup for topping. Press remaining mixture into a greased 8-in. baking dish. Bake at 350° for 13-15 minutes or until golden.

Combine butter, sugar, lime juice, cornmeal and salt in a heavy saucepan. Cook and stir over low heat until sugar is dissolved and cornmeal is softened, about 10 minutes. Remove from heat.

In a small bowl, lightly beat the egg yolks. Stir a small amount of hot lime mixture into the yolks; return all to the pan, stirring constantly. Cook and stir until a thermometer reads 160° and mixture coats the back of a metal spoon, about 20 minutes. Remove from the heat; stir in lime peel.

Pour over the crust; sprinkle with reserved coconut mixture. Bake at 350° for 18-20 minutes or until golden. Cool completely on a wire rack. Dust with confectioners' sugar. **Yield:** 16 bars.

Editor's Note: The cornmeal is used as a thickener in the filling.

Hearty Hamburger Soup

(Pictured below)

Diane Mrozinski, Essexville, Michigan

When I served this soup to my family the first time, I got a thumbs-up from everyone. You can substitute ground turkey for the beef, if you like, and easily double or triple the recipe to serve more people.

- 1/4 pound ground beef
- 1/4 cup chopped onion
- 1-1/2 cups water
- 1/4 cup thinly sliced carrot
- 1-1/2 teaspoons beef bouillon granules
- 1 can (5-1/2 ounces) V8 juice
- 1/4 cup frozen corn
- 1/4 cup frozen peas
- 1/4 cup sliced fresh mushrooms
- 1/4 cup sliced zucchini
- 1/8 teaspoon dried basil
- Dash pepper
- 1/2 cup cooked elbow macaroni

In a small saucepan, cook beef and onion over medium heat until meat is no longer pink; drain. Add the water, carrot and bouillon. Bring to a boil. Reduce the heat; simmer, uncovered, for 5 minutes.

Add the V8 juice, corn, peas, mushrooms, zucchini, basil and pepper. Simmer 6-8 minutes longer or until vegetables are tender. Add macaroni; heat through. **Yield:** 2 servings.

Skillet Pizzas

(Pictured above)

Cara Cobb, Abbeville, Georgia

Faced with a nearly empty fridge, I combined the ingredients I had on hand and created a quick pizza, using a tortilla for the crust. It tastes great served with a green salad and a glass of iced tea.

- 1/3 cup thinly sliced onion
- 1/3 cup julienned green pepper
- 2 teaspoons olive oil, *divided*
- 1 cup sliced fresh mushrooms
- 2 flour tortillas (6 inches)
- 28 slices pepperoni
- 1 cup chopped tomatoes
- 3/4 cup shredded Mexican cheese blend
- Crushed red pepper flakes, optional

In a skillet, saute onion and green pepper in 1 teaspoon oil until almost tender. Add mushrooms; cook 2-3 minutes longer. Remove and keep warm.

In the same skillet, lightly brown one tortilla in 1/2 teaspoon oil. Turn over; top with half of the pepperoni, tomatoes, onion mixture and cheese. Cover and cook until cheese is melted, about 2 minutes. Sprinkle with pepper flakes if desired. Repeat for second pizza. **Yield:** 2 servings.

Tangy Franks and Pears

Josephine Laughlin, Norwich, New York

This entree is one of my comfort foods. The combination of sweet fruit flavors and a touch of spicy meat is surprisingly compatible.

1 large potato, peeled, quartered and
   thinly sliced
1/2 cup chopped onion
1/2 cup chopped celery
1/4 cup butter
  4 hot dogs, cut into 1-inch pieces
  2 medium ripe pears, peeled and diced
1/2 cup golden raisins
1/2 cup apple juice
  2 tablespoons brown sugar
  1 tablespoon lemon juice
  1 teaspoon caraway seeds
1/4 teaspoon salt
1/4 teaspoon ground mustard

In a skillet, saute the potato, onion and celery in
butter until celery is tender. Add the remaining
ingredients; bring to a boil. Reduce heat; cover
and simmer for 20-25 minutes or until potatoes
are tender. **Yield:** 2 servings.

RHUBARB PUFF

(Pictured below)

Shirley Kasbee, Hadley, Pennsylvania

*I came up with this recipe one day when I had cooked
rhubarb left over and needed a dessert.*

1-1/2 cups chopped fresh *or* frozen rhubarb
  1/4 cup plus 1 teaspoon sugar, *divided*
    4 tablespoons water, *divided*
    2 teaspoons cornstarch
    1 egg yolk
    3 tablespoons sour cream
    2 egg whites

In a small saucepan, combine the rhubarb, 1/4 cup
sugar and 3 tablespoons water. Cook over medium heat for 10-12 minutes or until rhubarb is
crisp-tender, stirring occasionally. Combine corn-

starch and remaining water until smooth; stir into rhubarb mixture. Bring to a boil; cook and stir
for 1 minute or until thickened. Remove from the
heat; set aside.

In a bowl, combine egg yolk and sour cream until smooth. In a small mixing bowl, beat egg whites
until foamy. Add the remaining sugar; beat until
stiff peaks form. Fold into the egg yolk mixture.
Pour half into a greased 6-in. ovenproof skillet.

Spoon rhubarb mixture on top; spread with the
remaining egg mixture, sealing edges to sides of
skillet. Bake at 350° for 18-20 minutes or until
golden brown. **Yield:** 2 servings.

SESAME SIRLOIN STEAK

(Pictured above)

Paulette Barnett, Guelph, Ontario

*The first time I tried this recipe was at my in-laws for
Mother's Day. We've made a few adjustments to the
original recipe, only improving on the great taste.*

1/4 cup soy sauce
  2 tablespoons sesame seeds, toasted
  2 garlic cloves, minced
  2 tablespoons olive oil
  2 tablespoons brown sugar
1/4 teaspoon pepper
Dash to 1/8 teaspoon hot pepper sauce
3/4 pound boneless beef sirloin steak
   (about 3/4 inch thick)

In a large resealable plastic bag, combine the soy
sauce, sesame seeds, garlic, oil, brown sugar, pepper and hot pepper sauce. Pierce steak on both
sides with a fork; place in the bag. Seal and turn
to coat; refrigerate for 8 hours or overnight.

Drain and discard marinade. Grill the steak,
covered, over medium heat for 7-9 minutes on
each side or until meat reaches desired doneness
(for rare, a meat thermometer should read 140°;
medium, 160°; well-done, 170°). **Yield:** 2 servings.

TUNA NOODLE CASSEROLE

Lorraine Rafuse, New Ross, Nova Scotia

My mom made this tuna casserole through the years…a delicious family dish, but good for any occasion. I often serve it for a luncheon along with garlic bread and a salad. It's quick and easy to prepare, freezes well and makes a complete meal.

- 1 medium onion, chopped
- 2 teaspoons butter
- 1 tablespoon all-purpose flour
- 1/2 teaspoon salt
- 1/4 teaspoon pepper
- 1 cup milk
- 2 cups cooked wide egg noodles
- 1 can (6 ounces) tuna, drained and flaked
- 2/3 cup frozen peas, thawed
- 1/4 cup crushed cornflakes

In a saucepan, saute onion in butter until tender. Stir in the flour, salt and pepper until blended. Gradually add milk. Bring to a boil; cook and stir for 2 minutes or until thickened. Stir in the noodles, tuna and peas.

Transfer to a greased 1-qt. baking dish. Sprinkle with cornflakes. Bake, uncovered, at 350° for 30-35 minutes or until bubbly around the edges. **Yield:** 2 servings.

RICE SALAD IN TOMATO CUPS

Esther Pittello, Chicopee, Massachusetts

I created this recipe for a contest a long time ago. With an abundance of tomatoes in our garden each year, I had to come up with something new. I serve this as a side dish or lively lunch.

- 1 cup cooked rice
- 1 hard-cooked egg, chopped
- 3 to 4 tablespoons mayonnaise
- 1 tablespoon chopped celery
- 1 tablespoon chopped onion
- 1/4 teaspoon dried basil
- 1/4 teaspoon dried parsley flakes
- 1/8 teaspoon dried oregano
Dash pepper
- 2 medium tomatoes

In a bowl, combine the rice, egg, mayonnaise, celery, onion, basil, parsley, oregano and pepper; mix well.

Cut a thin slice off the top of each tomato. Scoop out and discard pulp, leaving a 1/2-in. shell. Cut a thin slice off bottom of tomatoes to level if necessary. Fill with rice salad. Cover and refrigerate for 1 hour or until serving. **Yield:** 2 servings.

PINEAPPLE BANANA BREAD

Grace Gibbons, Melbourne, Florida

This versatile bread can be enjoyed as a breakfast treat or simple dessert. My mother gave me the recipe. It was one of her church potluck favorites. It freezes well, too.

- 1 cup all-purpose flour
- 1/2 teaspoon baking soda
- 1/2 teaspoon salt
- 1/4 teaspoon ground cinnamon
- 1/8 teaspoon baking powder
- 1 egg
- 1/3 cup vegetable oil
- 2/3 cup sugar
- 2/3 cup mashed banana (about 1 medium)
- 1/2 teaspoon vanilla extract
- 1 can (8 ounces) crushed pineapple, drained
- 1/4 cup chopped walnuts

In a bowl, combine the flour, baking soda, salt, cinnamon and baking powder. Combine the egg, oil, sugar, banana and vanilla; mix well.

Add the banana mixture to the dry ingredients; stir just until moistened. Fold in pineapple and walnuts.

Pour into two greased and floured 5-3/4-in. x 3-in. x 2-in. loaf pans. Bake at 350° for 40-45 minutes or until a toothpick comes out clean. Cool for 5 minutes before removing from pans to wire racks. **Yield:** 2 mini loaves.

CHOCOLATE CHOW MEIN CLUSTERS

Tracey Anthonijsz, Midpines, California

Chocolate and peanuts are two of my favorite treats, and the combination in this recipe, along with butterscotch, gives this candy a special flavor. My mother made these for Christmas every year, but they're so easy to fix, you can enjoy them anytime.

- 1/2 cup semisweet chocolate chips
- 1/2 cup butterscotch chips
- 1/2 cup chow mein noodles
- 1/2 cup salted peanuts

In a microwave or heavy saucepan, melt the chocolate and butterscotch chips; stir until smooth. Stir in chow mein noodles and peanuts until well coated.

Drop by rounded tablespoonfuls onto a waxed paper-lined baking sheet. Refrigerate for 2 hours or until set. **Yield:** 8 clusters.

CRAB ALFREDO
(Pictured below)

Esther Pittello, Chicopee, Massachusetts

I improvised this recipe when I was looking for quick Lenten dishes, but it has become a favorite for my husband and me all year long.

> 1/4 cup chopped onion
> 1 tablespoon butter
> 1 cup sliced fresh mushrooms
> 1 cup prepared Alfredo sauce
> 2 tablespoons chicken broth
> 1 package (8 ounces) imitation crabmeat, flaked
> 2 cups hot cooked fettuccine *or* pasta of your choice

In a skillet, saute onion in butter until tender. Add mushrooms; cook and stir for 3 minutes or until tender. Stir in the sauce and broth until blended. Add the crab. Reduce heat; cook for 10 minutes or until heated through, stirring occasionally. Serve over pasta. **Yield:** 2 servings.

ORANGE CHICKEN STIR-FRY
(Pictured above right)

Bunny Bronson, Lake Placid, Florida

My husband loves this stir-fry, so we have it often. I'm delighted as we have six orange trees in our backyard.

> 2 boneless skinless chicken breast halves, cubed

> 2 green onions with tops, sliced
> 2 tablespoons vegetable oil
> 1/2 teaspoon cornstarch
> 1/2 cup orange juice
> 2 tablespoons soy sauce
> 1/4 teaspoon ground ginger
> Hot cooked rice
> 1 medium navel orange, peeled and sectioned
> 1/4 cup chopped walnuts
> 2 tablespoons minced fresh parsley

In a skillet or wok, cook the chicken and onions in oil until chicken juices run clear. In a small bowl, combine the cornstarch, orange juice, soy sauce and ginger until smooth. Pour over chicken mixture.

Bring to a boil; cook and stir for 1 minute or until thickened. Serve over rice. Top with the orange segments, walnuts and parsley. **Yield:** 2-3 servings.

ASPARAGUS SOUFFLE

Patricia Patton, Jal, New Mexico

I'm not sure where I found this recipe, but being an asparagus lover, I knew I'd like it. I've tried it out on several guests, and all have enjoyed it.

> 1 package (8 ounces) frozen cut asparagus, thawed and well drained
> 1/3 cup finely shredded cheddar cheese
> 1/3 cup mayonnaise

1/4 cup chopped onion
1 egg white

In a bowl, combine the asparagus, cheese, mayonnaise and onion. In a small mixing bowl, beat egg white on medium speed until soft peaks form. Fold into asparagus mixture. Transfer to a greased 2-1/2-cup baking dish.

Bake, uncovered, at 350° for 20-25 minutes or until lightly browned. **Yield:** 2 servings.

PEACHY ORANGE SHAKES

(Pictured below)

Helen Phillips, Horseheads, New York

I found this recipe in an old cookbook I bought at a garage sale. When I first read it, the memories of younger days and my first job in a soda fountain came back. I also liked the ingredients, and when I tried the shake, I decided it was a keeper.

1 can (8 ounces) sliced peaches
1 cup orange juice
2 cups vanilla ice cream, softened
1 tablespoon peach yogurt
1 tablespoon milk

Drain peaches, reserving syrup; save half of the peaches and syrup for another use. In a blender, combine orange juice, ice cream, yogurt, milk, half of the peaches and 1 tablespoon syrup (add any remaining syrup to the reserved peaches). Cover and process until smooth. Serve immediately in chilled glasses. **Yield:** 2-3 servings.

SWEET POTATO LOAVES

(Pictured above)

Joyce Randolph, Canton, Maine

My husband and I are missionaries in Brazil, where sweet potatoes are a staple food. I make this recipe often to share with the local people.

1/4 cup butter, softened
1/2 cup sugar
1 egg
1 cup all-purpose flour
1-1/2 teaspoons baking powder
1/2 teaspoon ground cinnamon
1/4 teaspoon ground ginger
1/4 teaspoon salt
1/2 cup cold mashed sweet potatoes
2 tablespoons milk
1/4 cup raisins

In a small mixing bowl, cream butter and sugar. Add egg; mix well. Combine the flour, baking powder, cinnamon, ginger and salt; add to creamed mixture just until blended (batter will be thick). Combine sweet potatoes and milk; stir into batter until blended. Fold in raisins.

Transfer to two greased 5-3/4-in. x 3-in. x 2-in. loaf pans. Bake at 350° for 35-40 minutes or until lightly browned and a toothpick inserted near the center comes out clean. Cool for 10 minutes before removing from pans to wire racks. **Yield:** 2 mini loaves.

Editor's Note: An 8-in. round baking pan may be used instead of the loaf pans. Bake for 20-25 minutes.

SHRIMP FETTUCCINE

Viola Walmer, Tequesta, Florida

This delicious recipe makes the perfect amount for two. It's become one of my husband's favorites—it's lighter but still very flavorful and satisfying.

- 1/2 cup ricotta cheese
- 1 tablespoon minced fresh parsley
- 1 teaspoon minced fresh basil
- 1 teaspoon minced chives
- 1 medium carrot
- 2 ounces uncooked fettuccine
- 1/2 cup fresh *or* frozen snow peas
- 1/2 cup sliced fresh mushrooms
- 1/2 pound uncooked medium shrimp, peeled and deveined
- 2 teaspoons butter
- 1 teaspoon cornstarch
- 1/4 cup orange juice
- 1 medium tomato, seeded and diced

Salt and pepper to taste

In a blender, combine the ricotta cheese, parsley, basil and chives; cover and process until smooth. Set aside.

Using a vegetable peeler, make long thin strips from the carrot. Cook the fettuccine according to package directions, adding the carrot strips during the last minute of cooking.

In a skillet, saute snow peas, mushrooms and shrimp in butter for 4-5 minutes or until shrimp turn pink. Combine the cornstarch and orange juice until smooth; stir into skillet. Bring to a boil; cook and stir for 2 minutes or until thickened. Add the tomato; cook 2 minutes longer or until heated through.

Drain fettuccine; toss with ricotta mixture. Add shrimp mixture and gently toss. Season with salt and pepper. **Yield:** 2 servings.

MINI SKILLET CORN BREAD

Ellen Pyle, Apple Springs, Texas

My husband says this recipe is close enough to the corn bread his mother used to make, so I consider it a winner. His criteria were to "put butter on the corn bread without it crumbling to pieces" and "to be able to break it up into a glass of milk without it turning to mush."

- 1 tablespoon butter
- 3/4 cup plus 2 tablespoons corn bread/muffin mix
- 1/4 cup cornmeal
- 1 egg
- 1/4 cup milk
- 1/2 teaspoon cider vinegar

Place butter in a 6-in. ovenproof skillet or baking dish. Melt in a 425° oven; tilt to coat bottom and sides. In a bowl, combine the corn bread mix and cornmeal.

In another bowl, beat the egg, milk and vinegar. Add to cornmeal mixture; stir until moistened. Pour into prepared skillet.

Bake, uncovered, for 12-15 minutes or until a toothpick inserted in the center comes out clean. **Yield:** 2 servings.

Editor's Note: This recipe was tested with half of an 8-1/2-ounce package of Jiffy corn bread/muffin mix.

BLUE CHEESE SALAD DRESSING

Margaret Krueger, New Berlin, Wisconsin

This tangy salad dressing can be ready to serve in 15 minutes or less. We like the blend of flavors.

- 1/2 cup plain yogurt
- 1/2 cup sour cream
- 1 tablespoon lemon juice
- 1 garlic clove, minced
- 1/8 teaspoon pepper
- 1/2 cup (2 ounces) crumbled blue cheese

In a small bowl, combine the yogurt, sour cream, lemon juice, garlic and pepper; whisk until smooth.

Stir in the blue cheese. Serve over salad greens. Store in the refrigerator. **Yield:** 1-1/3 cups.

BANANA SPLIT DESSERT

Stella Paukovich, Apollo, Pennsylvania

This refreshing dessert creates such a pretty picture, it's sure to be met with compliments. It has all the flavors of a banana split but fewer calories with whipped topping in place of ice cream. I really enjoy this little treat.

- 1 cup miniature marshmallows
- 1 can (8 ounces) crushed pineapple, drained
- 1 cup whipped topping
- 2 small firm bananas, split lengthwise

Chocolate syrup

- 2 maraschino cherries

In a bowl, combine the marshmallows, pineapple and whipped topping. Place banana halves in dessert dishes with two scoops of marshmallow mixture between.

Drizzle with chocolate syrup; top with a cherry. Serve immediately. **Yield:** 2 servings.

til no longer pink. Drain on paper towels.

Meanwhile, in a saucepan, saute the mushrooms, celery, onion and green pepper in butter. Add the tomato sauce, brown sugar, broth, lemon juice and garlic powder. Bring to a boil. Reduce heat; add the meatballs. Cover and simmer for 15 minutes or until heated through. Serve over noodles. **Yield:** 2 servings.

CITRUS FRUIT CUP

Mary Ann Marino, West Pittsburg, Pennsylvania

Try this tart and tasty salad for a refreshing midwinter lift. I love to prepare pretty dishes, and this salad is fancy, fast and almost sweet enough to be a dessert.

- 2 tablespoons sugar
- 2 tablespoons water
- 1 teaspoon grated lime peel
- 1 tablespoon olive oil
- 1 medium pink grapefruit, peeled and sectioned
- 1 medium navel orange, peeled and sectioned

In a saucepan, heat sugar and water over low heat until sugar is dissolved. Stir in the lime peel. Gradually whisk in oil. Bring to a boil. Reduce heat; simmer, uncovered, for 5 minutes. In a bowl, combine the grapefruit and orange sections. Pour the dressing over fruit; cover and refrigerate until chilled. **Yield:** 2 servings.

MEATBALLS WITH VEGETABLE SAUCE

(Pictured above)

Dorothy Stegall, Appleton, Wisconsin

This is such an easy way to do meatballs without all the mess of frying and turning each one. Best of all, they can be made ahead and frozen, then added to the tangy, vegetable-rich sauce and served over noodles or rice.

- 1 egg yolk, lightly beaten
- 1 tablespoon milk
- 3 tablespoons soft bread crumbs
- 2 tablespoons finely chopped onion
- 1/4 teaspoon salt
- 1/2 pound ground beef

SAUCE:
- 1/4 cup sliced fresh mushrooms
- 1/4 cup chopped celery
- 3 tablespoons chopped onion
- 3 tablespoons chopped green pepper
- 1 teaspoon butter
- 1/2 cup tomato sauce
- 2 tablespoons brown sugar
- 2 tablespoons beef broth
- 4 teaspoons lemon juice
- 1/8 teaspoon garlic powder

Hot cooked noodles

In a bowl, combine the first five ingredients. Crumble beef over mixture and mix well. Shape into 1-in. balls. Place 1 in. apart on a greased baking pan. Bake, uncovered, at 425° for 10-12 minutes or un-

SQUASH PASTA BAKE

Marguerite Shaeffer, Sewell, New Jersey

I was cooking summer squash for dinner when my grandchildren informed me they'd just had it the night before. To disguise the vegetables, I added pasta, spaghetti sauce and cheese, and the kids loved it! I often make it for lunch these days.

- 1/2 cup chopped yellow summer squash
- 1/2 cup chopped zucchini
- 1 teaspoon olive oil
- 1 cup cooked small pasta shells *or* small tube pasta
- 1 cup spaghetti sauce
- 3 tablespoons shredded mozzarella cheese

In a skillet, saute squash in oil for 2-3 minutes or until tender. Stir in pasta and spaghetti sauce; heat through. Transfer to a greased 3-cup baking dish. Sprinkle with cheese. Bake, uncovered, at 350° for 5-10 minutes or until heated through and cheese is melted. **Yield:** 2 servings.

PEPPERONI CAESAR SALAD

(Pictured below)

Nancy Stock, Minonk, Illinois

Here's a hearty salad that's just big enough for two. It makes a wonderful fast meal coupled with warm soup and a loaf of crusty bread.

> 3 cups torn lettuce
> 1/2 cup sliced pepperoni
> 1 small tomato, seeded and chopped
> 1/2 cup cubed avocado
> 2 hard-cooked eggs, sliced
> 3/4 cup salad croutons
> 1/4 cup Caesar salad dressing
> Shredded Parmesan cheese

On two salad plates, arrange the lettuce, pepperoni, tomato, avocado, eggs and croutons. Drizzle with salad dressing; sprinkle with the Parmesan cheese. **Yield:** 2 servings.

PEAR-FECT PORK SUPPER

(Pictured above right)

Lori Jameson, Chattaroy, Washington

This hearty dish nicely pairs sweet and savory flavors. It's different, colorful, and I can make the entire meal in the time it takes to cook the rice.

> 1 cup water
> 2 tablespoons raisins

> 3/4 teaspoon salt, *divided*
> 1/2 cup uncooked long grain rice
> 2 bone-in pork rib chops (3/4 inch thick)
> 1/8 teaspoon pepper
> 1-1/2 teaspoons vegetable oil
> 1 can (8-1/2 ounces) sliced pears
> 1 tablespoon cornstarch
> 1 tablespoon soy sauce
> 1/4 to 1/2 teaspoon dried thyme
> 1 medium sweet red pepper, cut into 3/4-inch pieces
> 1 small onion, cut into 3/4-inch pieces
> 1 garlic clove, minced

In a small saucepan, bring the water, raisins and 1/4 teaspoon salt to a boil. Stir in rice. Reduce heat; cover and simmer for 18-20 minutes or until rice is tender. Meanwhile, sprinkle pork chops with pepper and remaining salt. In a skillet, brown chops on both sides in oil over medium-high heat. Remove and keep warm.

Drain pears, reserving juice; set pears aside. Add enough water to juice to measure 1 cup. Combine cornstarch, pear juice, soy sauce and thyme until blended; set aside. In the drippings in the skillet, saute red pepper, onion and garlic for 2-3 minutes or until crisp-tender. Stir in pear juice mixture. Bring to a boil; cook and stir for 1-2 minutes or until thickened.

Return chops to skillet. Cook for 4 minutes. Add pears; cook 2 minutes longer or until pork is tender and pears are heated through. Serve with rice. **Yield:** 2 servings.

PORK MEATBALLS

Joan Newberry, Indiana, Pennsylvania

This recipe is one of my favorites. My mom used to make the moist, flavorful meatballs often.

    1 egg, lightly beaten
    1 slice bread, crumbled
    1 garlic clove, minced
1/4 cup grated Romano *or* Parmesan cheese
1/2 teaspoon salt
1/2 teaspoon dried parsley flakes
1/4 teaspoon pepper
3/4 pound ground pork
    1 can (14-1/2 ounces) beef broth

In a bowl, combine the first seven ingredients. Crumble meat over mixture and mix well. Shape into ten 2-in. balls.

In a saucepan, bring broth to a boil. Place meatballs in the broth. Reduce heat; cover and simmer for 15 minutes. Turn the meatballs; cook 15 minutes longer or until meat is no longer pink. Remove with a slotted spoon. **Yield:** 2 servings.

HOT GERMAN NOODLE SALAD

Roxie Wilcox, Bellville, Texas

Onion, herbs and bacon in a sweet-and-sour sauce make these noodles delicious and distinctive.

    1 cup uncooked wide egg noodles
    2 bacon strips, diced
1/2 cup chopped celery
    2 tablespoons chopped onion
    2 teaspoons all-purpose flour
1/2 teaspoon sugar
1/4 teaspoon salt
1/8 teaspoon ground mustard
1/3 cup water
    1 tablespoon cider vinegar
    1 tablespoon minced fresh parsley

Cook noodles according to package directions. Meanwhile, in a skillet, cook the bacon over medium heat until crisp. Remove with a slotted spoon.

In the drippings, saute celery and onion until tender. Stir in the flour, sugar, salt and mustard. Gradually stir in water. Bring to a boil; cook and stir for 1 minute or until thickened. Reduce the heat.

Drain noodles. Add the noodles, bacon, vinegar and parsley to the celery mixture. Cook for 2 minutes longer or until heated through. **Yield:** 2 servings.

CHEDDAR ZUCCHINI SLICES

Mrs. Bobby Tucker, Bethalto, Illinois

The microwave makes this side dish simple to prepare, and it's easy to adjust the quantity to serve more people.

    2 small zucchini, halved lengthwise and
        sliced (2 cups)
    1 tablespoon water
1/4 teaspoon salt
Dash pepper
1/3 cup shredded cheddar cheese
1/3 cup sour cream

Place zucchini and water in a microwave-safe dish. Microwave, uncovered, on high for 3-4 minutes or until crisp-tender. Add the salt, pepper and cheese. Cook 1-2 minutes longer or until cheese is melted. Dollop with sour cream. **Yield:** 2 servings.

Editor's Note: This recipe was tested in an 850-watt microwave.

RICH CHEESECAKE BARS

Tammy Helle, St. Louis, Missouri

When I provide snacks for adult Bible class and Sunday school, these gooey bars are a favorite.

    1 package (9 ounces) yellow cake
        mix
    3 tablespoons butter, softened
    2 eggs
    1 package (3 ounces) cream cheese,
        softened
    2 cups confectioners' sugar

In a mixing bowl, combine the dry cake mix, butter and 1 egg; mix well. Spread into a greased 9-in. square baking pan. In a small mixing bowl, combine the cream cheese, confectioners' sugar and remaining egg; spread evenly over batter.

Bake at 350° for 30-35 minutes or until a toothpick comes out clean. Cool on a wire rack. Store in the refrigerator. **Yield:** 2 dozen.

GRATE FOR CHEESE

For easier cleanup, spray your grater with nonstick cooking spray before grating cheese.

tender. Remove meat and vegetables to a serving platter and keep warm. Pour drippings and loosened browned bits into a measuring cup. Skim fat and discard bay leaf.

In a saucepan, combine cornstarch and the remaining water until smooth. Gradually stir in the drippings. Bring to a boil; cook and stir for 2 minutes or until thickened. Serve with meat and vegetables. **Yield:** 2 servings.

DEVILED CHICKEN THIGHS
(Pictured below)

Bernice Morris, Marshfield, Missouri

When I make this dish, I invite my next-door neighbor over for supper. It's just enough for the two of us. This tasty chicken is tender and moist, with a bit of crunch from the cashews.

>   1 teaspoon butter, softened
>   1 teaspoon cider vinegar
>   1 teaspoon prepared mustard
>   1 teaspoon paprika
> Dash pepper
>   2 boneless skinless chicken thighs
>   (about 4 ounces *each*)
>   3 tablespoons soft bread crumbs
>   2 tablespoons chopped cashews

In bowl, combine the butter, vinegar, mustard, paprika and pepper. Spread over chicken thighs. Place in a greased 11-in. x 7-in. x 2-in. baking dish. Sprinkle with bread crumbs.

Bake, uncovered, at 400° for 15 minutes. Sprinkle with the cashews. Bake 7-12 minutes longer or until chicken juices run clear and topping is golden brown. **Yield:** 2 servings.

VEAL SHANK FRICASSEE
(Pictured above)

Jean Wright, Clarkston, Washington

This recipe is from a cookbook my mother gave me in 1944, when I was 14. Inside the front cover, she wrote, "When and if Jean ever gets married." Well, this recipe, along with many others from the same book, has pleased my family for over 55 years.

>   2 tablespoons all-purpose flour
>   2 teaspoons salt
>   1/2 teaspoon dried thyme
>   1/2 teaspoon dried parsley flakes
>   1/8 teaspoon pepper
>   1/8 teaspoon cayenne pepper
>   2 veal shanks (about 1 pound)
>   1 tablespoon vegetable oil
>   1-1/2 cups water, *divided*
>   1 medium onion, chopped
>   1 celery rib, chopped
>   1 bay leaf
>   4 medium carrots, cut into 1-inch slices
>   2 medium potatoes, peeled and cut
>   into 1-inch cubes
>   2 tablespoons cornstarch

In a shallow dish, combine the first six ingredients. Add veal shanks; turn to coat. In a Dutch oven or large skillet, brown veal in oil over medium heat. Pour 1-1/4 cups water into pan; add onion, celery and bay leaf. Bring to a boil over medium heat. Reduce heat; cover and simmer for 1 hour.

Add carrots and potatoes; cover and cook 30 minutes longer or until meat and vegetables are

CRUNCHY KRAUT SALAD

(Pictured above)

Mrs. J.B. Culwell, Arlington, Texas

Anyone who likes sauerkraut will enjoy this salad. I serve it as a side dish with ham, any kind of sausage or a sandwich.

   1 can (14 ounces) sauerkraut, drained
1/2 cup chopped celery
1/2 cup chopped green pepper
1/4 cup chopped onion
1/2 cup sugar
1/4 cup white vinegar
1/2 teaspoon celery seed

In a serving bowl, combine the sauerkraut, celery, green pepper and onion; set aside. In a saucepan, bring sugar and vinegar to a boil; cook and stir for 1 minute or until sugar is dissolved.

Remove from the heat; cool slightly. Pour over sauerkraut mixture; sprinkle with celery seed. Toss to coat. Refrigerate for at least 1 hour. **Yield: 2-3 servings.**

HERBED LONDON BROIL

Sharon Patnoe, Elkins, Arkansas

I serve this well-seasoned steak quite often. I got the recipe years ago from my stepfather. It's good whether you grill or broil the meat.

1/4 cup chopped onion
1/4 cup lemon juice
   2 tablespoons vegetable oil
1/4 teaspoon *each* celery seed, salt, dried thyme and oregano
1/4 teaspoon dried rosemary, crushed
   1 garlic clove, minced
Dash pepper
   1 beef flank steak (1/2 to 3/4 pound)

In a large resealable bag, combine the onion, lemon juice, oil and seasonings; add steak. Seal bag and turn to coat; refrigerate for several hours or overnight, turning once.

Drain and discard marinade. Grill steak, uncovered, over medium heat for 6-7 minutes on each side or until meat reaches desired doneness (for rare, a meat thermometer should read 140°; medium, 160°; well-done, 170°). Slice thinly across the grain. **Yield: 2 servings.**

GINGERED TEA

(Pictured below)

Connie Lapp, Honey Brook, Pennsylvania

This is a wonderful tea when home alone on a rainy day or when the chill of fall fills the air. It always gives me a boost of energy, plus its taste is so soothing.

   1 cup water
   2 teaspoons honey
3/4 teaspoon ground ginger
   3 individual tea bags
3/4 cup milk

In a small saucepan, bring water to a boil. Add honey and ginger. Reduce heat; cover and simmer for 10 minutes. Remove from the heat; add the tea bags.

Cover and steep for 5-7 minutes. Discard the tea bags. Stir in milk; heat through (do not boil). **Yield: 2 servings.**

Meals in Minutes

Put impressive spreads together for your family's table!

Check Out This Fast and Filling Fare

FAST FOOD is the answer when Elizabeth Freise of Kansas City, Missouri gets extra busy. And without question, her favorite kind comes from her very own kitchen.

"I work second shift and arrive home fairly late from my job at a college library," Elizabeth explains. Rather than reading through complex recipes, she'd rather check out quick dishes that shorten her meal-making efforts.

Quick menus, such as the one Elizabeth shares here, are guaranteed best-sellers among busy cooks. The meal presented on this page is ready to eat in 30 minutes or less.

"With fully cooked sausage, pre-chopped veggies and instant rice, my Spicy Cajun Stew practically makes itself. It's my favorite skillet dinner," she notes. "Sometimes, I put the ingredients in my slow cooker, switch it on and go. When I get home, I can sit down to dinner, or carry it to a potluck with friends.

"My Green Bean Salad is ready on the spot, too. It has only a few on-hand fixings to toss together. With a hint of garlic, it stands up beside a highly flavored main dish. Plus, the lemon dressing refreshes the palate."

As she dives into dessert, Elizabeth concedes she feels like a kid again. "I invented Mandarin Fluff as an easy, grown-up version of the frozen cream-filled pops we all enjoyed as children," she says. "The mandarin oranges and whipped topping re-create the tangy orange and ice cream flavors. One bite cools the heat from the rest of the meal."

Since fetching dinner has become so easy, she has ample time for other pet projects, Elizabeth says. "The time I save in the kitchen, I use for flower gardening, creative writing, crafting and walking with 'Marlo,' my energetic German shepherd."

SPICY CAJUN STEW

1 package (16 ounces) fully cooked kielbasa *or* Polish sausage, cut into 1/4-inch slices
2 cans (10 ounces *each*) diced tomatoes and green chilies, undrained
1 can (14-1/2 ounces) chicken broth
1 package (10 ounces) frozen chopped spinach, thawed and drained
1/2 to 3/4 cup uncooked instant rice

In a large skillet, saute the sausage until lightly browned; drain. Add tomatoes and broth. Bring to a boil. Stir in spinach. Return to a boil; cook for 2 minutes. Stir in rice. Cover; remove from heat. Let stand 5 minutes. Stir with a fork. **Yield:** 5 servings.

GREEN BEAN SALAD

1/2 cup water
3 cups frozen cut green beans
3 to 4 tablespoons lemon juice
1 garlic clove, minced
1/2 teaspoon salt
Dash pepper
2 tablespoons olive oil
2 large tomatoes, cut into wedges

In a saucepan, bring water to a boil; add beans. Return to a boil; cook 5 minutes (beans will be crisp-tender). Immediately rinse in cold water. In a small bowl, combine lemon juice, garlic, salt and pepper; whisk in oil. Place beans and tomatoes on salad plates; drizzle with dressing. **Yield:** 5 servings.

MANDARIN FLUFF

2 cans (15 ounces each) mandarin oranges, well drained
1 carton (8 ounces) frozen whipped topping, thawed
1/2 cup chopped pecans

Place oranges in a bowl. Fold in whipped topping. Before serving, fold in pecans. **Yield:** 5-6 servings.

Create a Family Fiesta with Fun And Flavorful Foods

ALL THE TIME in the world is a luxury Patty Burk seldom has. But that doesn't keep her from inviting guests to her table all the way from Japan.

"So far, my husband, Tom, our children and I have been the host family to six international students," she shares from Nanaimo, British Columbia. Luckily, much of what she needs for a fast no-fuss supper is found as close as her kitchen cupboard.

The recipes Patty shares here are on the table in 30 minutes or less.

"Perfect for guests or family meals, Salsa Chicken is full of color and flavor. The simple sauce is tasty over pork chops, too," Patty adds. "Some mornings, I put the ingredients in the slow cooker. That way, it's ready when we walk in the door that evening.

"My quick rice side dish gets a zippy twist from lemon-pepper seasoning. It complements the Salsa Chicken and many other types of Mexican dishes quite nicely."

For a fun-looking dessert or a refreshing treat, Patty relies on limes. "I cut the fruit in half and remove the pulp," she says.

"Then my children, Emily, Jon and Ethan, fill the lime cups with a variety of ice cream and sherbet flavors. They even request these sundaes for birthday parties. Kids love them!

"We always manage to sit down together and have our dinner as a family," Patty says. "Talk around our table ranges from the kids' Celtic dance classes and Tom's floor hockey team to my volunteer work and our visiting students' progress with English."

Inevitably, Patty's quick dishes elicit one hearty international response—"Yum!"

SALSA CHICKEN

1-1/2 pounds boneless skinless chicken
     breasts, cut into thin strips
1 tablespoon vegetable oil

1 medium green pepper, cut into strips
2 cups salsa

In a large skillet, saute chicken in oil for 3 minutes. Add the green pepper; cook for 3 minutes or until peppers are crisp-tender. Stir in the salsa and bring to a boil. Reduce the heat; simmer, uncovered, for 3 minutes or until the chicken juices run clear. **Yield:** 4 servings.

LEMON-PEPPER RICE

2 cups water
1 to 2 teaspoons lemon-pepper
    seasoning
2 cups uncooked instant rice

In a saucepan, bring water and lemon-pepper to a boil. Stir in rice. Remove from the heat; cover and let rice stand for 5 minutes. Fluff with a fork. **Yield:** 4 servings.

LIME SUNDAES

4 large limes
1 cup lime sherbet
1 cup vanilla ice cream
Fresh mint, optional

Cut limes in half lengthwise; scoop out pulp and save for another use. Fill each lime half with 2 tablespoons of sherbet and ice cream.

Return to the freezer until serving. Garnish with mint if desired. **Yield:** 4 servings.

IDEAS FROM PATTY

- "If you don't have canned salsa, mix green peppers, onions, mushrooms and chili seasoning with tomato or mushroom soup," Patty suggests. "Sweet and spicy peach salsa is also great with chicken."
- For a change of pace, serve Salsa Chicken over a healthy portion of pasta.
- Patty recommends you make your own rice seasoning from basil, sage, thyme, oregano, dill, garlic or other favorite herb blends.
- To dress up her sundaes a bit more, Patty adds a dollop of whipped cream and a maraschino cherry to each.

Three Cooks Share Fast Favorites for A Delicious Meal

WHEN the first crocus opens and the first robin sings, the kitchen is the last place you want to be. Instead, spring into action and breeze through these quick-to-fix dishes.

Ready in 30 minutes, the menu we've put together here features recipes from three cooks who give "fast food" a flavorful new meaning.

Tammy Messing of Ruth, Michigan shares Skillet Barbecued Pork Chops. "Between keeping up with our three children and helping my carpenter husband, Jeff, build our new home, I don't have time to stand around the stove," she notes.

"On days I volunteer at church or shuttle between after-school activities, I'm glad this dinner comes together in one skillet. The sauce makes the chops so moist and tender. I also simmer it up with other meats like beef or venison steaks."

From Kansas City, Missouri, Elizabeth Freise sent the recipe for her Broccoli Garbanzo Salad, a fun and different side dish.

"This salad goes well with Mexican and Italian food," she says. "It's a nice change of pace from lettuce—and does not take much prep work.

"To make it a main dish, add broiled chicken strips, your favorite cheese and extra veggies," she suggests.

In Arkansaw, Wisconsin, Brenda Drier serves Chocolate Rice Dessert as a fast finish to a meal. "Even with calves to feed and chores to finish, I can plan this quick treat for supper," shares the dairy farm wife.

"Fresh pineapple chunks are a nice addition to this no-fuss rice parfait," Brenda says. "My mom made this dessert often when I was a girl. Now I prepare it for my children and grandkids."

SKILLET BARBECUED PORK CHOPS

- 4 boneless pork loin chops (1/2 inch thick)
- 1 teaspoon seasoned salt
- 1 tablespoon butter
- 1 medium onion, chopped
- 1/2 cup water
- 1/2 cup packed brown sugar
- 1 cup honey barbecue sauce
- 1 tablespoon Worcestershire sauce
- 2 teaspoons cornstarch
- 1 tablespoon cold water

Sprinkle the pork chops with seasoned salt. In a large skillet, brown chops on both sides in butter over medium-high heat. Remove chops.

In the drippings, saute onion until golden brown. Add the water, brown sugar, barbecue sauce and Worcestershire sauce. Return chops to the skillet. Bring to a boil. Reduce heat; cover and simmer for 15 minutes or until meat juices run clear. Remove chops; keep warm.

Combine cornstarch and cold water until smooth; stir into skillet. Bring to a boil; cook and stir for 2 minutes or until thickened. Serve over pork. **Yield:** 4 servings.

BROCCOLI GARBANZO SALAD

- 1 package (12 ounces) broccoli florets
- 1 can (15 ounces) garbanzo beans *or* chickpeas, rinsed and drained
- 1 cup pitted ripe olives, drained
- 1/3 to 1/2 cup Italian salad dressing

Place broccoli in a steamer basket over 1 in. of boiling water in a saucepan. Cover and steam for 5-6 minutes or until tender. Rinse with cold water; drain and place in a bowl.

Add the garbanzo beans and olives. Drizzle with dressing; toss to coat. Refrigerate until serving. **Yield:** 4-6 servings.

CHOCOLATE RICE DESSERT

- 4-1/2 teaspoons sugar
- 1 teaspoon ground cinnamon
- 1/8 teaspoon salt
- 3 cups cooked long grain rice, warmed
- 1/4 cup hot fudge sauce *or* chocolate ice cream topping
- 1/4 cup whipped topping
- 4 maraschino cherries

In a bowl, combine the sugar, cinnamon and salt. Add rice and mix well. Divide among four dessert dishes or parfait glasses.

Top with hot fudge sauce. Dollop with whipped topping and garnish with the cherries. **Yield:** 4 servings.

Bring Bountiful Veggies to Your Dinner Table Tonight!

IN THE MARKET for quick and simple recipes? You'll soon be sold on Melody Smaller's approach to cooking.

"My days stay full running a discount general store in the front of our home here in Fowler, Colorado," Melody notes.

And after closing her business for the day, she wastes no time shopping for something fast, filling and flavorful to whip up for dinner. Quick dishes, such as those Melody shares here, are just the ticket for time-conscious cooks.

"I created these speedy Veggie Beef Patties using ingredients I had on hand," she explains. "They make a nice entree for a dinner or potluck. Or, you can serve them with barbecue sauce on a bun for a casual lunch or cookout.

"Zucchini Lettuce Salad is a great way to use up an abundant crop of squash," says Melody. Shredding the veggies is a breeze with a food processor. Topped with bottled dressing and cheese, this colorful side makes such a flavorful addition to any meal.

To round out the dinner, Melody stirs up Paprika Cheese Biscuits. "My husband, Tom, loves their cheddar flavor," Melody says. "They're so tender, I eat them as a snack."

As for Melody's customers, they sometimes leave the store with more than they bargained for. She's always happy to pass along a labor-saving recipe, free of charge.

VEGGIE BEEF PATTIES

1/4 cup grated carrot
1/4 cup finely chopped onion
1/4 cup finely chopped green
    pepper
1 pound ground beef
Salt and pepper to taste

In a bowl, combine the carrot, onion and green pepper. Crumble beef over mixture and mix well. Shape into four patties. Season with the salt and pepper. Pan-fry the patties over medium heat until the meat is no longer pink. **Yield:** 4 servings.

ZUCCHINI LETTUCE SALAD

2 cups shredded leaf lettuce
1/2 cup shredded zucchini
1/2 cup sliced ripe olives
1/4 cup chopped red onion
1/2 cup Italian salad dressing
1/4 cup shredded Parmesan cheese

In a serving bowl, combine the lettuce, zucchini, olives and onion.

Drizzle with the dressing; sprinkle with the Parmesan cheese. Serve immediately. **Yield:** 4 servings.

PAPRIKA CHEESE BISCUITS

2-1/4 cups biscuit/baking mix
1/2 cup shredded cheddar cheese
2/3 cup milk
1 tablespoon butter, melted
1/2 teaspoon paprika

In a bowl, combine the biscuit mix and cheese. With a fork, stir in milk just until moistened. Turn onto a floured surface; knead 10 times.

Roll dough to 1/2-in. thickness; cut with a 2-1/2-in. biscuit cutter. Place on an ungreased baking sheet. Brush with butter; sprinkle with the paprika.

Bake at 450° for 8-10 minutes or until golden brown. **Yield:** 8 biscuits.

MORE GREAT IDEAS

- "To lighten up the burgers, you can substitute ground turkey for beef," Melody suggests. "You could try stuffing them with a vegetable-rice mix or mushrooms and cheese."
- To shake up her salad, try homemade vinegar and oil dressing. Add some chopped tomatoes, pimientos or red peppers to boost the color.
- "For a romantic candlelit dinner, cut the biscuits out with metal heart-shaped cookie cutters," Melody adds.

Timeless Recipes Make Mealtime Special

HER PLATE is as full as it's ever been, says octegenarian Jean Komlos of Plymouth, Michigan. But that doesn't mean she spends every day in the kitchen.

"If I'm not working on an afghan, I'm busy with my card club or walking a frisky terrier or sheltie as our neighborhood dog-sitter," says Jean. "I can't see taking time to decide what to cook when there are other fun things to do."

Quick menus, such as the one Jean shares here, are fast friends to cooks of any age.

Broiled Turkey Tenderloins are perfect for weekday meals or special dinners with her grandchildren, Jean notes. "The simple sauce gets its tang from citrus, a little kick from cayenne and subtle sweetness from molasses. It keeps well in the refrigerator, so it can be made ahead. I often fix extra to use later with other meats.

"My Cheesy Chive Potatoes are a speedy side dish that complements most any entree," she continues. "Feta cheese adds a rich zesty flavor. A neighbor supplies me with garden-fresh chives, but you can use frozen or dried chives for more convenience."

For dessert, Jean puts together a parfait that stacks up as a fuss-free favorite. "Cherry yogurt, chocolate syrup and whipped topping blend into a yummy fluff. It's lovely with the alternating layers of fruit," she shares. "I serve it as a light ending to a meal. It's also a perfect brunch item or snack when unexpected company stops in."

BROILED TURKEY TENDERLOINS

3/4 cup orange juice concentrate
1/3 cup molasses
1/4 cup ketchup
3 tablespoons prepared mustard
2 tablespoons soy sauce
1/2 teaspoon garlic powder
1/4 teaspoon cayenne pepper
1/8 teaspoon ground cumin
3 turkey breast tenderloins
(about 1-1/2 pounds), cut
lengthwise in halves

In a saucepan, whisk the first eight ingredients; bring to a boil. Set aside 3/4 cup for serving. Brush tenderloins on both sides with remaining sauce.

Broil 6 in. from the heat for 5 minutes, basting once. Turn and broil 5-8 minutes longer or until juices run clear. Serve with the reserved sauce. **Yield:** 6 servings.

CHEESY CHIVE POTATOES

6 medium potatoes, peeled and cubed
1/2 cup milk
1/2 cup crumbled feta cheese
1 tablespoon butter
1/2 teaspoon salt
1/8 teaspoon pepper
2 tablespoons minced chives

Place potatoes in a large saucepan and cover with water. Bring to a boil. Reduce heat; cover and boil for 10-15 minutes or until tender.

Drain and add milk, feta cheese, butter, salt and pepper; mash. Stir in chives. **Yield:** 6 servings.

CHERRY CHOCOLATE DESSERT

1 carton (8 ounces) cherry yogurt
1/2 cup chocolate syrup
1 carton (8 ounces) frozen whipped topping, thawed
2 cups sliced strawberries *or* bananas
Mint sprigs

In a large bowl, combine yogurt and chocolate syrup; fold in whipped topping. Set aside 12 strawberry slices.

In six dessert dishes, place half of the remaining fruit; top with half of the yogurt mixture. Repeat layers. Garnish with reserved strawberries and mint sprigs. **Yield:** 6 servings.

OTHER OPTIONS TO TRY

- "Try substituting chicken for the turkey in my main dish," Jean recommends. "To give it an Oriental twist, serve the tenderloins over instant rice."
- To put a different spin on Jean's spuds, use shredded cheddar cheese in place of feta or opt for sour cream instead. Can't find chives? Parsley or dill make snappy stand-ins.

This Dinner Combination Will Bring Compliments

PLAYING beat the clock daily at dinner? You can get ahead of the game in no time flat while serving something simple and deliciously satisfying.

Marlene Wiczek of Little Falls, Minnesota shares hearty Sirloin Steak Sandwiches. "My husband, Bill, and I raise black Angus on our hobby farm. So beef is big on our menu," she notes.

"I keep several of these easy steak sandwiches in the freezer. When family or friends stop over, I heat them through, add a side of baked beans or fruit salad, and we have an instant picnic. For a tasty variation, replace the steak with grilled turkey, garnish with sliced tomatoes and layer the ingredients onto a hoagie bun.

"This is a fun sandwich to pack into a brown bag lunch. If a microwave is available, warm it just enough to melt the cheese," Marlene suggests.

From Orrville, Ohio, reader Krista Musser sent a no-fuss spud recipe that bowls over her husband and son. "My Swiss Potato Soup is bubbling on the stovetop faster than Scott and our son, Donald, can ask what's for dinner," she laughs.

"This recipe can also be made in the microwave. Or, I may start simmering the ingredients in the slow cooker in the morning. Then, when I get home from work, I add the yummy finishing touches—shredded Swiss cheese and crisp bits of bacon."

In Lapeer, Michigan, Heidi Wilcox pays attention to the little things—whether tending to the six children at her in-home day care or sweetening up supper for her own two kids.

"Since I usually have all the ingredients on hand, Pound Cake Cobbler is as easy as pie to assemble," Heidi says. "Often, I'll change the canned filling to another fruit flavor. Try raspberry, peach, apricot or my personal favorite, strawberry."

▰▰▰▰▰▰▰▰▰▰▰▰
SIRLOIN STEAK SANDWICHES

     1 boneless beef sirloin steak (1 pound)
     4 onion rolls, split
 1/4 cup mayonnaise
     2 to 4 tablespoons prepared mustard
     4 teaspoons prepared horseradish
     4 slices Swiss cheese

Grill steak, uncovered, over medium heat for 5-8 minutes on each side or until meat reaches desired doneness (for rare, a meat thermometer should read 140°; medium, 160°; well-done, 170°). Spread cut side of roll tops with mayonnaise, mustard and horseradish. Slice steak diagonally; place on roll bottoms. Top with cheese and roll tops. **Yield:** 4 servings.

▰▰▰▰▰▰▰▰▰▰▰▰
SWISS POTATO SOUP

     5 bacon strips, diced
     1 medium onion, chopped
     2 cups water
     4 medium potatoes, peeled and cubed
 1-1/2 teaspoons salt
 1/8 teaspoon pepper
 1/3 cup all-purpose flour
     2 cups milk
     1 cup (4 ounces) shredded Swiss cheese

In a saucepan, cook bacon until crisp; remove to paper towels with a slotted spoon. Drain, reserving 1 tablespoon drippings. Saute onion in drippings until tender. Add water, potatoes, salt and pepper. Bring to a boil. Reduce heat; simmer, uncovered, for 12 minutes or until potatoes are tender.

Combine flour and milk until smooth; gradually stir into potato mixture. Bring to a boil; cook and stir for 2 minutes or until thickened and bubbly. Remove from the heat; stir in cheese until melted. Garnish with bacon. **Yield:** 4 servings.

▰▰▰▰▰▰▰▰▰▰▰▰
POUND CAKE COBBLER

     1 frozen pound cake (10-3/4 ounces), thawed
     1 can (21 ounces) cherry *or* blueberry pie filling
 1/3 cup water
 1/2 teaspoon almond extract
 Whipped topping
     2 tablespoons sliced almonds, toasted

Cut cake into 1-in. cubes. Place in a microwave-safe 1-1/2-qt. dish or 9-in. pie plate. In a small bowl, combine the pie filling, water and extract; spoon over cake. Cover and microwave on high for 3-5 minutes or until heated through. Spoon onto dessert plates; garnish with whipped topping and almonds. **Yield:** 4 servings.

Editor's Note: This recipe was tested in an 850-watt microwave.

Our Most Memorable Meals

These six meals bring back memories of the good, old-fashioned dinners that families shared together.

Go Nuts Over This Old-Fashioned Spread

TANGY ROUND STEAK STRIPS

Kathleen Roberts, St. Augustine, Florida

I like to fix this dish for a party or a buffet dinner. It adapts easily for any number and makes a delicious entree served over hot egg noodles.

> 2 pounds boneless beef round steak, cut into 2-1/2-inch strips
> 1 medium onion, chopped
> 1/2 cup French salad dressing
> 1 envelope Stroganoff sauce mix
> 1-1/2 cups water
> 1 jar (4-1/2 ounces) sliced mushrooms, drained
> 1 celery rib, chopped
> 1 teaspoon Worcestershire sauce
> Hot cooked noodles

In a large skillet, saute beef and onion in salad dressing until meat is no longer pink. Combine sauce mix and water until blended; stir into beef mixture. Stir in the mushrooms, celery and Worcestershire sauce.

Bring to a boil. Reduce heat; cover and simmer for 60-70 minutes or until meat is tender. Serve over noodles. **Yield:** 6-8 servings.

CIRCUS PEANUT GELATIN

Ruthanne Mengel, Demotte, Indiana

Circus Peanuts were one of the most talked-about candies in my hometown's old-fashioned candy shop. When I saw this gelatin recipe, I knew I had to try it. Kids love its cool fruity taste, and older folks enjoy the trip down memory lane.

> 44 Circus Peanut candies, *divided*
> 1 cup boiling water, *divided*
> 2 packages (3 ounces *each*) orange gelatin
> 2 cans (8 ounces *each*) crushed pineapple, undrained
> 1 carton (8 ounces) frozen whipped topping, thawed

Cut 32 candies into small pieces; place in a microwave-safe bowl. Add 1/4 cup of boiling water. Cover and microwave on high for 1 minute. Stir; microwave 1 minute longer. Stir until smooth.

In a large bowl, dissolve gelatin in remaining boiling water. Stir in candy mixture and pineapple. Refrigerate until partially set. Fold in whipped topping. Pour into a 13-in. x 9-in. x 2-in. dish coated with nonstick cooking spray. Refrigerate until firm. Cut into squares; top each with a Circus Peanut. **Yield:** 12 servings.

Editor's Note: This recipe was tested in an 850-watt microwave.

POPPY SEED SALAD DRESSING

Gay Nell Nicholas, Henderson, Texas

My ladies group at church printed a cookbook several years ago, and this recipe was in the book. I serve it over mixed greens, drizzle it over sliced tomatoes and cucumbers and use it as a dressing for coleslaw.

> 3/4 cup sugar
> 1/3 cup cider vinegar
> 4-1/2 teaspoons grated onion
> 3 teaspoons ground mustard
> 1 teaspoon poppy seeds
> 1/2 teaspoon salt
> 1 cup vegetable oil

In a small bowl, combine the first six ingredients. Slowly add oil, while whisking briskly. Cover and refrigerate until serving. **Yield:** 1-3/4 cups.

MARMALADE DATE PASTRIES

Nancy Lewis, Warwick, Rhode Island

These pretty pastries take a little time to put together but are worth the effort. They have a delicious, melt-in-your-mouth flavor.

   1 **package (11 ounces) pie crust mix**
   1 **package (3 ounces) cream cheese**
   1 **tablespoon milk**
  24 **pitted dates**
 1/2 **cup orange marmalade**
Confectioners' sugar

Place the pie crust mix in a bowl. Cut in cream cheese until mixture resembles coarse crumbs.

Add the milk and stir to form a ball. Cover and refrigerate for 30 minutes.

Divide dough in half. On a lightly floured surface, roll out each portion into a 12-in. x 9-in. rectangle. Cut into 3-in. squares. Cut dates in half lengthwise; fill each with 1/2 teaspoon marmalade. Place a date in the center of each pastry square. Moisten corners with water; bring corners together, pinching dough to seal.

Place on greased baking sheets. Bake at 400° for 9-11 minutes or until lightly browned. Cool on wire racks. Dust with confectioners' sugar. **Yield:** 2 dozen.

Reel in the Compliments with This Hearty Meal

POTATO FISH SKILLET

Jeff Brown, Colon, Michigan

I've been fixing this stir-fry for years, often using bass since we live on a lake where bass are quite common. When I first tried the recipe, my wife declared it a winner.

        4 medium red potatoes, cubed
        6 tablespoons butter
        2 tablespoons olive oil
        1 pound grouper *or other lean fish, cut*
            into 3/4-inch pieces
      1/2 cup all-purpose flour
        2 cups sliced fresh mushrooms
      1/2 cup chopped celery
      1/4 cup chopped onion
        3 garlic cloves, minced
    4-1/2 teaspoons lemon juice
Salt and pepper to taste

In a large skillet, stir-fry potatoes in butter and oil for 8-10 minutes or until lightly browned. Coat fish with flour; add to the skillet. Cover and cook for 4 minutes, stirring occasionally.

Add the mushrooms, celery, onion and garlic. Cover and cook 4-6 minutes longer or until fish flakes easily with a fork. Sprinkle with lemon juice, salt and pepper. **Yield:** 4 servings.

HONEY MUSTARD CARROTS

Jean Dandrea, Burkesville, Kentucky

After tasting this side dish at a restaurant, I created a similar recipe by trial and error in my own kitchen. Since we have six beehives, I like to use honey in many of my recipes.

        2 pounds carrots, julienned
        2 tablespoons honey
        2 tablespoons Dijon mustard
      1/2 to 3/4 teaspoon ground cumin
      1/4 teaspoon ground cinnamon
        2 tablespoons butter
      1/4 teaspoon salt
      1/8 teaspoon pepper
        1 tablespoon minced fresh parsley

Place 1 in. of water in a large saucepan; add carrots. Bring to a boil. Reduce heat; cover and simmer for 3 minutes or until tender. In a small bowl, combine honey, mustard, cumin and cinnamon. Drain carrots well; stir in butter, salt and pepper. Add honey mixture; heat through. Sprinkle with parsley. **Yield:** 6 servings.

CREAMY ASPARAGUS SOUP

Pat Stevens, Granbury, Texas

After trying several different recipes for asparagus soup, I put together the best ingredients from each for my favorite version. This soup is great year-round and adds an elegant touch to special-occasion meals.

        2 medium leeks (white portion only),
            sliced
       12 green onions, chopped
        2 tablespoons olive oil
        1 tablespoon butter
    2-1/2 pounds fresh asparagus, cut into 1-inch
            pieces
        4 cups chicken broth
        1 cup half-and-half cream
      1/2 teaspoon salt
      1/8 teaspoon pepper

In a large saucepan, saute leeks and onions in oil and butter until tender. Add the asparagus and broth. Bring to a boil. Reduce heat; simmer, uncovered, until vegetables are tender. Remove from the heat. Set aside 1 cup of asparagus pieces.

In a blender, process the remaining asparagus mixture in batches until smooth; return to the pan. Stir in the cream, salt and pepper. Cook over low heat until heated through. Garnish with reserved asparagus pieces. **Yield:** 6 servings.

PINEAPPLE MERINGUE CAKE

Carol Forbes, Norwalk, Connecticut

This was my grandmother's favorite recipe, made only for special occasions. She never measured anything and her food was always great, but I think she had to be a little more exact with this cake.

      1/2 cup butter, softened
    1-1/4 cups sugar, *divided*
        4 eggs, *separated*
        1 teaspoon vanilla extract
      1/2 cup plus 2 tablespoons all-purpose flour
        1 teaspoon baking powder
      1/4 teaspoon salt
      1/4 cup milk
      3/4 cup chopped walnuts

FILLING:

- 1 cup heavy whipping cream
- 1/4 teaspoon vanilla extract
- 1 can (8 ounces) crushed pineapple,
  well drained

In a small mixing bowl, cream butter and 1/2 cup sugar. Add egg yolks and vanilla; mix well. Combine the flour, baking powder and salt; add to creamed mixture alternately with milk. Spread batter over the bottom of two greased and floured 9-in. round baking pans (batter will be about 1/4 in. thick); set aside.

In another mixing bowl, beat egg whites on medium speed until soft peaks form. Gradually add remaining sugar, 1 tablespoon at a time, beating on high until stiff glossy peaks form and sugar is dissolved. Spread meringue evenly over batter; sprinkle with walnuts. Bake at 350° for 20-25 minutes or until meringue is lightly browned. Cool in pans for 5 minutes; loosen edges of cakes from pans with a knife. Using two large spatulas, carefully remove cakes from pans; cool completely, meringue side up, on wire racks.

In a chilled mixing bowl, beat the cream and vanilla until stiff peaks form. Fold in pineapple. Transfer one cake layer to a serving plate, meringue side up. Carefully spread filling over meringue; top with the remaining cake layer. Store in the refrigerator. **Yield:** 10-12 servings.

HAM VEGETABLE STRATA

Diane Meyer, Geneseo, New York

Ever since my niece gave me this recipe, I've shared it with many friends. The crunchy golden brown topping and colorful ingredients present a tantalizing dish.

- 1 small zucchini, cut into 1/4-inch slices
- 2 cups broccoli florets
- 1/2 cup shredded carrot
- 12 slices white bread, crusts removed
- 1 cup cubed fully cooked ham
- 1 can (8 ounces) mushroom stems and pieces, drained
- 1 cup (4 ounces) shredded sharp cheddar cheese
- 1 cup (4 ounces) shredded Swiss cheese
- 12 eggs
- 2-1/2 cups milk
- 1/4 cup chopped onion
- 1/2 teaspoon ground mustard
- 1/4 teaspoon salt
- 1/8 teaspoon pepper
- 1-1/2 cups crushed cornflakes
- 1/4 cup butter, melted

In a small saucepan, cook the zucchini, broccoli and carrot in a small amount of water until tender; drain. Cut bread in half diagonally; place half of the pieces in a greased 13-in. x 9-in. x 2-in. baking dish. Top with half of the vegetables, ham, mushrooms and cheeses. Repeat layers.

In a bowl, beat the eggs, milk, onion, mustard, salt and pepper; pour over the top. Cover and refrigerate for 8 hours or overnight.

Remove from the refrigerator 30 minutes before baking. Toss cornflakes and butter; sprinkle over the casserole. Bake, uncovered, at 350° for 50 minutes or until a knife inserted near the center comes out clean. Let stand for 10 minutes before cutting. **Yield:** 12-16 servings.

ZIPPY PRALINE BACON

Myrt Pflannkuche, Pell City, Alabama

We live on a lake and have many overnight guests, so I serve brunch often. I'm always looking for recipes to enhance the usual eggs and bacon. My husband came home from a men's brunch raving about this one, and the hostess shared the recipe. Make more than you think you need...everybody wants seconds.

- 1 pound sliced bacon
- 3 tablespoons brown sugar
- 1-1/2 teaspoons chili powder
- 1/4 cup finely chopped pecans

Line two 15-in. x 10-in. x 1-in. baking pans with foil. Arrange bacon in a single layer in pans. Bake at 425° for 10 minutes; drain. Combine the brown sugar and chili powder; sprinkle over bacon. Sprinkle with pecans. Bake 5-10 minutes longer or until bacon is crisp. Drain on paper towels. **Yield:** 6-8 servings.

MANDARIN FRUIT SALAD

Misty Frazier, Kennewick, Washington

When a friend brought this salad to a picnic, every bit of it was devoured. I never would have thought apple pie filling in a fruit salad would produce such delicious results.

- 2 cans (11 ounces *each*) mandarin oranges, drained
- 1 can (21 ounces) apple pie filling
- 1 can (20 ounces) pineapple chunks, drained
- 3 medium firm bananas, sliced
- 2 cups halved fresh strawberries

In a large bowl, combine all ingredients. Cover and refrigerate for 2 hours or until chilled. **Yield:** 10-12 servings.

ORANGE LEMONADE

C. Mason, Wamego, Kansas

This cool fruit drink is so refreshing on warm summer days. Fresh orange and lemon juice give it a terrific citrus flavor.

- 1 cup sugar
- 1 cup hot water
- 1 tablespoon grated lemon peel
- 2 teaspoons grated orange peel
- 3 cups cold water
- 2 cups orange juice
- 1/4 cup lemon juice

In a saucepan, combine the first four ingredients. Bring to a gentle boil; boil for 8-10 minutes or un-

til thickened. Remove from the heat. Strain and discard lemon and orange peel. Cool to room temperature. Transfer to a pitcher; stir in the cold water and juices. Chill. Serve over ice. **Yield:** 7 servings.

Savor the Flavor Of Yesteryear

▰▰▰▰▰▰▰▰▰▰
SAUERBRATEN PATTIES

Chris Christoffers, Lake Worth, Florida

My mother made this family favorite back in the '20s when chopped meat was only pennies a pound.

          2 eggs
          1 cup water, *divided*
          1 cup seasoned bread crumbs
      1/4 cup chopped onion
      3/4 teaspoon poultry seasoning
      3/4 teaspoon salt
      1/4 teaspoon pepper
  1-1/2 pounds ground beef
          1 cup beef broth
      1/4 cup red wine vinegar
          1 to 2 tablespoons brown sugar
        10 whole cloves
          1 bay leaf
        12 gingersnaps, crumbled

In a large bowl, combine eggs, 3/4 cup water, bread crumbs, onion, poultry seasoning, salt and pepper. Crumble beef over mixture; mix well. Shape into eight patties.

In a skillet, brown patties on both sides; drain. Add broth, vinegar, brown sugar, cloves, bay leaf, gingersnaps and remaining water. Bring to a boil over medium heat. Reduce heat; cover and simmer for 1 hour or until meat is no longer pink. Discard cloves and bay leaf. **Yield:** 6-8 servings.

▰▰▰▰▰▰▰▰▰▰
GERMAN POTATO CASSEROLE

Dara Luburgh, Sparta, New Jersey

I bring this dish to an annual Oktoberfest party. Everyone likes it, which ensures our invitation each year.

          5 pounds red potatoes, peeled and cut
              into 1/2-inch cubes
          1 pound sliced bacon, diced
          8 hard-cooked eggs, chopped
          1 large onion, chopped
      1/2 teaspoon salt
      1/2 teaspoon pepper
  1-1/2 cups mayonnaise
          3 tablespoons cider vinegar
          2 tablespoons Worcestershire sauce
          1 pound process cheese (Velveeta), cubed

Place potatoes in a Dutch oven and cover with water. Bring to a boil. Reduce heat; cover and cook for 15-20 minutes or until tender. Drain. In a skillet, cook bacon over medium heat until crisp. Using a slotted spoon, remove to paper towels; drain, reserving 1 tablespoon drippings.

In a large bowl, gently toss potatoes, bacon, eggs, onion, salt and pepper. Combine mayonnaise, vinegar, Worcestershire sauce and reserved bacon drippings; add to potato mixture and toss to coat.

Divide half of mixture between one greased 13-in. x 9-in. x 2-in. baking dish and one 9-in. square baking dish. Top with half of cheese cubes. Repeat layers. Bake, uncovered, at 350° for 40-45 minutes or until golden and bubbly. **Yield:** 16-20 servings.

Editor's Note: Reduced-fat or fat-free mayonnaise is not recommended for this recipe.

▰▰▰▰▰▰▰▰▰▰
GREEN BEAN FETA SALAD

Cheryl Martinetto, Grand Rapids, Minnesota

I sampled this salad at my sister-in-law's home years ago. The tasty salad complements lots of entrees.

  1-1/2 pounds fresh green beans, cut
              into 1-inch pieces
      2/3 cup olive oil
      1/3 cup white wine vinegar
          1 garlic clove, minced
          1 teaspoon dill weed
      1/2 teaspoon salt
      1/4 teaspoon pepper
          1 cup coarsely chopped pecans
      1/2 cup chopped red onion
          1 cup crumbled feta cheese

Place beans in a large saucepan and cover with water; bring to a boil. Cook, uncovered, for 8-10 minutes or until crisp-tender. Drain; rinse with cold water. Place beans in a bowl; cover and refrigerate for at least 1 hour.

In a jar with a tight-fitting lid, combine next six ingredients; shake well. Add nuts and onion to beans; add dressing and toss to coat. Sprinkle with cheese. Serve immediately with a slotted spoon. **Yield:** 6 servings.

▰▰▰▰▰▰▰▰▰▰
STRAWBERRY CHOCOLATE MERINGUE

Mary Lou Smarsh, Laurel, Montana

This special-occasion dessert features my family's favorite fruit. Strawberries go great with chocolate.

          3 egg whites
      1/4 teaspoon cream of tartar
          1 teaspoon vanilla extract

1 cup sugar
1/2 cup finely chopped almonds, toasted
FILLING:
   1 package (3 ounces) cream cheese,
     softened
1/2 cup packed brown sugar
1/2 cup baking cocoa
   2 tablespoons milk
1/2 teaspoon vanilla extract
   1 cup heavy whipping cream, whipped
   3 cups whole fresh strawberries
   2 squares (1 ounce *each*) semisweet
     chocolate, chopped
   2 teaspoons shortening

Place egg whites in a mixing bowl; let stand at room temperature for 30 minutes. Add cream of tartar and vanilla; beat on medium speed until soft peaks form. Gradually beat in sugar, 1 tablespoon at a time, until stiff peaks form. Fold in almonds.

Line a baking sheet with parchment paper. Trace a 9-in. circle on the paper. Spoon meringue evenly over circle, forming a 1-1/4-in. rim. Bake at 300° for 45 minutes. Turn oven off and (do not open door); let meringue dry for 1 hour. Cool on baking sheet on a wire rack. When completely cool, remove from parchment paper.

In a bowl, beat cream cheese and brown sugar until smooth and fluffy. Beat in cocoa, milk and vanilla. Fold in cream. Spoon into meringue shell. Top with berries. Melt chocolate and shortening; drizzle over berries. **Yield:** 8-10 servings.

Enjoy Family Pleasing Fare that Draws Raves

▰▰▰▰▰▰▰▰▰▰▰
SAUCY PORK CHOPS WITH VEGETABLES

Mildred Sherrer, Fort Worth, Texas

These savory chops served with mashed potatoes satisfy any hearty appetite. It is a very colorful dish and is nice to serve to guests, too.

  6 pork chops (1/2 inch thick)
  1 cup sliced carrots
  1 medium green pepper, cut into strips
  1 medium onion, chopped
  1 can (10-3/4 ounces) condensed golden
    mushroom soup, undiluted
  1/4 cup water
  1/2 to 3/4 teaspoon rubbed sage
Hot cooked noodles *or* rice

In a large skillet coated with nonstick cooking spray, brown pork chops on both sides. Remove and set aside. Saute the carrots, green pepper and onion until crisp-tender, stirring to loosen any browned bits from pan. Stir in the soup, water and sage. Return chops to the pan. Cover and simmer for 15-20 minutes or until meat is tender. Serve over noodles or rice. **Yield:** 6 servings.

▰▰▰▰▰▰▰▰▰▰▰
LIGHT WHEAT BREAD

Holly Shirk, Grantville, Pennsylvania

I bake bread twice a week because my family loves it. But I wanted a simple, foolproof recipe. After experimenting with several, I came up with this light-colored wheat bread.

  4 to 5 cups all-purpose flour
  1/2 cup whole wheat flour
  1 tablespoon sugar
  1 tablespoon salt
  2 packages (1/4 ounce *each*) active dry
    yeast
  1-3/4 cups water
  1 tablespoon butter

In a mixing bowl, combine 2-1/2 cups all-purpose flour, whole wheat flour, sugar, salt and yeast. In a saucepan, heat water and butter to 120°-130°.

Add to the dry ingredients; beat until smooth. Stir in enough remaining all-purpose flour to form a stiff dough. Turn onto a floured surface; knead until smooth and elastic, about 6-8 minutes. Cover and let rest for 20 minutes.

Divide dough in half; shape into loaves. Place in two greased 8-in. x 4-in. x 2-in. loaf pans. Cover and refrigerate for up to 12 hours. Remove from the refrigerator; let stand in a warm place for 30 minutes. Bake at 400° for 30-35 minutes or until golden brown. Remove from pans to wire racks to cool. **Yield:** 2 loaves.

Editor's Note: To bake without refrigeration, cover dough and let rise in a warm place until doubled, about 1 hour. Bake as directed.

▰▰▰▰▰▰▰▰▰▰▰
HOT CURRIED FRUIT

Carole Martin, Vernon, Alabama

This colorful, delicious side dish is a favorite with baked ham but also works well with traditional turkey and other poultry entrees. Curry gives interesting flavor, and it's a nice substitute for cranberry sauce.

  2 cans (8 ounces *each*) pineapple chunks
  1 can (15-1/4 ounces) peach halves
  1 can (15 ounces) pear halves
  2 tablespoons cornstarch
  2 tablespoons brown sugar
  1 tablespoon sugar
  1 teaspoon curry powder
  1 jar (14 ounces) spiced apple rings,
    drained
  1 jar (6 ounces) maraschino cherries,
    drained

Drain the pineapple, peaches and pears, reserving juices; set the fruit aside. In a saucepan, combine the cornstarch, sugars and curry powder. Gradually stir in reserved juices until smooth.

Bring to a boil; cook and stir for 2 minutes or until thickened. Stir in apple rings and reserved fruit; heat through. Remove from the heat; stir in cherries. **Yield:** 8-10 servings.

▰▰▰▰▰▰▰▰▰▰▰
COCONUT CARROT CAKE

Shirley Braithewaite, Onaway, Alberta

I found this recipe in a cookbook years ago. It's easy to make, and my family loves its moistness. It's very impressive when prepared in three layers.

  4 cups all-purpose flour
  2 cups sugar
  2 teaspoons baking powder
  2 teaspoons ground cinnamon

1-1/2 teaspoons baking soda
1 teaspoon salt
1 cup vegetable oil
4 eggs
1 can (8 ounces) crushed pineapple
2 cups grated carrots
1-1/2 cups flaked coconut
FROSTING:
1 package (8 ounces) cream cheese, softened
1/2 cup butter, softened
1 teaspoon vanilla extract
2-1/2 cups confectioners' sugar
Orange paste food coloring
Parsley sprig

In a mixing bowl, combine the first six ingredients. Add oil and eggs; beat until well blended. Drain the pineapple, reserving juice. Stir in the pineapple, carrots and coconut to batter (batter will be thick). Transfer to three greased and floured 9-in. round baking pans. Bake at 350° for 35-40 minutes or until a toothpick inserted near the center comes out clean. Cool for 10 minutes before removing from pans to wire racks.

For frosting, in a mixing bowl, beat cream cheese, butter and vanilla until fluffy. Gradually add confectioners' sugar and enough of the reserved pineapple juice if needed to achieve desired spreading consistency. Tint 1/4 cup frosting orange; place in a small resealable plastic bag. Cut a small hole in a corner of the bag; set aside.

Place one cake layer on a serving plate; spread with a third of the white frosting. Repeat layers twice. With orange frosting, pipe carrots on top; add parsley sprig for carrot top. Cover and store in the refrigerator. **Yield:** 12-14 servings.

Tasty Holiday Meal

■■■■■■■■■■■■■■

TURKEY WITH HERB STUFFING
(Also pictured on front cover)

Ruth Warner, Grand Junction, Colorado

This old family recipe was brought West by my great-great-grandmother, who rode in a covered wagon.

- 2 cups finely chopped onions
- 1 cup finely chopped celery with leaves
- 1/2 cup butter
- 1 package (12 ounces) unseasoned bread cubes
- 1 teaspoon *each* dried basil, thyme and savory
- 1/2 teaspoon salt
- 1/4 teaspoon pepper
- 1 can (14-1/2 ounces) chicken broth
- 1 turkey (12 to 14 pounds)

Additional butter, melted

Saute onions and celery in butter until tender. Transfer to a large bowl. Add bread cubes, seasonings and broth; toss to mix. Loosely stuff turkey. Place remaining stuffing in a greased 1-1/2-qt. baking dish; refrigerate. Skewer openings of turkey; tie drumsticks together with kitchen string. Place on a rack in a roasting pan. Brush with melted butter.

Bake, uncovered, at 325° for 3-1/2 to 4 hours or until a meat thermometer reads 180° for turkey and 165° for stuffing. Bake additional stuffing, covered, for 45-60 minutes or until heated through.

When turkey begins to brown, baste with drippings (if turkey browns too quickly, cover loosely with foil). Cover turkey; let stand 20 minutes before removing stuffing and carving. **Yield:** 6-8 servings (10 cups stuffing).

■■■■■■■■■■■■■■

SAUCY GREEN BEANS

Hazel Holley, Samson, Alabama

A special cooked sauce added to fresh green beans makes this a unique and hearty side dish.

- 2 pounds fresh green beans
- 1/3 cup chopped onion
- 1/4 cup butter
- 3 tablespoons all-purpose flour
- 1 tablespoon sugar
- 1-1/4 cups milk
- 1 cup (8 ounces) sour cream
- 3 tablespoons minced fresh parsley
- 3 tablespoons white vinegar

Salt and pepper to taste
- 6 bacon strips, cooked and crumbled

Place beans in a large saucepan; cover with water. Bring to a boil. Cook, uncovered, for 8-10 minutes or until crisp-tender. In another saucepan, saute onion in butter. Stir in flour and sugar until blended. Gradually add milk. Bring to a boil; cook and stir 2 minutes or until thickened.

Reduce heat; stir in sour cream, parsley and vinegar until blended. Drain beans; place in a serving bowl. Season with salt and pepper. Top with sauce and bacon. **Yield:** 10-12 servings.

■■■■■■■■■■■■■■

APPLE SWEET POTATO BAKE

Opal Sanders, Glouster, Ohio

Mother never used a recipe, so I finally duplicated this comfort food after many tries.

- 5 medium sweet potatoes (2-1/2 pounds)
- 4 cups sliced peeled tart apples
- 3/4 cup apple juice concentrate
- 1-1/2 cups plus 2 tablespoons cold water, *divided*
- 1/4 cup sugar
- 1/4 cup packed brown sugar
- 1/2 teaspoon salt
- 7-1/2 teaspoons cornstarch
- 1/4 cup butter, cubed

Place potatoes in a large saucepan or Dutch oven; cover with water. Bring to a boil; cover and cook for 30-45 minutes or until tender. Drain. When cool enough to handle, peel and slice potatoes.

Place apples in a large saucepan and cover with water. Cover and cook over medium heat for 7-8 minutes or until crisp-tender; drain. Place apples and potatoes in a greased 2-1/2-qt. baking dish.

In a saucepan, combine concentrate, 1-1/2 cups water, sugars and salt. Combine cornstarch with remaining water until smooth; stir into concentrate mixture. Bring to a boil; cook and stir 2 minutes or until thickened. Remove from heat; stir in butter until melted. Pour over potato mixture. Bake, uncovered, at 325° for 30-35 minutes or until heated through. **Yield:** 12 servings.

■■■■■■■■■■■■■■

CHOCOLATE PINEAPPLE TRIFLE

Gloria Vrabel, Webster, Massachusetts

We have this every Christmas. Sometimes I serve individual helpings in stemmed goblets for an elegant look.

1 package (16 ounces) angel food cake mix
1/2 cup sugar
2 tablespoons cornstarch
4 cups cold milk, *divided*
3 eggs, lightly beaten
1 can (20 ounces) crushed pineapple, drained
1 teaspoon vanilla extract
1 package (5.9 ounces) instant chocolate pudding mix
1/3 cup water
2 teaspoons rum extract
2 cups heavy whipping cream
2 tablespoons confectioners' sugar
Pineapple chunks and grated chocolate

Prepare and bake cake according to package directions. Cool completely. Meanwhile, combine sugar and cornstarch in a large saucepan. Gradually whisk in 2 cups of milk. Bring to a boil; cook and stir 2 minutes or until thickened. Remove from heat. Stir 1/2 cup hot mixture into the eggs; return all to the pan, stirring constantly. Bring to a gentle boil; cook and stir 2 minutes longer.

Remove from heat; stir in pineapple and vanilla. Pour into a bowl; press a piece of waxed paper or plastic wrap on top of pudding. Refrigerate, without stirring, until cooled. Meanwhile, place remaining milk in a bowl. Whisk in chocolate pudding mix for 2 minutes or until thickened. Chill.

To assemble, cut cooled cake into 1-in. cubes. Place a third of the cake in a 3-1/2-qt. trifle dish. Combine water and rum extract; drizzle a third over the cake. Top with pineapple pudding, a third of the cake and a third of the rum mixture. Layer with the chocolate pudding and remaining cake and rum mixture. Cover and chill.

Just before serving, beat cream and confectioners' sugar until stiff peaks form; spread over cake. Garnish with pineapple and chocolate. **Yield:** 10-12 servings.

General Recipe Index

✓Recipe includes Nutritional Analysis and Diabetic Exchanges

A

APPETIZERS & SNACKS

Cold Appetizers
Chutney Stuffed Eggs, 7
Deviled Ham Stuffed Eggs, 8
Fancy Fruit Pizza, 7

Dips & Spreads
Cheesy Beef Taco Dip, 6
Cheesy Corn Dip, 16
Festive Cheese Beach Ball, 10
Hot Cheese Spread, 12
Layered Three-Cheese Spread, 6
Mexican Corn Dip, 13
Party Cheese Balls, 5
Peanut Butter Chocolate Fondue, 5
✓Smoked Salmon Spread, 8
Tasty Cheese Spread, 17
✓Western Black Bean Dip, 8

Hot Appetizers
Green Bean Fritters, 17

Snacks & Mixes
Caramel Crunch, 9
Pecan Cheddar Snacks, 134
Sugared Pecans, 12
Sweet 'n' Salty Party Mix, 5

APPLES
Apple Mallow Salad, 59
Apple Oven Pancake, 19
Apple Pear Pie, 124
Apple-Smothered Pork Chops, 48
Apple Sweet Potato Bake, 174
Cider Pork Chop Dinner, 51
Cranberry Apple Crisp, 108
Maple-Apple Baked Beans, 88
Orange Applesauce Cupcakes, 104
Sandra's Apple-Rhubarb Pie, 108

APRICOTS
Apricot-Date Mini Loaves, 31
Apricot Pineapple Jam, 23

ARTICHOKES
Artichoke Cheese Oven Omelet, 32
Artichoke Spinach Salad, 74
Tossed Salad with Artichokes, 70

ASPARAGUS
Asparagus Salad, 137
Asparagus Souffle, 142
Creamy Asparagus Soup, 166

B

BANANAS
✓Banana Cupcakes, 124
Banana Nut Bars, 94
Banana Pancakes, 31
Banana Shakes, 12
Banana Split Dessert, 145
Banana Sundae Sauce, 105
Banana Upside Down Cake, 111
Chocolate Banana Cream Pie, 116
✓Chocolate Banana Smoothies, 13
Chocolate Banana Split Cupcakes, 105
Chocolate Chip Banana Cream Pie, 111
Creamy Banana Crepes, 30
Fruited Cabbage Salad, 78
Gelatin Banana Split, 60
Honey Banana Punch, 9
Peanut Butter Banana Pudding, 100
Pineapple Banana Bread, 140
✓Sour Cream Banana Bread, 28
Triple Layer Banana Cake, 110

BARS & BROWNIES
Banana Nut Bars, 94
Blueberry Bars, 97
Fruit 'n' Nut Spice Bars, 94
Fudgy Walnut Brownies, 92
Lime Coconut Bars, 137
Mini Brownie Treats, 109
Peaches 'n' Cream Bars, 95
Peanut Butter Cereal Bars, 92
Rich Cheesecake Bars, 148

BEANS
Beans and Biscuits, 48
Broccoli Garbanzo Salad, 157
Corn and Black Bean Salad, 77
Green Bean Feta Salad, 170
Green Bean Fritters, 17
Green Bean Salad, 153
Maple-Apple Baked Beans, 88
Marinated Lima Bean Salad, 64
Mini Green Bean Casserole, 131
Saucy Green Beans, 174
Savory Green Beans, 88
Tangy Bean Soup, 72
✓Western Black Bean Dip, 8

BEEF & CORNED BEEF
Barbecued Round Steak, 51
✓Deviled Swiss Steak, 41
Herbed London Broil, 151
Potato Roast Beef Salad, 77
Red-Eye Beef Roast, 47
Reuben Sandwiches, 65
Sesame Sirloin Steak, 139
Sirloin Steak Sandwiches, 162
Spiced Beef Pot Roast, 52
Stuffed Round Steak, 53
Tangy Franks and Pears, 138
Tangy Round Steak Strips, 164

BEVERAGES
Banana Shakes, 12
✓Chocolate Banana Smoothies, 13
Citrus Iced Tea, 6
Fruity Thirst Quencher, 15
Frosted Ruby Punch, 11
Gingered Tea, 151
Grape Juice Crush, 15
Honey Banana Punch, 9
Mint Cocoa Mix, 16
Orange Lemonade, 168
Orange Spiced Tea, 16
Peaches 'n' Cream Smoothies, 14
Peachy Orange Shakes, 143
Peanut Butter Milkshakes, 13
Pear Cooler, 15
Punch Delight, 15
Raspberry Mint Cooler, 14
Strawberry Punch, 11

BISCUITS & SCONES
Currant Jelly Scones, 20
Omelet Biscuit Cups, 28
Paprika Cheese Biscuits, 158

🎗 BLUE-RIBBON RECIPES

Appetizers & Beverages
Caramel Crunch, 9
Cheesy Beef Taco Dip, 6
Deviled Ham Stuffed Eggs, 8
Honey Banana Punch, 9
Mexican Corn Dip, 13
Mint Cocoa Mix, 16
Party Cheese Balls, 5
Raspberry Mint Cooler, 14

Breads & Rolls
Bacon-Onion Crescent Buns, 31
Orange-Hazelnut Spiral Rolls, 26
Herbed Garlic Bread, 12
Maple Oatmeal Bread, 33

Brunch Dishes
Apple Oven Pancake, 19
Artichoke Cheese Oven Omelet, 32
Breakfast Pizza, 19
Creamy Banana Crepes, 30
Ham 'n' Corn Fritters, 26
Italian Sausage Strata, 25
Sausage Garden Quiche, 19

Cakes, Pies & Desserts
Banana Sundae Sauce, 105

Chocolate Banana Split
   Cupcakes, 105
Chocolate Chip Banana
   Cream Pie, 111
Chocolate Chipper Pie Mix, 123
Chocolate Orange Cupcakes, 101
Coconut Peach Pie, 126
Cream Cheese Chocolate
   Cupcakes, 104
Cream-Filled Pumpkin Cupcakes, 99
Eggnog Cake, 107
Grandma's Chocolate Cake, 106
Hawaiian Cream Pie, 112
Heavenly Surprise Cupcakes, 99
Lemon Icebox Dessert, 117
Lemon Sparkle Cupcakes, 100
Orange Applesauce Cupcakes, 104
Peanut Butter Banana Pudding, 100
Peanut Butter Layer Cake, 106
Raspberry Mocha Torte, 118
Shoofly Cupcakes, 100
Triple Layer Banana Cake, 110
Walnut Carrot Cake, 125
Walnut Glory Cake, 122

Cookies, Bars & Candies
Banana Nut Bars, 94
Chunky Peanut Brittle, 91
Oat Pecan Cookie Mix, 93

Main Dishes
Apple-Smothered Pork Chops, 48
Barbecue Lasagna, 40
Beef Cabbage Roll-Ups, 37
Chicken Italian, 53
Corn Bread Taco Bake, 42
Crawfish-Stuffed Pork
   Tenderloins, 44
Creamed Ham in Toast Cups, 46
Creole Flounder with Seafood
   Sauce, 40
Macaroni 'n' Cheese Pizza, 36
Picante Cranberry Meatballs, 50
Southwestern Pizza, 46
Swordfish with Sauteed
   Vegetables, 52
Vegetable Beef Potpie, 36
Zesty Onion Burgers, 63

Salads
Apple Mallow Salad, 59
Artichoke Spinach Salad, 74
Black-Eyed Pea Salad, 56
Corn and Black Bean Salad, 77
Corn Medley Salad, 56
Tossed Salad with Artichokes, 70
Wild Rice Seafood Salad, 56

Side Dishes & Condiments
Christmas Pickles, 82
Cranberry Sweet Potato Bake, 81
Creamy Veggie Vermicelli, 83
Hearty Corn Pudding, 86
Mushroom Wild Rice Bake, 83
Nutty Brussels Sprouts, 81

Savory Green Beans, 88
Soup & Chili
Creamy Corn Crab Soup, 70
Hearty Chili Mac, 55

BREADS (also see Biscuits
& Scones; Rolls; Yeast Breads)
Apricot-Date Mini Loaves, 31
Corn Bread Salad, 68
Corn Bread Taco Bake, 42
Cranberry Bread Pudding, 120
Herbed Garlic Bread, 12
Mini Skillet Corn Bread, 145
Pineapple Banana Bread, 140
Pineapple Bread Pudding, 114
Raisin Sweet Potato Bread, 32
✓Sour Cream Banana Bread, 28
Sweet Potato Loaves, 143

C

CABBAGE & SAUERKRAUT
Beef Cabbage Roll-Ups, 37
Cabbage-Cucumber Gelatin Cups, 73
Cranberry Kraut Meatballs, 39
Crunchy Kraut Salad, 151
Fruited Cabbage Salad, 78
Old-Fashioned Coleslaw, 132
Reuben Sandwiches, 65
✓Turkey Cabbage Soup, 68

CAKES, CUPCAKES
& TORTES
✓Banana Cupcakes, 124
Banana Upside Down Cake, 111
Cappuccino Cupcakes, 123
Caramel Chocolate Cake, 118
Caramel Pear Cake, 113
Chocolate Banana Split Cupcakes, 105
Chocolate Orange Cupcakes, 101
Chocolate Zucchini Cake, 126
Coconut Carrot Cake, 172
Cream Cheese Chocolate Cupcakes, 104
Cream-Filled Pumpkin Cupcakes, 99
Cupcake Cones, 112
Eggnog Cake, 107
Grandma's Chocolate Cake, 106
Heavenly Surprise Cupcakes, 99
Lemon Sparkle Cupcakes, 100
Orange Applesauce Cupcakes, 104
Peach Coffee Cake, 27
Peanut Butter Cupcakes, 119
Peanut Butter Layer Cake, 106
Pineapple-Cherry Nut Cake, 115
Pineapple Meringue Cake, 166
Pound Cake Cobbler, 162
Raspberry Mocha Torte, 118
Raspberry Swirl Cupcakes, 115
Shoofly Cupcakes, 100
Triple Layer Banana Cake, 110
Walnut Carrot Cake, 125
Walnut Glory Cake, 122

CANDIES
Caramel Nut Marshmallows, 92
Chocolate Chow Mein Clusters, 140
Chunky Peanut Brittle, 91
Crunchy Chocolate Cups, 96

CARROTS
Carrot Cookies, 96
Carrot Mushroom Medley, 85
Coconut Carrot Cake, 172
Coconut Carrot Casserole, 84
Honey Mustard Carrots, 166
Walnut Carrot Cake, 125

CASSEROLES
Main Dishes
Beans and Biscuits, 48
Ham Vegetable Strata, 168
No-Bake Lasagna, 134
Pepperoni Cheese Bake, 21
Pineapple Ham Casserole, 49
✓Sausage Egg Bake, 21
Tuna Noodle Casserole, 140
Side Dishes
Apple Sweet Potato Bake, 174
Asparagus Souffle, 142
Brown Rice Vegetable Casserole, 82
Coconut Carrot Casserole, 84
German Potato Casserole, 170
Hearty Corn Pudding, 86
Mini Green Bean Casserole, 131
Mushroom Wild Rice Bake, 83
Scalloped Corn, 81
Squash Pasta Bake, 146
Sweet Potato Cranberry Bake, 84
Turnip Casserole, 84

CHEESE
Artichoke Cheese Oven Omelet, 32
Blue Cheese Salad Dressing, 145
Cheddar Waldorf Salad, 64
Cheddar Zucchini Slices, 148
Cheesy Beef Taco Dip, 6
Cheesy Chive Potatoes, 161
Cheesy Corn Dip, 16
Cream Cheese Chocolate Cupcakes, 104
Cream Cheese Cutouts, 96
Cubed Parmesan Potatoes, 137
Festive Cheese Beach Ball, 10
Green Bean Feta Salad, 170
Hot Cheese Spread, 12
Layered Three-Cheese Spread, 6
Macaroni 'n' Cheese Pizza, 36
Paprika Cheese Biscuits, 158
Party Cheese Balls, 5
Pecan Cheddar Snacks, 134
Pepperoni Cheese Bake, 21
Spinach Feta Strata, 27
Swiss Potato Soup, 162
Tasty Cheese Spread, 17

CHEESECAKE

✓Caramel Chocolate Cheesecake Bites, 124
Chilled Cranberry Cheesecake, 113
Hawaiian Cheesecake, 109
Rich Cheesecake Bars, 148

CHERRIES

Cherry Chocolate Chip Cookies, 95
Cherry Chocolate Dessert, 161
Danish Cherry Rhubarb Dessert, 119
Pineapple-Cherry Nut Cake, 115
Pound Cake Cobbler, 162

CHICKEN & FOWL

Chicken and Pear Tossed Salad, 59
Chicken Italian, 53
Country Chicken, 43
Deviled Chicken Thighs, 150
Farmhouse Chicken Soup, 62
Fruity Chicken Salad, 130
Hawaiian Chicken Salad, 68
Hearty Chicken Strata, 41
Jambalaya, 50
Layered Three-Cheese Spread, 6
Lemonade Chicken, 35
Orange Chicken Stir-Fry, 142
Orange-Honey Cashew Chicken, 130
Salsa Chicken, 154
Strawberry Chicken Salad, 69
✓Tossed Chicken Salad, 75
Zippy Chicken Corn Chowder, 57

CHOCOLATE

Cappuccino Cupcakes, 123
Caramel Chocolate Cake, 118
✓Caramel Chocolate Cheesecake Bites, 124
Cherry Chocolate Chip Cookies, 95
Cherry Chocolate Dessert, 161
Chocolate Banana Cream Pie, 116
✓Chocolate Banana Smoothies, 13
Chocolate Banana Split Cupcakes, 105
Chocolate Chip Banana Cream Pie, 111
Chocolate Chip Pudding Parfaits, 135
Chocolate Chipper Pie Mix, 123
Chocolate Chow Mein Clusters, 140
Chocolate Mousse, 131
Chocolate Orange Cupcakes, 101
Chocolate Pineapple Trifle, 174
Chocolate Rice Dessert, 157
Chocolate Zucchini Cake, 126
Chunky Peanut Brittle, 91
Cream Cheese Chocolate Cupcakes, 104
Crunchy Chocolate Cups, 96
Frozen Chocolate Crunch, 114
Fudgy Walnut Brownies, 92
Grandma's Chocolate Cake, 106
Mini Brownie Treats, 109
Mint Cocoa Mix, 16
Old-Fashioned Cocoa Pudding, 121
Peanut Butter Chocolate Fondue, 5
Pineapple Chocolate Chip Cookies, 97
Strawberry Chocolate Meringue, 170

COCONUT

Coconut Carrot Cake, 172
Coconut Carrot Casserole, 84
Coconut Custard Pudding, 123
Coconut Peach Pie, 126
Lime Coconut Bars, 137
Pecan Coconut Pie, 114

CONDIMENTS

Christmas Pickles, 82
Fruited Cranberry Relish, 129
Hot Curried Fruit, 172
Hot Curried Fruit Sauce, 89

COOKIES

Carrot Cookies, 96
Cherry Chocolate Chip Cookies, 95
Cream Cheese Cutouts, 96
Frosted Creams, 93
Hedgehog Cookies, 132
Linzer Heart Cookies, 91
Oat Pecan Cookie Mix, 93
Pineapple Chocolate Chip Cookies, 97
Spiced Spritz Cookies, 91

CORN & CORNMEAL

Cheesy Corn Dip, 16
Corn and Bacon Pancakes, 32
Corn and Black Bean Salad, 77
Corn Bread Salad, 68
Corn Bread Taco Bake, 42
Corn Medley Salad, 56
Corn Pudding Stuffed Tomatoes, 87
Corny Eggs, 25
Corny Rice, 87
Creamy Corn Crab Soup, 70
Ham 'n' Corn Fritters, 26
Hearty Corn Pudding, 86
Mexican Corn Dip, 13
Mini Skillet Corn Bread, 145
Scalloped Corn, 81
Sunday Best Corn, 86
✓Sweet Corn Blintzes, 20
Zesty Corn Salad, 67
Zippy Chicken Corn Chowder, 57

CRANBERRIES

Chilled Cranberry Cheesecake, 113
Cranberry Apple Crisp, 108
Cranberry Bread Pudding, 120
Cranberry Kraut Meatballs, 39
Cranberry Sweet Potato Bake, 81
Cranberry Velvet Freeze, 57
Cranberry Waldorf Gelatin, 69
Frosted Ruby Punch, 11
Fruited Cranberry Relish, 129
Picante Cranberry Meatballs, 50
Sweet Potato Cranberry Bake, 84

CUCUMBERS

Cabbage-Cucumber Gelatin Cups, 73
Cucumber Tomato Salad, 67
Dilly Cucumber Salad, 56
✓Gazpacho Salad, 76

D

DESSERTS (*also see specific kinds*)

Banana Split Dessert, 145
Banana Sundae Sauce, 105
Cherry Chocolate Dessert, 161
Chocolate Pineapple Trifle, 174
Chocolate Rice Dessert, 157
Cranberry Apple Crisp, 108
Cream Puff Ghosts, 127
Danish Cherry Rhubarb Dessert, 119
Frozen Chocolate Crunch, 114
Gelatin Banana Split, 60
Lemon Icebox Dessert, 117
Lime Sundaes, 154
Marmalade Date Pastries, 164
Peaches 'n' Cream Gelatin, 60
Pound Cake Cobbler, 162
Rhubarb Puff, 139
Strawberry Chocolate Meringue, 170

E

EGGS & EGGNOG

Artichoke Cheese Oven Omelet, 32
Asparagus Souffle, 142
Bacon 'n' Egg Gravy, 131
Breakfast Pizza, 19
Chutney Stuffed Eggs, 7
Corny Eggs, 25
Deviled Eggs, 132
Deviled Ham Stuffed Eggs, 8
Easter Lettuce Salad, 63
Egg Salad Tuna Wraps, 76
Eggnog Cake, 107
Eggnog Gelatin Mold, 61
Ham Vegetable Strata, 168
Hearty Potato Omelet, 21
Italian Sausage Strata, 25
Omelet Biscuit Cups, 28
Pepperoni Cheese Bake, 21
Pineapple Meringue Cake, 166
Potato Vegetable Quiche, 29
✓Sausage Egg Bake, 21
Sausage Garden Quiche, 19
✓Simple Souffle, 33
✓Special Egg Salad, 58
Spinach Feta Strata, 27
Strawberry Chocolate Meringue, 170

F

FISH & SEAFOOD

Baked Orange Roughy, 49
Catfish Creole, 48

Crab Alfredo, 142
Crawfish-Stuffed Pork Tenderloins, 44
Creamy Corn Crab Soup, 70
Creole Flounder with Seafood
    Sauce, 40
Crispy Salmon Steaks, 137
Egg Salad Tuna Wraps, 76
Jambalaya, 50
Potato Fish Skillet, 166
Shrimp Creole, 42
Shrimp Fettuccine, 145
✓Smoked Salmon Spread, 8
Snowcapped Salmon, 45
Swordfish with Sauteed Vegetables, 52
Tuna Noodle Casserole, 140
Wild Rice Seafood Salad, 56

FRUIT
Citrus Fruit Cup, 146
Fancy Fruit Pizza, 7
Fresh Fruit Salad, 63
Fruit 'n' Nut Spice Bars, 94
Fruited Cabbage Salad, 78
Fruited Cranberry Relish, 129
Fruity Chicken Salad, 130
Fruity Thirst Quencher, 15
Hot Curried Fruit, 172
Hot Curried Fruit Sauce, 89

G

GRILLED & BROILED RECIPES
Broiled Turkey Tenderloins, 161
Creole Flounder with Seafood
    Sauce, 40
Crispy Salmon Steaks, 137
Grilled Herbed Pork Roast, 42
Herbed London Broil, 151
Lemonade Chicken, 35
✓Mushroom Pizza Burgers, 70
Pork Tenderloin with Herb Sauce, 47
✓Pork with Sour Cream Salsa, 37
Sesame Sirloin Steak, 139
Sirloin Steak Sandwiches, 162
Swordfish with Sauteed
    Vegetables, 52

GROUND BEEF
Barbecue Lasagna, 40
Beans and Biscuits, 48
Beef Cabbage Roll-Ups, 37
Beef-Stuffed Potatoes, 38
Cheesy Beef Taco Dip, 6
Corn Bread Taco Bake, 42
Cranberry Kraut Meatballs, 39
Hearty Chili Mac, 55
Hearty Hamburger Soup, 138
Italian Beef Patties, 76
Macaroni 'n' Cheese Pizza, 36
Meatballs with Vegetable Sauce, 146
Microwave Meat Loaf, 35
✓Mushroom Pizza Burgers, 70

Pantry Chili, 66
Picante Cranberry Meatballs, 50
✓Root Vegetable Beef Stew, 38
Sauerbraten Patties, 170
✓Sloppy Joes, 73
Slow Cooker Chili, 74
Taco Sandwich, 66
Taco Soup, 79
Vegetable Beef Potpie, 36
Veggie Beef Patties, 158
Zesty Onion Burgers, 63

H

HAM & BACON
Bacon 'n' Egg Gravy, 131
Bacon-Onion Crescent Buns, 31
Bacon Potato Chowder, 67
Corn and Bacon Pancakes, 32
Creamed Ham in Toast Cups, 46
Deviled Ham Stuffed Eggs, 8
Ham 'n' Corn Fritters, 26
Ham and Sweet Potato Salad, 62
Pineapple Ham Casserole, 49
✓Sweet and Sour Ham, 44
Zippy Praline Bacon, 168

I

ICE CREAM & SHERBET
Banana Sundae Sauce, 105
Frosted Ruby Punch, 11
Lime Sundaes, 154
Peach Ice Cream, 122
Peaches 'n' Cream Smoothies, 14
Peanut Butter Milkshakes, 13

J

JAM & JELLY
Apricot Pineapple Jam, 23
Orange Jelly, 24
Orange Pear Jam, 22
Orange Pineapple Marmalade, 22
Peach Raspberry Jam, 22
Surprise Raspberry Jam, 24

L

LAMB
Rack of Lamb, 129

LEMONS & LIMES
Baked Lemon Pudding, 121
Buttermilk Lemon Pie, 116
Citrus Iced Tea, 6
Lemon Icebox Dessert, 117
Lemon-Pepper Rice, 154
Lemon Sparkle Cupcakes, 100
Lemonade Chicken, 35
Lime Coconut Bars, 137
Lime Sundaes, 154
Orange Lemonade, 168

M

MEAT LOAF & MEATBALLS
Cranberry Kraut Meatballs, 39
Meatballs with Vegetable Sauce, 146
Microwave Meat Loaf, 35
Picante Cranberry Meatballs, 50
Pork Meatballs, 148

MEAT PIE & PIZZAS
Macaroni 'n' Cheese Pizza, 36
Roasted Garlic Tomato Pizza, 45
Skillet Pizzas, 138
Southwestern Pizza, 46
Vegetable Beef Potpie, 36

MICROWAVE RECIPES
Caramel Nut Marshmallows, 92
Cheddar Zucchini Slices, 148
Cubed Parmesan Potatoes, 137
Microwave Meat Loaf, 35
Peanut Butter Cereal Bars, 92
Pound Cake Cobbler, 162

MUSHROOMS
Carrot Mushroom Medley, 85
Eggplant with Mushroom
    Stuffing, 135
✓Mushroom Pizza Burgers, 70
Mushroom Wild Rice Bake, 83

N

NUTS & PEANUT BUTTER
Banana Nut Bars, 94
Caramel Crunch, 9
Caramel Nut Marshmallows, 92
Chunky Peanut Brittle, 91
Fruit 'n' Nut Spice Bars, 94
Fudgy Walnut Brownies, 92
Hedgehog Cookies, 132
Linzer Heart Cookies, 91
Mandarin Peanut Rice Salad, 66
Nutty Brussels Sprouts, 81
Oat Pecan Cookie Mix, 93
Orange-Hazelnut Spiral Rolls, 26
Orange-Honey Cashew Chicken, 130
Peanut Butter Banana Pudding, 100
Peanut Butter Cereal Bars, 92
Peanut Butter Chocolate Fondue, 5
Peanut Butter Cupcakes, 119
Peanut Butter Layer Cake, 106
Peanut Butter Milkshakes, 13
Pecan Cheddar Snacks, 134
Pecan Chess Pie, 117
Pecan Coconut Pie, 114
Pineapple-Cherry Nut Cake, 115
Sugared Pecans, 12
Walnut Carrot Cake, 125
Walnut Glory Cake, 122
Walnut Oat Pie, 127
Zippy Praline Bacon, 168

O

ORANGES
Chocolate Orange Cupcakes, 101
Citrus Fruit Cup, 146
Mandarin Fluff, 153
Mandarin Fruit Salad, 168
Mandarin Peanut Rice Salad, 66
Marmalade Date Pastries, 164
Orange Applesauce Cupcakes, 104
Orange Chicken Stir-Fry, 142
Orange-Hazelnut Spiral Rolls, 26
Orange-Honey Cashew Chicken, 130
Orange Jelly, 24
Orange Lemonade, 168
Orange Pear Jam, 22
Orange Pineapple Marmalade, 22
Orange Spiced Tea, 16
Peachy Orange Shakes, 143
Punch Delight, 15
Tossed Salad with Citrus Dressing, 64

OVEN ENTREES (also see
Casseroles; Meat Loaf &
Meatballs; Meat Pie & Pizzas;
Microwave Recipes)
Apple-Smothered Pork Chops, 48
Baked Orange Roughy, 49
Barbecue Lasagna, 40
Beef Cabbage Roll-Ups, 37
Beef-Stuffed Potatoes, 38
Catfish Creole, 48
Chicken Italian, 53
Corn Bread Taco Bake, 42
Crawfish-Stuffed Pork Tenderloins, 44
Deviled Chicken Thighs, 150
Hearty Chicken Strata, 41
Italian Beef Patties, 76
Pork Roast with Tangy Sauce, 43
Rack of Lamb, 129
Red-Eye Beef Roast, 47
Shaker Pork Sandwiches, 74
Snowcapped Salmon, 45
Stuffed Round Steak, 53

P

PANCAKES, BLINTZES & CREPES
Apple Oven Pancake, 19
Banana Pancakes, 31
Corn and Bacon Pancakes, 32
Creamy Banana Crepes, 30
✓Sweet Corn Blintzes, 20

PASTA & NOODLES
Barbecue Lasagna, 40
Crab Alfredo, 142
Creamy Veggie Vermicelli, 83
Hearty Chili Mac, 55
Hot German Noodle Salad, 148
Macaroni 'n' Cheese Pizza, 36
Macaroni Salad, 73
No-Bake Lasagna, 134
Pepperoni Caesar Pasta Salad, 72
Shrimp Fettuccine, 145
Squash Pasta Bake, 146
Tuna Noodle Casserole, 140

PEACHES
Coconut Peach Pie, 126
Hot Curried Fruit, 172
Peach Coffee Cake, 27
Peach Ice Cream, 122
Peach Raspberry Jam, 22
Peaches 'n' Cream Bars, 95
Peaches 'n' Cream Gelatin, 60
Peaches 'n' Cream Smoothies, 14
Peachy Orange Shakes, 143

PEARS
Apple Pear Pie, 124
Caramel Pear Cake, 113
Chicken and Pear Tossed Salad, 59
Hot Curried Fruit, 172
Minted Pears, 129
Orange Pear Jam, 22
Pear Cooler, 15
Pear Crunch Pie, 104
Pear-fect Pork Supper, 147
Tangy Franks and Pears, 138

PIES
Apple Pear Pie, 124
Buttermilk Lemon Pie, 116
Caramel Pear Cake, 113
Chocolate Banana Cream Pie, 116
Chocolate Chip Banana Cream Pie, 111
Chocolate Chipper Pie Mix, 123
Coconut Peach Pie, 126
Crustless Pumpkin Pie, 108
Hawaiian Cream Pie, 112
Pear Crunch Pie, 104
Pecan Chess Pie, 117
Pecan Coconut Pie, 114
Sandra's Apple-Rhubarb Pie, 108
Walnut Oat Pie, 127

PINEAPPLE
Aloha Pork Chops, 35
Apricot Pineapple Jam, 23
Chocolate Pineapple Trifle, 174
Hawaiian Cheesecake, 109
Hawaiian Chicken Salad, 68
Hawaiian Cream Pie, 112
Hot Curried Fruit, 172
Mandarin Fruit Salad, 168
Orange Pineapple Marmalade, 22
Pineapple Banana Bread, 140
Pineapple Bread Pudding, 114
Pineapple-Cherry Nut Cake, 115
Pineapple Ham Casserole, 49

Pineapple Meringue Cake, 166
✓Sweet and Sour Ham, 44

PORK (also see Ham & Bacon; Sausage)
Aloha Pork Chops, 35
Apple-Smothered Pork Chops, 48
Cider Pork Chop Dinner, 51
Crawfish-Stuffed Pork Tenderloins, 44
Grilled Herbed Pork Roast, 42
Pear-fect Pork Supper, 147
Pork Barbecue Sandwiches, 132
Pork Meatballs, 148
Pork Roast with Tangy Sauce, 43
Pork Tenderloin with Herb Sauce, 47
✓Pork with Sour Cream Salsa, 37
Saucy Pork Chops with Vegetables, 172
Shaker Pork Sandwiches, 74
Skillet Barbecued Pork Chops, 157

POTATOES & SWEET POTATOES
Apple Sweet Potato Bake, 174
Bacon Potato Chowder, 67
Beef-Stuffed Potatoes, 38
Cheesy Chive Potatoes, 161
Cranberry Sweet Potato Bake, 81
Creamy Potatoes 'n' Peas, 88
Cubed Parmesan Potatoes, 137
Double-Crust Potato Pie, 84
French Potato Salad, 78
German Potato Casserole, 170
Ham and Sweet Potato Salad, 62
Hearty Potato Omelet, 21
Oven Potatoes, 85
Potato Fish Skillet, 166
Potato Roast Beef Salad, 77
Potato Vegetable Quiche, 29
Raisin Sweet Potato Bread, 32
Sweet Potato Cranberry Bake, 84
Sweet Potato Loaves, 143
Swiss Potato Soup, 162
Warm Potato Salad, 134

PUDDING & MOUSSE
Baked Lemon Pudding, 121
Chocolate Chip Pudding Parfaits, 135
Chocolate Mousse, 131
Coconut Custard Pudding, 123
Corn Pudding Stuffed Tomatoes, 87
Cranberry Bread Pudding, 120
Hearty Corn Pudding, 86
Old-Fashioned Cocoa Pudding, 121
Peanut Butter Banana Pudding, 100
Pineapple Bread Pudding, 114
Raspberry Rice Pudding, 121

PUMPKIN
Cream-Filled Pumpkin Cupcakes, 99
Cream Puff Ghosts, 127
Crustless Pumpkin Pie, 108

R

RAISINS & DATES
Apricot-Date Mini Loaves, 31
Marmalade Date Pastries, 164
Raisin Sweet Potato Bread, 32

RASPBERRIES
Linzer Heart Cookies, 91
Peach Raspberry Jam, 22
Raspberry Mint Cooler, 14
Raspberry Mocha Torte, 118
Raspberry Rice Pudding, 121
Raspberry Swirl Cupcakes, 115
Surprise Raspberry Jam, 24

RHUBARB
Danish Cherry Rhubarb Dessert, 119
Rhubarb Puff, 139
Sandra's Apple-Rhubarb Pie, 108

RICE & BARLEY
Brown Rice Vegetable Casserole, 82
Chocolate Rice Dessert, 157
Corny Rice, 87
Hearty Rice Salad, 75
Lemon-Pepper Rice, 154
Mandarin Peanut Rice Salad, 66
Mushroom Wild Rice Bake, 83
Raspberry Rice Pudding, 121
Rice Salad in Tomato Cups, 140
Wild Rice Seafood Salad, 56
Wild Rice Turkey Salad, 71

ROLLS
Bacon-Onion Crescent Buns, 31
Orange-Hazelnut Spiral Rolls, 26

S

SALADS & DRESSINGS
Coleslaw
Old-Fashioned Coleslaw, 132
Dressings
Blue Cheese Salad Dressing, 145
Honey Mustard Salad Dressing, 129
Poppy Seed Salad Dressing, 164
✓Zesty Buttermilk Salad Dressing, 79
Fruit & Gelatin Salads
Apple Mallow Salad, 59
Cabbage-Cucumber Gelatin Cups, 73
Cheddar Waldorf Salad, 64
Circus Peanut Gelatin, 164
Citrus Fruit Cup, 146
Cranberry Velvet Freeze, 57
Cranberry Waldorf Gelatin, 69
Eggnog Gelatin Mold, 61
Fresh Fruit Salad, 63
Gelatin Banana Split, 60
Mandarin Fluff, 153
Mandarin Fruit Salad, 168
Peaches 'n' Cream Gelatin, 60
Seven-Layer Gelatin Salad, 61

Green Salads
Artichoke Spinach Salad, 74
Chicken and Pear Tossed Salad, 59
Easter Lettuce Salad, 63
Fruited Cabbage Salad, 78
Pepperoni Caesar Salad, 147
Tossed Salad with Artichokes, 70
Tossed Salad with Citrus Dressing, 64
Zucchini Lettuce Salad, 158
Main-Dish Salads
Fruity Chicken Salad, 130
Ham and Sweet Potato Salad, 62
Hawaiian Chicken Salad, 68
✓Special Egg Salad, 58
Strawberry Chicken Salad, 69
✓Tossed Chicken Salad, 75
Wild Rice Turkey Salad, 71
Pasta & Rice Salads
Hearty Rice Salad, 75
Hot German Noodle Salad, 148
Macaroni Salad, 73
Mandarin Peanut Rice Salad, 66
Pepperoni Caesar Pasta Salad, 72
Rice Salad in Tomato Cups, 140
Wild Rice Seafood Salad, 56
Potato Salads
French Potato Salad, 78
Potato Roast Beef Salad, 77
Warm Potato Salad, 134
Vegetable Salads
Asparagus Salad, 137
Black-Eyed Pea Salad, 56
Broccoli Garbanzo Salad, 157
Corn and Black Bean Salad, 77
Corn Bread Salad, 68
Corn Medley Salad, 56
Crunchy Kraut Salad, 151
Cucumber Tomato Salad, 67
Dilly Cucumber Salad, 56
✓Gazpacho Salad, 76
Green Bean Feta Salad, 170
Green Bean Salad, 153
Marinated Lima Bean Salad, 64
Marinated Veggie Salad, 78
Zesty Corn Salad, 67

SANDWICHES
Bacon 'n' Egg Gravy, 131
Egg Salad Tuna Wraps, 76
Pork Barbecue Sandwiches, 132
Reuben Sandwiches, 65
Shaker Pork Sandwiches, 74
Sirloin Steak Sandwiches, 162
✓Sloppy Joes, 73
✓Special Egg Salad, 58
Super Bowl Stromboli, 55
Taco Sandwich, 66

SAUSAGE
Breakfast Pizza, 19
Chicken Italian, 53

Italian Sausage Strata, 25
Jambalaya, 50
✓Sausage Egg Bake, 21
Sausage Garden Quiche, 19
Spicy Cajun Stew, 153

SIDE DISHES (*also see Casseroles*)
Carrot Mushroom Medley, 85
Cheddar Zucchini Slices, 148
Cheesy Chive Potatoes, 161
Corn Pudding Stuffed Tomatoes, 87
Corny Rice, 87
Cranberry Sweet Potato Bake, 81
Creamy Potatoes 'n' Peas, 88
Creamy Veggie Vermicelli, 83
Cubed Parmesan Potatoes, 137
Double-Crust Potato Pie, 84
Eggplant with Mushroom Stuffing, 135
Honey Mustard Carrots, 166
✓Italian-Style Peas, 81
Lemon-Pepper Rice, 154
Maple-Apple Baked Beans, 88
Nutty Brussels Sprouts, 81
Oven Potatoes, 85
Saucy Green Beans, 174
Savory Green Beans, 88
Sunday Best Corn, 86
Turkey with Herb Stuffing, 174

SKILLET & STOVETOP SUPPERS
Aloha Pork Chops, 35
Barbecued Round Steak, 51
Cider Pork Chop Dinner, 51
Country Chicken, 43
Crab Alfredo, 142
Jambalaya, 50
Mini Skillet Corn Bread, 145
Orange Chicken Stir-Fry, 142
Orange-Honey Cashew
  Chicken, 130
Pear-fect Pork Supper, 147
Pork Barbecue Sandwiches, 132
Potato Fish Skillet, 166
Reuben Sandwiches, 65
✓Root Vegetable Beef Stew, 38
Salsa Chicken, 154
Saucy Pork Chops with Vegetables, 172
Sauerbraten Patties, 170
Shrimp Creole, 42
Shrimp Fettuccine, 145
Skillet Barbecued Pork Chops, 157
Skillet Pizzas, 138
✓Sloppy Joes, 73
Spiced Beef Pot Roast, 52
✓Sweet and Sour Ham, 44
Tangy Franks and Pears, 138
Tangy Round Steak Strips, 164
Veal Shank Fricassee, 150
Veggie Beef Patties, 158
Zesty Onion Burgers, 63

SLOW COOKER RECIPES
✓Deviled Swiss Steak, 41
Slow Cooker Chili, 74
Tangy Bean Soup, 72

SOUPS, STEW & CHILI
Bacon Potato Chowder, 67
Chilled Blueberry Soup, 65
Creamy Asparagus Soup, 166
Creamy Corn Crab Soup, 70
Hearty Chili Mac, 55
Hearty Hamburger Soup, 138
Farmhouse Chicken Soup, 62
Pantry Chili, 66
✓Root Vegetable Beef Stew, 38
Slow Cooker Chili, 74
Spicy Cajun Stew, 153
Swiss Potato Soup, 162
Taco Soup, 79
Tangy Bean Soup, 72
✓Turkey Cabbage Soup, 68
Zippy Chicken Corn Chowder, 57

STRAWBERRIES
Strawberry Chicken Salad, 69
Strawberry Chocolate Meringue, 170
Strawberry Punch, 11

T

TIPS
A Basketful of Corn Tips, 86
A Host of Cupcake Hints, 101
Appealing Banana Tips, 110
Chicken Salad Savers, 75
Delightful Drink Ideas, 10
Frying Tips, 17
Glazed to Perfection, 89
Grate for Cheese, 148
Great Ground Beef Tips, 39
Helpful Bread-Spread Tips, 24
Keeping Cabbage Crisp, 132
Mind the Marinade, 47
Parsley Pointers, 5
Second-Day Salad Tips, 71
Tasty Toast, 107
Yeast Bread Basics, 55

TOMATOES
Corn Pudding Stuffed Tomatoes, 87
Cucumber Tomato Salad, 67
✓Gazpacho Salad, 76
Rice Salad in Tomato Cups, 140
Roasted Garlic Tomato Pizza, 45
Surprise Raspberry Jam, 24

TURKEY
Broiled Turkey Tenderloins, 161
✓Turkey Cabbage Soup, 68
Turkey with Herb Stuffing, 174
Wild Rice Turkey Salad, 71

V

VEGETABLES
Brown Rice Vegetable Casserole, 82
Creamy Potatoes 'n' Peas, 88
Creamy Veggie Vermicelli, 83
Eggplant with Mushroom
    Stuffing, 135
Ham Vegetable Strata, 168
Marinated Veggie Salad, 78
Meatballs with Vegetable Sauce, 146
Nutty Brussels Sprouts, 81
✓Root Vegetable Beef Stew, 38
Saucy Pork Chops with
    Vegetables, 172
Swordfish with Sauteed
    Vegetables, 52
Turnip Casserole, 84
Vegetable Beef Potpie, 36
Veggie Beef Patties, 158

Y

YEAST BREADS
Light Wheat Bread, 172
Maple Oatmeal Bread, 33
Super Bowl Stromboli, 55
Zucchini Yeast Bread, 28

Z

ZUCCHINI & SQUASH
Cheddar Zucchini Slices, 148
Chocolate Zucchini Cake, 126
Squash Pasta Bake, 146
Zucchini Lettuce Salad, 158
Zucchini Yeast Bread, 28

Alphabetical Recipe Index

✓*Recipe includes Nutritional Analysis and Diabetic Exchanges*

A

Aloha Pork Chops, 35
Apple Mallow Salad, 59
Apple Oven Pancake, 19
Apple Pear Pie, 124
Apple-Smothered Pork Chops, 48
Apple Sweet Potato Bake, 174
Apricot-Date Mini Loaves, 31
Apricot Pineapple Jam, 23
Artichoke Cheese Oven Omelet, 32
Artichoke Spinach Salad, 74
Asparagus Salad, 137
Asparagus Souffle, 142

B

Bacon 'n' Egg Gravy, 131
Bacon-Onion Crescent Buns, 31
Bacon Potato Chowder, 67
Baked Lemon Pudding, 121
Baked Orange Roughy, 49
✓Banana Cupcakes, 124
Banana Nut Bars, 94
Banana Pancakes, 31
Banana Shakes, 12
Banana Split Dessert, 145
Banana Sundae Sauce, 105
Banana Upside Down Cake, 111
Barbecue Lasagna, 40
Barbecued Round Steak, 51
Beans and Biscuits, 48
Beef Cabbage Roll-Ups, 37
Beef-Stuffed Potatoes, 38
Black-Eyed Pea Salad, 56
Blue Cheese Salad Dressing, 145
Blueberry Bars, 97
Breakfast Pizza, 19

Broccoli Garbanzo Salad, 157
Broiled Turkey Tenderloins, 161
Brown Rice Vegetable Casserole, 82
Buttermilk Lemon Pie, 116

C

Cabbage-Cucumber Gelatin Cups, 73
Cappuccino Cupcakes, 123
Caramel Chocolate Cake, 118
✓Caramel Chocolate Cheesecake
    Bites, 124
Caramel Crunch, 9
Caramel Nut Marshmallows, 92
Caramel Pear Cake, 113
Carrot Cookies, 96
Carrot Mushroom Medley, 85
Catfish Creole, 48
Cheddar Waldorf Salad, 64

Cheddar Zucchini Slices, 148
Cheesy Beef Taco Dip, 6
Cheesy Chive Potatoes, 161
Cheesy Corn Dip, 16
Cherry Chocolate Chip Cookies, 95
Cherry Chocolate Dessert, 161
Chicken and Pear Tossed Salad, 59
Chicken Italian, 53
Chilled Blueberry Soup, 65
Chilled Cranberry Cheesecake, 113
Chocolate Banana Cream Pie, 116
✓Chocolate Banana Smoothies, 13
Chocolate Banana Split Cupcakes, 105
Chocolate Chip Banana Cream Pie, 111
Chocolate Chip Pudding Parfaits, 135
Chocolate Chipper Pie Mix, 123
Chocolate Chow Mein Clusters, 140
Chocolate Mousse, 131
Chocolate Orange Cupcakes, 101
Chocolate Pineapple Trifle, 174
Chocolate Rice Dessert, 157
Chocolate Zucchini Cake, 126
Christmas Pickles, 82
Chunky Peanut Brittle, 91
Chutney Stuffed Eggs, 7
Cider Pork Chop Dinner, 51
Circus Peanut Gelatin, 164
Citrus Fruit Cup, 146
Citrus Iced Tea, 6
Coconut Carrot Cake, 172
Coconut Carrot Casserole, 84
Coconut Custard Pudding, 123
Coconut Peach Pie, 126
Corn and Bacon Pancakes, 32
Corn and Black Bean Salad, 77
Corn Bread Salad, 68
Corn Bread Taco Bake, 42
Corn Medley Salad, 56
Corn Pudding Stuffed Tomatoes, 87
Corny Eggs, 25
Corny Rice, 87
Country Chicken, 43
Crab Alfredo, 142
Cranberry Apple Crisp, 108
Cranberry Bread Pudding, 120
Cranberry Kraut Meatballs, 39
Cranberry Sweet Potato Bake, 81
Cranberry Velvet Freeze, 57
Cranberry Waldorf Gelatin, 69
Crawfish-Stuffed Pork Tenderloins, 44
Cream Cheese Chocolate
    Cupcakes, 104
Cream Cheese Cutouts, 96
Cream-Filled Pumpkin Cupcakes, 99
Cream Puff Ghosts, 127
Creamed Ham in Toast Cups, 46
Creamy Asparagus Soup, 166
Creamy Banana Crepes, 30

Creamy Corn Crab Soup, 70
Creamy Potatoes 'n' Peas, 88
Creamy Veggie Vermicelli, 83
Creole Flounder with Seafood Sauce, 40
Crispy Salmon Steaks, 137
Crunchy Chocolate Cups, 96
Crunchy Kraut Salad, 151
Crustless Pumpkin Pie, 108
Cubed Parmesan Potatoes, 137
Cucumber Tomato Salad, 67
Cupcake Cones, 112
Currant Jelly Scones, 20

D
Danish Cherry Rhubarb Dessert, 119
Deviled Chicken Thighs, 150
Deviled Eggs, 132
Deviled Ham Stuffed Eggs, 8
✓Deviled Swiss Steak, 41
Dilly Cucumber Salad, 56
Double-Crust Potato Pie, 84

E
Easter Lettuce Salad, 63
Egg Salad Tuna Wraps, 76
Eggnog Cake, 107
Eggnog Gelatin Mold, 61
Eggplant with Mushroom Stuffing, 135

F
Fancy Fruit Pizza, 7
Farmhouse Chicken Soup, 62
Festive Cheese Beach Ball, 10
French Potato Salad, 78
Fresh Fruit Salad, 63
Frosted Creams, 93
Frosted Ruby Punch, 11
Frozen Chocolate Crunch, 114
Fruit 'n' Nut Spice Bars, 94
Fruited Cabbage Salad, 78
Fruited Cranberry Relish, 129
Fruity Chicken Salad, 130
Fruity Thirst Quencher, 15
Fudgy Walnut Brownies, 92

G
✓Gazpacho Salad, 76
Gelatin Banana Split, 60
German Potato Casserole, 170
Gingered Tea, 151
Grandma's Chocolate Cake, 106
Grape Juice Crush, 15
Green Bean Feta Salad, 170
Green Bean Fritters, 17
Green Bean Salad, 153
Grilled Herbed Pork Roast, 42

H
Ham 'n' Corn Fritters, 26

Ham and Sweet Potato Salad, 62
Ham Vegetable Strata, 168
Hawaiian Cheesecake, 109
Hawaiian Chicken Salad, 68
Hawaiian Cream Pie, 112
Hearty Chicken Strata, 41
Hearty Chili Mac, 55
Hearty Corn Pudding, 86
Hearty Hamburger Soup, 138
Hearty Potato Omelet, 21
Hearty Rice Salad, 75
Heavenly Surprise Cupcakes, 99
Hedgehog Cookies, 132
Herbed Garlic Bread, 12
Herbed London Broil, 151
Honey Banana Punch, 9
Honey Mustard Carrots, 166
Honey Mustard Salad Dressing, 129
Hot Cheese Spread, 12
Hot Curried Fruit, 172
Hot Curried Fruit Sauce, 89
Hot German Noodle Salad, 148

I
Italian Beef Patties, 76
Italian Sausage Strata, 25
✓Italian-Style Peas, 81

J
Jambalaya, 50

L
Layered Three-Cheese Spread, 6
Lemon Icebox Dessert, 117
Lemon-Pepper Rice, 154
Lemon Sparkle Cupcakes, 100
Lemonade Chicken, 35
Light Wheat Bread, 172
Lime Coconut Bars, 137
Lime Sundaes, 154
Linzer Heart Cookies, 91

M
Macaroni 'n' Cheese Pizza, 36
Macaroni Salad, 73
Mandarin Fluff, 153
Mandarin Fruit Salad, 168
Mandarin Peanut Rice Salad, 66
Maple-Apple Baked Beans, 88
Maple Oatmeal Bread, 33
Marinated Lima Bean Salad, 64
Marinated Veggie Salad, 78
Marmalade Date Pastries, 164
Meatballs with Vegetable Sauce, 146
Mexican Corn Dip, 13
Microwave Meat Loaf, 35
Mini Brownie Treats, 109
Mini Green Bean Casserole, 131
Mini Skillet Corn Bread, 145

Mint Cocoa Mix, 16
Minted Pears, 129
✓Mushroom Pizza Burgers, 70
Mushroom Wild Rice Bake, 83

N

No-Bake Lasagna, 134
Nutty Brussels Sprouts, 81

O

Oat Pecan Cookie Mix, 93
Old-Fashioned Cocoa Pudding, 121
Old-Fashioned Coleslaw, 132
Omelet Biscuit Cups, 28
Orange Applesauce Cupcakes, 104
Orange Chicken Stir-Fry, 142
Orange-Hazelnut Spiral Rolls, 26
Orange-Honey Cashew Chicken, 130
Orange Jelly, 24
Orange Lemonade, 168
Orange Pear Jam, 22
Orange Pineapple Marmalade, 22
Orange Spiced Tea, 16
Oven Potatoes, 85

P

Pantry Chili, 66
Paprika Cheese Biscuits, 158
Party Cheese Balls, 5
Peach Coffee Cake, 27
Peach Ice Cream, 122
Peach Raspberry Jam, 22
Peaches 'n' Cream Bars, 95
Peaches 'n' Cream Gelatin, 60
Peaches 'n' Cream Smoothies, 14
Peachy Orange Shakes, 143
Peanut Butter Banana Pudding, 100
Peanut Butter Cereal Bars, 92
Peanut Butter Chocolate Fondue, 5
Peanut Butter Cupcakes, 119
Peanut Butter Layer Cake, 106
Peanut Butter Milkshakes, 13
Pear Cooler, 15
Pear Crunch Pie, 104
Pear-fect Pork Supper, 147
Pecan Cheddar Snacks, 134
Pecan Chess Pie, 117
Pecan Coconut Pie, 114
Pepperoni Caesar Pasta Salad, 72
Pepperoni Caesar Salad, 147
Pepperoni Cheese Bake, 21
Picante Cranberry Meatballs, 50
Pineapple Banana Bread, 140
Pineapple Bread Pudding, 114
Pineapple-Cherry Nut Cake, 115
Pineapple Chocolate Chip Cookies, 97
Pineapple Ham Casserole, 49

Pineapple Meringue Cake, 166
Poppy Seed Salad Dressing, 164
Pork Barbecue Sandwiches, 132
Pork Meatballs, 148
Pork Roast with Tangy Sauce, 43
Pork Tenderloin with Herb Sauce, 47
✓Pork with Sour Cream Salsa, 37
Potato Fish Skillet, 166
Potato Roast Beef Salad, 77
Potato Vegetable Quiche, 29
Pound Cake Cobbler, 162
Punch Delight, 15

R

Rack of Lamb, 129
Raisin Sweet Potato Bread, 32
Raspberry Mint Cooler, 14
Raspberry Mocha Torte, 118
Raspberry Rice Pudding, 121
Raspberry Swirl Cupcakes, 115
Red-Eye Beef Roast, 47
Reuben Sandwiches, 65
Rhubarb Puff, 139
Rice Salad in Tomato Cups, 140
Rich Cheesecake Bars, 148
Roasted Garlic Tomato Pizza, 45
✓Root Vegetable Beef Stew, 38

S

Salsa Chicken, 154
Sandra's Apple-Rhubarb Pie, 108
Saucy Green Beans, 174
Saucy Pork Chops with Vegetables, 172
Sauerbraten Patties, 170
✓Sausage Egg Bake, 21
Sausage Garden Quiche, 19
Savory Green Beans, 88
Scalloped Corn, 81
Sesame Sirloin Steak, 139
Seven-Layer Gelatin Salad, 61
Shaker Pork Sandwiches, 74
Shoofly Cupcakes, 100
Shrimp Creole, 42
Shrimp Fettuccine, 145
✓Simple Souffle, 33
Sirloin Steak Sandwiches, 162
Skillet Barbecued Pork Chops, 157
Skillet Pizzas, 138
✓Sloppy Joes, 73
Slow Cooker Chili, 74
✓Smoked Salmon Spread, 8
Snowcapped Salmon, 45
✓Sour Cream Banana Bread, 28
Southwestern Pizza, 46
✓Special Egg Salad, 58
Spiced Beef Pot Roast, 52
Spiced Spritz Cookies, 91

Spicy Cajun Stew, 153
Spinach Feta Strata, 27
Squash Pasta Bake, 146
Strawberry Chicken Salad, 69
Strawberry Chocolate Meringue, 170
Strawberry Punch, 11
Stuffed Round Steak, 53
Sugared Pecans, 12
Sunday Best Corn, 86
Super Bowl Stromboli, 55
Surprise Raspberry Jam, 24
Sweet 'n' Salty Party Mix, 5
✓Sweet and Sour Ham, 44
✓Sweet Corn Blintzes, 20
Sweet Potato Cranberry Bake, 84
Sweet Potato Loaves, 143
Swiss Potato Soup, 162
Swordfish with Sauteed Vegetables, 52

T

Taco Sandwich, 66
Taco Soup, 79
Tangy Bean Soup, 72
Tangy Franks and Pears, 138
Tangy Round Steak Strips, 164
Tasty Cheese Spread, 17
✓Tossed Chicken Salad, 75
Tossed Salad with Artichokes, 70
Tossed Salad with Citrus Dressing, 64
Triple Layer Banana Cake, 110
Tuna Noodle Casserole, 140
✓Turkey Cabbage Soup, 68
Turkey with Herb Stuffing, 174
Turnip Casserole, 84

V

Veal Shank Fricassee, 150
Vegetable Beef Potpie, 36
Veggie Beef Patties, 158

W

Walnut Carrot Cake, 125
Walnut Glory Cake, 122
Walnut Oat Pie, 127
Warm Potato Salad, 134
✓Western Black Bean Dip, 8
Wild Rice Seafood Salad, 56
Wild Rice Turkey Salad, 71

Z

✓Zesty Buttermilk Salad Dressing, 79
Zesty Corn Salad, 67
Zesty Onion Burgers, 63
Zippy Chicken Corn Chowder, 57
Zippy Praline Bacon, 168
Zucchini Lettuce Salad, 158
Zucchini Yeast Bread, 28